MIND & MEDICINE MONOGRAPHS

Editor

MICHAEL BALINT, M.D., PH.D., M.SC.

1

Psychotherapeutic Techniques in Medicine

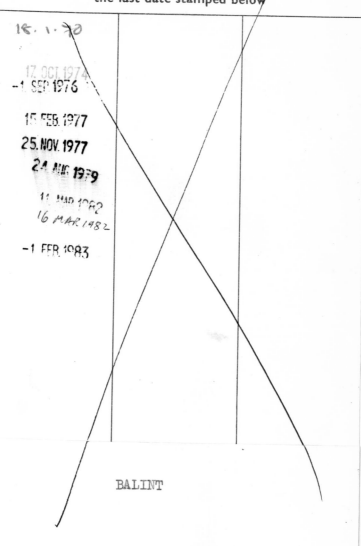

Psychotherapeutic Techniques in Medicine

MICHAEL & ENID BALINT

TAVISTOCK PUBLICATIONS

First published in 1961
by Tavistock Publications (1959) Limited
11 New Fetter Lane, London E.C.4
and printed in Great Britain
in 10 point Times Roman by
C. Tinling & Co. Ltd., Liverpool, London, and Prescot

ALSO BY MICHAEL BALINT

Primary Love and Psychoanalytic Technique (1952)
Problems of Human Pleasure and Behaviour (1957)
The Doctor, His Patient and The Illness (1957)
Thrills and Regressions (1959)

CONTENTS

v

PREFACE

Almost all the clinical material in this book comes from various research-cum-training seminars on psychological problems in medical practice. When we devised and started our first seminar of this kind at the Tavistock Clinic in 1949, we hoped that both the training and the research aspects of our work would materially benefit by the combination. Since that date over two hundred doctors have taken part in such seminars led by us or our colleagues, and we are certain that many of them would agree that this has been the case. Their aim when joining the seminar was to get some training, and while being trained they co-operated in the research, some results of which form the body of this book. Recently the Cassel Hospital and the Family Planning Association have organized seminars on the same principle, and we have drawn considerably on their experience.

We are greatly indebted to all the doctors who have participated in the seminars led either jointly or individually by the two of us, because it was their observations that provided the clinical basis for this book. We wish to express our gratitude to all of them; unfortunately the list of their names would be too long, but we wish to thank individually those doctors who allowed us to use their clinical observations as illustrations for our ideas or as bases for our conclusions: Dr. M. B. Clyne, Dr. S. Dawkins, Dr. B. R. Finlay, Dr. J. C. Foster, Dr. A. J. Hawes, Dr. D. M. Hill, Dr. A. Lask, Dr. J. E. Lennard-Jones, Dr. R. M. Lloyd-Thomas, Dr. R. E. D. Markillie, Dr. V. J. Marmery, Dr. P. R. Saville, and Dr. G. Tintner. Thanks are also due to the staff of the Family Discussion Bureau for their permission to quote three of their cases, and to Mr. A. Pollock for the permission to use his report on a psychological test.

Two research projects were supported by grants from the Tavistock Institute of Human Relations and from the Family Planning Association, each of them defraying the expenses of recording one seminar. Almost all the case histories used in this book were taken from these records. We wish to express our gratitude to these two organizations for their continuing support and to this gratitude we would add our hope that some other organization or fund will find our research work worthy of the financial help which we need so urgently.

Sincere thanks are due to our secretary, Miss Doris Young, who not only recorded and transcribed the discussions of one seminar but kept all our notes in order, typed and collated the various pieces of manuscript, and was in general responsible for all the administrative work connected with the compilation of this book. It was her able and conscientious help that enabled us to complete this book in a relatively short time. We also wish to thank our other secretary, Mrs. Linda Martin, for her understanding and reliable work. She was responsible for the recording and transcribing of the Family Planning Association seminar.

Dr. Richard Bayliss, a Member of the Advisory Board of this Monograph Series, kindly read the whole of the typescript and we are greatly indebted for his sympathetic interest and many helpful suggestions. Mr. John Harvard-Watts undertook the editing of our manuscript, which was no mean task. We owe him sincere thanks for his unsparing and understanding help.

We also wish to thank two of our colleagues, Dr. A. J. Hawes and Dr. J. L. Wilson, who helped us with the correction of the text and the reading of the proofs.

And lastly, we wish to acknowledge the courtesy of the Editors of the following periodicals: *Deutsche Medizinische Wochenschrift, Journal of the Hillside Hospital, The Lancet, The Medical World, Psyche*, and *Revue de Médecine Psychosomatique*, for allowing us to use in this book material previously published by them.

INTRODUCTION

The status of psychotherapy in medicine is equivocal in more than one respect. Its enthusiasts claim that it is one of the most important therapeutic methods available; its enemies claim that it has no scientific justification whatsoever. Somewhere in between the two, medicine proper reluctantly admits that there may be some slender empirical basis to justify its use, especially if it is administered in conjunction with some other therapy, such as placebos, physiotherapy, etc. Psycho-analysis considers psychotherapy a poor substitute, really a kind of watered-down psycho-analysis. Academic psychiatry has very limited use for it in comparison with its interest in physical and chemical therapeutic methods. Because of this equivocal status hardly any doctor identifies himself with it; though some may practise psychotherapy, they style themselves psychiatrists, psycho-analysts, and so on.

The same ambiguous situation faces us when we inquire what the specific methods of medical psychotherapy are; what sort of professional skill is required from those who intend to practise it; and in what way and where these skills may be acquired. Although psychology, and even psychopathology on dynamic lines, may be taught by some teaching hospitals, we do not know of any which would offer a systematic course in psychotherapy to its students. True, some of the larger American Universities now have a Department of Psycho-analysis in which systematic courses in psycho-analysis are offered to postgraduate students intending to specialize as psychiatrists or psycho-analysts, but apparently it is not thought necessary to train medical undergraduates in psychotherapy.

What are the facts about psychotherapy? Has it a right to a place in medicine? Have any psychotherapeutic methods a scientific basis and can they be taught? If so, what are these methods and who should teach them? Our book attempts to examine these questions, not theoretically, but on the basis of concrete clinical material.

There seems little doubt that a considerable proportion of the complaints about which patients consult their doctors are not primarily or solely related to physical causes but originate from emotional problems. For our purposes it is irrelevant to establish what the exact proportions are; in any case, the figures found in the literature vary widely probably because they depend as much on the personality and prejudices of the examiner as on the patient material examined.[1] Still, it is worth recording that the lowest figures speak of about 10%, whereas the highest go as far as 60%-80% or even higher. But if we accept a conservative estimate, say, about 25% of all patients —which according to our experience is probably too low—we are faced with the inevitable conclusion that medicine must develop reliable methods for coping with this problem.

This development, initiated by the increasing weight of the evidence mentioned above, is already on its way throughout the whole scientific world, and will influence not only everyday medical practice but also, equally inevitably, the medical curriculum. Signs are increasing that the present traditional distribution of time, energy, and attention among the demands of the various medical and pre-medical sciences is felt to be unsatisfactory. More and more voices are heard advocating that roughly comparable amounts of time and energy—of both students and teaching staff—should be allocated to the study of the structure and function of the human body and of the human mind. The protagonists of this revolutionary idea have become so daring that on occasion they have questioned the wisdom of spending so much time in the traditional sanctum of medicine, the anatomy school, and have advocated—and in a few medical schools succeeded in—curtailing the time spent in the study of anatomy and substituting for it the study of normal and abnormal psychology.

The same demand, and with even more force, can be made for allocating comparable time and energy—of both students and teaching staff—to the study of pharmacotherapeutic and psychotherapeutic techniques. Of course this cannot be achieved tomorrow. We have too few teachers trained in psychotherapy and too little is known about this subject; therefore for many years to come a considerable part of the time available will have to be given to research and to the training of future teachers.

If medicine refuses to accept responsibility for this aspect of its task a number of other professions are more than willing to claim it, some of them on the basis of a long-standing tradition, others because their members have received during their training a fair amount of

[1] To test the reliability of such assessment we tried—with several groups of doctors at the Tavistock Clinic—the following experiment: Each doctor in turn was asked to report about all the patients who consulted him during a pre-arranged surgery. After each report every member of the group had to assess the organic versus neurotic aetiology of the case on an eleven-point scale—0: purely organic, 10: purely neurotic. In spite of the fact that we knew each other fairly well and that any widely diverging assessment had to be explained, we had to give up these experiments since the assessments seemed to depend much more on the assessor's personality and preconceived ideas than on the nature of the cases reported.

instruction in some sort of psychotherapeutic work. The oldest among these professions is the priesthood, which has developed a special science called pastoral psychology on the basis of its experience in this field. Some of the lawyers, in particular criminologists, on the one hand, and those specializing in family and divorce affairs, on the other, show an increasing interest in this subject. A number of specialized social workers are already doing some kinds of psychotherapeutic work, some of it of a very good standard—to cite a few examples, hospital almoners, probation officers, health visitors, and, above all, psychiatric social workers. And last, particularly since the war, more and more psychologists have turned their interest towards these problems.

The question that arises is: what sort of psychotherapy should be taught by the teaching hospitals? Here we would suggest *not* the psychotherapy most commonly employed nowadays, based chiefly on a good bedside manner, some sympathy, and some common sense, the principal methods of which are sedatives, tranquillizers, and so-called 'reassurance'. The usefulness of these as 'therapeutic' techniques is just as limited in psychological as in organic medicine. What are needed for the present as well as the future medical generation are therapeutic methods amounting to *proper professional skills*, just as in any other branch of medicine. These professional skills, of course, need to be based on something more positive than common sense, sympathy, or empiricism; they must be based on proper and critical medical research.

A further point must be mentioned here, namely, that psychotherapeutic techniques must, in our opinion, be based chiefly on personal skill and cannot be acquired by book learning. Remarkably enough, this simple truth, which is accepted as self-evident in surgery, obstetrics, radiology, and so on, requires special emphasis in our field. Knowledge can be learned from books and lectures; skill must be acquired by doing the thing, and its price in psychotherapy must always be *a limited though considerable change of one's own personality*.[1] Without this, psychotherapy, so-called, is a well-intentioned, amateurish exercise; it is this change of personality that raises it to a professional level.

Reading this book will, therefore, neither bestow on anyone this professional skill, nor transform any doctor into a psychotherapist. Why did we bother, then, to write it? Our chief aim was to give a first orientation in this field, by differentiating *professional* psychotherapy, whether carried out by a psychiatrist or a non-

---

[1] cf. M. Balint (1957). *The Doctor, His Patient and The Illness* London: Pitman Med. Publ. Co.; New York: Int. Univ. Press. Appendix I. Training.

psychiatrist, from what we have called *common-sense* psychotherapy. Our method will be to present concrete clinical material to show that psychotherapy requires a special skill with technical considerations of its own. We hope that in this way it will emerge clearly what kind of skill is demanded from the psychotherapist in order to tackle the problems confronting him. Then we shall offer some tentative solutions which we hope may help doctors to cope with the problems they encounter. We are fully aware, however, that all that we can offer is far from constituting the textbook of psychotherapy that is so much needed. In our opinion, knowledge in this field is as yet insufficient to allow of a truly systematic treatment.

While maintaining that real training in psychotherapy can be achieved only by practical work under proper supervision, we think this book may serve some useful purpose (*a*) in providing a first orientation for those who have no access to training centres such as exist in London, (*b*) in offering some guidance to psychiatrists who consider starting similar seminars in new centres, (*c*) in helping our colleagues taking part in our seminars by clarifying certain ideas and, last but not least, (*d*) in having compelled us to express in more precise form some of our rather vague ideas about processes taking place during psychotherapy and during training for psychotherapy.

An additional aim of ours was to stimulate interest among psychiatrists, and especially among psycho-analysts, in these problems by showing their immense importance for the whole of medicine.

As we stated above, present knowledge of psychotherapy is insufficient to allow of its systematic treatment in a textbook. We feel that we psycho-analysts must accept part of the blame for this unsatisfactory situation. In 1956, on the occasion of the centenary of Freud's birth, his Budapest Congress Paper 'Advances in Psycho-analytic Therapy'[1] was very widely quoted to show that already in 1918 Freud correctly predicted the coming demand for psychotherapy for the broad masses. The address ends with another correct prediction: that whatever form this new psychotherapy will take, a most important ingredient in its composition will be pure psycho-analysis. However, the address contains yet another passage, which, because of its vivid imagery, has made a profound and lasting impression on the workers in this field—'It is very probable, too, that the large-scale application of our therapy will compel us to alloy the pure gold of analysis freely with the copper of direct suggestion; and hypnotic influence, too, might find a place in it again . . .'

[1] Delivered at the Fifth Psycho-analytic Congress, Budapest, 1918. Standard Edition, Volume XVII.

The fact is that this valuable alloy between the pure gold of psycho-analysis and some baser metal has not yet been found, however great the need for it may have been. One reason for the failure is perhaps the 'hubris' inherent in this metaphor. Although it is questionable whether Freud himself meant these words to be taken in a literal sense, it is a fact that psycho-analysts—and not only psycho-analysts—have behaved as if these words represented letters patent conferring precedence and privileges upon them, the sole possessors of the pure gold; while every other ingredient—that has been contributed by a fellow professional worker—has been considered *ipso facto* as something of incomparably lower value. Psycho-analysts, in consequence, felt uneasy if they experimented with methods other than pure analysis; for them it was almost as if they had either betrayed their sacred cause, or tried to fob off one of their patients with something that they themselves considered inferior; thus if, in spite of all these feelings, they tried their hands at any other method of psychotherapy, they had to do it in a manner so condescending as to spoil any chance of a fruitful co-operation with their non-analytic colleagues. Non-analysts, on the other hand, approached this problem with an admission, both insincere and ambivalent, of inferiority. The price for the collaboration with analysts was invariably the unconditional acceptance of the principle that psycho-analysis, being far superior to everything else in psycho-therapy, has the final answer for every problem. It is no wonder that in this uneasy atmosphere no proper collaborative research could be done, and in its place there developed the ambivalent sterility of the teacher-pupil relationship, in which the analyst invariably assumed the role of the superior mentor. The result has been ambivalent admiration of the analyst's superior skill leading either to therapeutic inhibition, or to a poor form of watered-down analytic technique of which both mentor and pupil were rightly ashamed.

This book is yet another proof of the usefulness of an entirely different approach—that which we have adopted for all our researches in this field. Although we have not discarded one grain of the pure gold of analytic findings, we have come to accept openly its various limitations, above all those imposed upon its techniques by the setting in which analytic treatment is carried out. Because of this new attitude we encountered no major difficulties in our research; in fact, it was a simple consequence of our policy to welcome as our equals our various non-analytic colleagues in medicine, whose clinical and therapeutic experiences in the vast fields beyond the confines of the analytic setting evidently had to be considered as contributions just as valid and valuable as our own analytic findings. We hope that this book will truly reflect the spirit of equality that characterized our whole research work.

Contrary to Freud's expectations, the methods worked out, and subsequently used in practice by our various research teams, do not make any use of either direct suggestion or hypnotic influence. In making this statement we do not wish to pass judgement on the validity or practicability of these methods, we only wish to state the fact that we did not use either of them. Instead, as will be evident from our description, we tried to develop the specific psychotherapeutic potentialities inherent in each of the various medical settings studied by us —admittedly strongly influenced by our own analytic orientation. Still, we think that our findings may offer solutions for some of the innumerable problems of psychotherapy for the broad masses. Should this claim prove correct, then our book may be a contribution to the building up of a systematic psychotherapy that might be taught to students at teaching hospitals.

The scope of this book has by intention been restricted to psychotherapy and psychodiagnosis by medical practitioners. This does not mean that we have disregarded experiences in other fields of medicine or psychotherapy, but only that we have concentrated our attention on the limited field chosen for this book. Before discussing why we adopted this policy, we think that we ought to defend ourselves against a possible charge of professional jealousy or prejudice. One of us (E.B.), though a psycho-analyst, has had wide experience in social casework and is still active in that field; the other (M.B.) has always stood out for equal status in psycho-analysis for medical and non-medical analysts and was for many years actively engaged in training social workers for psychotherapy.

The principal reason for our choice of this limited field was that for the last few years we have been extensively engaged in a joint study of psychotherapy by non-psychiatrists in the framework of the training-cum-research seminars for general practitioners and specialists at the Tavistock Clinic. Although our chief aim with both specialists and general practitioners has been to awaken in them an awareness and understanding of the psychological and emotional factors active in their patients' illnesses and thus, so to speak, help them to become better doctors in their own field, they were at liberty, and were even encouraged, to undertake—in selected cases—proper psychotherapy. This has always been accepted as a welcome venture, and considerable time has been spent by the seminars in discussing and evaluating in their dynamic aspects the various events occurring during psychotherapy. As mentioned, we do not intend to disregard our experiences with other non-medical professional workers but will refer to them only occasionally when we need to illustrate a special aspect of the context.

This book is, in fact, a companion volume to *The Doctor, His Patient and The Illness*, which was written by one of us (M.B.), and published in 1957. Both books are based on the training-cum-research method worked out by the two of us, the principle of which is the study of the interaction between the patient and his therapist in a group setting in which every member has full and continuing responsibility for his patients. The earlier book drew solely on experiences with general practitioners, whereas the present one uses in addition experiences with various specialists, with doctors in charge of the Family Planning Association's special clinics, and with a group of psycho-analysts engaged in a research on 'focal' therapy. The previous book aimed at demonstrating the importance for the whole of medicine and in particular for general medical practice of the doctor-patient interaction; the scope of the present one is more restricted: it deals with some technical and theoretical aspects of psychotherapeutic work by non-psychiatrists.

This book contains four largely independent parts. The first discusses the influence of the setting in which psychotherapy is carried out on the methods used, and the results obtained. Our aim is to show that psychiatrists as well as psycho-analysts are not really acquainted with the great psychotherapeutic possibilities inherent in the various forms of medical practice, and thus their contribution to these fields is often ill-founded and even misguided. On the other hand, a research undertaken jointly by psychiatrists and non-psychiatric medical practitioners is a highly promising venture.

The second part, under the title 'Some Common Problems in Psychotherapy', discusses the everyday problems that the doctor encounters, such as how he should start his psychotherapeutic venture, what he should look out for, what sort of pitfalls he ought to try to avoid and, lastly, the place of psychotherapy in medicine.

The first two parts of the book are designed to awaken interest in non-psychiatrist medical psychotherapy. We hope that psychiatrists will find in them proof that this field merits their attention, and that doctors in general, who under the pressure of their everyday experience have come to realize that many of their patients are in need of psychiatric help, will be encouraged to acquire the appropriate skills.

The third part, being more technical and more abstract, may awaken less general interest, but we hope that even the beginner may gain some insight into professional psychotherapeutic techniques and will, in this way, be encouraged to abandon the sort of psychotherapy we mentioned earlier—that which is based on a good bedside manner, common sense, and reassurance.

Our aim in writing this was to give a tentative survey of psycho-therapeutic methods which may be classified as proper professional skills and which, perhaps, could be taught in the future at our medical schools. We think that a fair amount of clinical experience in our field will be needed to understand the full implications of the problems discussed in this part but we hope that the general direction of our train of thought will not be missed.

The basis of every kind of psychotherapeutic intervention is the psychiatric interview. The fourth part of our book is an attempt at summing up the results that our research has brought to light in this particular field and at pointing out the many unsolved problems that await study and solution.

To preserve the anonymity of the patients whose case histories are used in this book, we have adopted the same method that was found useful in the previous volume. The doctors' names are not mentioned and only the masculine pronoun has been used to describe them, except in Case 2, in which the sex of the doctor was of importance in the development of the doctor-patient relationship. Although we have done our best to make the individual patients mentioned unrecognizable—by identifying them only by a symbol and by disguising whenever possible their external circumstances—all such attempts must stop at a certain point, otherwise the reported case history will differ so greatly from the original one as to amount to a falsification. In consequence, all the essential features of the case, and in particular its psychological details, had to be carefully preserved.

This unfortunately means that a patient may recognize himself, should he happen to read his case history. In order to lessen this risk only the histories of patients who were thought unlikely to read this book were chosen. In spite of all our precautions it is possible that by some ill-luck this publication may occasion inconvenience, distress, or even pain to one or another of the patients. In this event, all we can do is to express our sincere regret and give the assurance that it is highly improbable that the individual concerned will be identifiable by anyone except himself.

PART I

THE INFLUENCE OF THE SETTING

B

CHAPTER 1

Psychotherapy by Non-Psychiatrists

Psychotherapy by non-psychiatrists has become fashionable since the last war; convincing evidence for it is the yearly increasing number of books and papers on this topic. In the field of medicine most of them deal only with psychotherapy in general medical practice. In this chapter, for the sake of simplicity, we shall follow this example but we would stress that everything that we say will apply, *mutatis mutandis*, to all branches of medical practice.

Remarkably, most of these publications, whether by general practitioners or by psychiatrists, are based on a preconceived notion—half true, half untrue—that has, in our view, obstructed real progress in our field. This preconception, expressed somewhat bluntly, runs roughly as follows:

'General practitioners know but little about psychiatry and especially about psychotherapy, so they are well advised to be highly cautious; psychiatrists, on the other hand, know a good deal about both areas and it is their duty and their privilege to advise general practitioners what to do and what not to do in this field.'

This assertion is to a large extent based on over-simplification and prejudice; thus it is far from being the whole truth. Our first aim will be to disentangle truth from half-truth and then to show some of the paths which open up to both general practitioners and psychiatrists after the obstacles created by this half-true idea have been removed.

Let us start our discussion with that part of the opinion just quoted which is true. It is generally agreed that the traditional medical training does not equip the future general practitioner with adequate knowledge and skill in psychotherapy. True, in recent years more and more teaching hospitals have become aware of this situation—particularly in America, but much less so in Great Britain—and have made some attempt to remedy it; with few exceptions, however, these attempts can only be described as half-hearted or even as face-saving devices. To prove this we refer to the recent survey by the College of General Practitioners printed in the *British Medical*

3

Journal, 6th September 1958, which showed that not one of the teaching hospitals in Great Britain offered a systematic course in psychotherapy to its medical students. A further fact of ominous significance is that it was the College of General Practitioners that showed interest in this problem and carried out the survey, and not one of the psychiatric organizations.

This is more deplorable since there is a general consensus that a high proportion of the patients seen in general practice are in need of some psychotherapy. As psychiatrists simply cannot, through numerical insufficiency, undertake the enormous amount of therapeutic work needed by these patients, the general practitioner is forced to shoulder the lion's share of it. Since he did not receive adequate training in this field, the only way in which he can respond to this need is through the acquisition, by trial and error, of some simple or common-sense psychotherapeutic skill. Unfortunately this is no simple task, and the fond hope that doctors may develop some common-sense empirical psychotherapeutic technique that will then enable them to deal adequately with the psychological problems presented by their patients seldom proves to be fully justified. The use of empirical methods picked up from everyday life or established during everyday medical practice would be looked on with suspicion in any other sphere of medicine, and they should be accorded no higher status in psychotherapy. We shall return to this topic in Parts II and III.

The first part of the opinion quoted above has thus proved tolerably correct up to this point, but is its second part equally true—namely, that psychiatrists know about psychotherapy and can teach general practitioners what to do and what not to do? It is common knowledge that some psychiatrists do not like using psychotherapy, and whenever possible resort to other methods, chemical and physical, such as drugs and the various shock treatments. It is fair to assume that such psychiatrists will not know a great deal about psychotherapy. But what about the rest? Do they possess a system of psychotherapy? Are psychiatrists agreed among themselves about what to do and what not to do in any given case requiring psychotherapeutic help? There is, we fear, no general agreement on these questions.

Perhaps it may be agreed that the psychotherapeutic method that has been worked out most systematically is that of psycho-analysis; but we have to ask whether its techniques and criteria are applicable to every kind of psychotherapy, and, if applied, whether they will yield the same results as they would in a properly handled analytic situation. Though we, the authors, are psycho-analysts, we do not think so. To prove this point, let us compare the methods and

4

results of psycho-analysis proper with those of group therapy conducted on psycho-analytic lines. Anyone who has had some experience with these two methods will agree that the therapeutic results achieved by the two are utterly different, though it is rather difficult to describe exactly in what this difference consists.

Our description will seem rather crude and vague, and is far from being fully validated; it is only intended to give some idea as to the directions in which these differences may be found. Perhaps one might be justified in saying that after a successful psycho-analytic treatment a patient is *definitely less neurotic (or psychotic) but perhaps not necessarily really mature*; on the other hand, after a successful treatment by group methods the patient is *not necessarily less neurotic but inevitably more mature*.

The reasons for these differences lie in the differing therapeutic settings in which the patient's problems are approached. During psycho-analysis the patient receives full and undivided attention in a very close and intense two-person relationship. The whole situation is centred continuously on him, every attention, every interest, is focused on him and his problems; nothing matters except what concerns him. This initiates in the patient powerful regressive tendencies, both in his relationships to objects and in his instinctual strivings. These regressive desires, emotions, urges, etc.—usually described as 'pre-genital transference'—constitute a highly important part of the material that is worked through during analytic treatment. This pre-genital (regressive) transference—as correctly expressed by the term itself—is an important factor in determining the patient's relationship to his analyst, although its intensity diminishes towards the end of the treatment when, as a rule, it gives way to a more mature relationship. Ideally, this latter should be free from any regressive elements, since the patient is supposed to have worked through his transference before finishing his treatment. This, however, is an extrinsic factor to the analytic treatment; intrinsically the analytic situation does not depend on the patient's maturity.

In the group therapy setting, during the whole of the therapeutic venture, every patient must accustom himself to the idea of fair shares, which is anything but easy. Any one patient gets some, but not all, of the attention; he must share it with his fellow members in roughly similar proportions. As the other members of the group are inevitably always present and their interests must also be taken into account all the time, there is much less possibility of developing a primitive two-person relationship between the therapist and the patient. The group as a whole may regress in their behaviour towards the therapist, but the individual patient cannot but progress towards accepting other people as his equals. Moreover, and this is a highly important point too, all the time the patient must witness other people's frustration and misery, suffering and distress, and cannot merely be engrossed in his own. This goes even further, because accepting other people's claims for help and actually helping them with their problems is part and parcel of the general atmosphere of the group situation, and every patient soon learns that his own progress is linked with that of his 'neighbours' in the group. All this is a most startling experience and under its influence, instead of regressing, the patient progresses towards maturity, at any rate in so far as he is sincerely concerned about other people's needs and suffering.

Of course, psycho-analysis proper, on the one hand, and psycho-analytically oriented group therapy, on the other, are based on the same kind of theoretical foundations, and the therapist understands and even interprets the material produced in much the same way. To quote one example instead of many: he refrains from giving advice, reassurance, or directives in both forms of treatment for the same reasons, and in their place interprets the wish for them in terms of, say, the Oedipus conflict or of still more primitive relationships. In spite of this the results are definitely different. If this difference and the explanation just suggested are accepted as valid, a number of important conclusions are inevitable. Some of them are simple and plausible; nevertheless, we think they ought to be stated explicitly.

It appears that various psychotherapies initiate different therapeutic processes in the patient, and in consequence most probably affect different parts, or layers, of the mind. One of us has discussed this topic in a separate paper,[1] so a brief reference will suffice here. Moreover, though the clinical differences observed as reactions to the various forms of psychotherapy are undoubtedly determined, on the one hand, by the patient's personality and illness and, on the other, by the therapist's skill, knowledge, and personality, these are not all that matters. *The setting in which the psychotherapy is carried out appears to have an important bearing on the therapeutic processes and the therapeutic results.*

We all know that the psychotherapist must vary his techniques according to his patient's age, illness, and personality. These variations are openly and amply discussed in the various textbooks and publications in psycho-analysis and psychotherapy. We know also that therapeutic techniques vary to some extent, and even widely, with the therapist's personality. This factor has received more and more attention in recent years, usually under the heading of 'counter-

[1] M. Balint (1958). 'The Three Areas of the Mind'. *Int. J. Psycho-Anal.* **39**, Part V.

transference' or 'the use of counter-transference in psychotherapy'. What we propose here is something different: that is, *the influence of the setting*, in which the psychotherapy is carried out, on the techniques used and the results that may be achieved.

In the last ten years we have been—fully or partly—responsible for various research projects in the Tavistock Clinic in which several of these settings have been studied. Perhaps the most important among them is the setting within general practice, in which the psychotherapy is carried out by the family doctor.[1] Another setting is that of the Family Discussion Bureau,[2] in which specially trained social workers try to help people with marital problems. Recently we started a research group studying the psychotherapeutic techniques of specialists, mainly non-psychiatric. In yet another project we are examining the techniques used and the results achieved when analysts accept patients for a therapy planned with limited aims, that is, cases in which for some reason or other right at the outset the therapeutic aims and/or the time available for achieving them have to be limited.[3] Another setting under study is that in the special clinics of the Family Planning Association. Here doctors with considerable experience in gynaecology and contraceptive techniques endeavour to help their women patients to achieve a better adjustment in their married lives. And lastly, there are the two mainstays of our therapeutic potential, namely, psycho-analysis proper and group therapy on psycho-analytic lines.

None of these projects is yet concluded. Still, we have established some facts which highlight the different potentialities of the various settings. Thus, this part of our book should be taken as a progress report on a comparative study of the various forms of psychotherapies included in our studies, i.e. on the differences inherent in, and inseparable from, their various settings.

Let us start with the difference between psychotherapy in general practice and psycho-analysis. The psycho-analyst undertakes the treatment of a patient for a limited period only. This period may be very long, lasting for several years, none the less it is always limited. That is, if at all possible, there should be no contact between the therapist and the patient either before or after the treatment. We know only too well how difficult conditions may become—for instance during analytic training—when the relationship does not end with the termination of the analysis proper. So in an ideal case

[1] cf. M. Balint (1957). *The Doctor, His Patient and The Illness.*

[2] A preliminary report on this scheme was published by the staff of the Bureau (1955). *Social Casework in Marital Problems.* London: Tavistock Publications.

[3] An interim report on this project—on 'focal therapy'—is being prepared by the research team.

it is desirable that, after the successful conclusion of the therapy, analyst and patient part for good.

The whole atmosphere is utterly different in general practice.[1] There, usually, the doctor has for quite a time known not only the patient, but also a number of his relatives, in some cases even for several generations. After a successful psychotherapy doctor and patient do not part but revert to the former relationship between them. In fact to part for good would be a loss to both, as the essence of general practice is the continuing relationship binding together the doctor and his clientele. The more they know about each other, the better the prospects will be of a mutually satisfactory relationship in health and in illness.

Psychiatrists and psycho-analysts know but little about the therapeutic possibilities and the professional hazards of this on-going relationship, as their everyday experience does not extend to this field. Moreover, a general practitioner sees his patients in all sorts of circumstances, in his surgery,[2] at the patient's home, in the street, at a neighbour's house; may meet him at the local church, pub, cinema, or in some other social setting; sees him dressed, half-dressed, and completely undressed; examines the various parts of the patient's body and is even allowed to inspect and to touch the parts not usually exposed for inspection. It is certain that this intimate contact has highly important psychological implications and therapeutic potentialities, but psychiatrists in general, and certainly psycho-analysts, have practically no experience with these important dynamic factors.

Further, should any trouble arise between a psycho-analyst and his patient, as a rule it is inadvisable for the analyst to get in touch with any relative or friend in order to try to overcome the difficulty in an indirect way. What may be done only in highly exceptional circumstances by the psycho-analyst is a matter of course in general practice. The doctor not only knows the patient's nearest relatives, friends, and neighbours, but constantly and openly keeps up a very intimate relationship with them and uses the opportunities thereby provided—again openly and admittedly—both to get information about his patient and to help him through these indirect ways. In our research seminars we have studied numerous cases in which this could be, or even had to be, done to the great benefit of the patient in difficulty.

Now, let us turn away from the psycho-analyst in his somewhat esoteric and secluded atmosphere to the psychiatrist and the other

[1] *The Doctor, His Patient and The Illness*, Chapters XIII and XVIII.
[2] 'Office' in America.

specialists. The difference in psychological climate between the general practitioner's and the specialist's practice appears to be equally great. The specialist sees the patient for a still more limited period than the psycho-analyst. This period in the case of a non-psychiatric consultant rarely amounts to more than one, or at most a few, interviews; consequently, should he intend to influence his patient psychotherapeutically he must find methods of a highly concentrated type that enable him to do so during this short contact—the only time available to him. His relationship to his patient is spectacular, highly intense—but transient. Compared with this, the general practitioner's relationship to his patient is everyday, friendly, and above all lasting.

Psychiatric specialists come somewhere between these two extremes. They may act in the same way as other consultants do, seeing the patient only for a short diagnostic period, or they may adopt a kind of intermediate role, accepting the patient for some length of psycho-therapeutic treatment. Both of these happen in practice, but, whatever the form may be, their relationship to the patient is never as lasting as the general practitioner's.

Now looking back on the whole field from this angle, one may say that the general practitioner, of all types of doctor, has the most strings to his bow. He occupies the safest position and may take considered risks with his patients—risks which would be inadvisable, or even rash, for any of his specialist colleagues. If he is a good doctor, true to his calling, his relationship to his patient is strong and many-sided enough to overcome a host of difficulties.

Let us suppose he makes a mistake. The patient may perhaps stay away for some time, but sooner or later he will probably come back either because his supply of medicine has run out, or because he has got some slight malaise, e.g. a cold, or in order to consult the doctor about his child, his wife, or even his grandfather. Even if the patient himself refuses to see him for some time, the doctor may continue the treatment, for instance, when seeing the wife for ante-natal examinations or while inoculating one of the children. If need be, the doctor may even drop in casually at the patient's house after visiting one of the neighbours in the same street.

No such possibilities exist for the specialist, or for the psycho-analyst. If their relationship with the patient has been broken off, whether by the patient or through their own mistakes, they can hardly do anything but wait—and hope.

To put the same idea in another way, one may say that the general practitioner is a part of the patient's real life. The patient meets him in the street; he knows where the doctor's wife shops, how many children he has, whether he smokes a pipe, is a teetotaller, and so on. A specialist, on the other hand, and especially a psycho-analyst, belongs to an utterly different world and, as a rule, great care is taken to keep the two worlds apart. Doubtless the specialist is always an important stranger, a V.I.P., and the relationship between patient and specialist is seldom real—it belongs much more to the world of fantasies. This is an important difference and explains, perhaps, why at times specialists can achieve results which strike the general practitioner as almost miraculous; but also—and conversely—why general practitioners can manage situations that no specialist would even attempt. Details of both types of case will be discussed in Chapters 2 and 3.

Thus, the claim, quoted at the beginning of this chapter, that psychiatrists know a great deal about psychotherapy and can teach general practitioners how to do it appears somewhat ill-founded or, at any rate, grossly exaggerated. The two techniques appear to differ considerably; and if a psychiatrist or a psycho-analyst were to try to impart to a general practitioner his technique, however well proved in his own practice, he would create mainly havoc.

On the other hand, there undoubtedly exist a number of identical technical problems in the various forms of psychotherapy. These problems, one may assume, are better known to the professional psychotherapist, foremost among them to the psycho-analyst, than to the general practitioner or to the non-psychiatric specialist. These identical problems will be discussed in Parts II and III of this book. We hope that in this way our book will faithfully reflect the spirit of our research work; one part describing what we—psycho-analysts and psychiatrists—have learnt from our colleagues, and the other what they have been able to learn from us.

CHAPTER 2

The Setting in General Practice

A systematic study of the specific psychological characteristics of general medical practice is not a simple task, largely because of its versatility, to which reference was made in the previous chapter. By comparison, the setting within which the specialist works is fairly constant, while that of the psycho-analyst may safely be called standardized. We expect that some of our analyst colleagues will find this statement unacceptable and will cite the immense variations often occurring during one analytic session. We certainly have not overlooked this fact, nor do we wish to minimize its importance; our contention, however, is that the *setting* in which the variations occur is fairly standardized and one important task of analytic technique is to keep the setting constant, whereas non-analytic doctors—foremost among them general practitioners—have to accept immensely varying conditions for their therapeutic work. In the next chapter we shall to some extent discuss the specialist's world.

Although we have now for more than ten years studied the 'psychological problems in general practice'—as our seminars have been styled in the medical press—we are still far from claiming a systematic knowledge of this field. Thus, instead of a systematic survey we shall pick out only two aspects of general practice which, in our view, differentiate it from the other branches of medicine. To have a safe foundation we shall base all our conclusions on concrete clinical material.

The two aspects to be discussed are: (*a*) what may happen if a doctor is able to maintain a steady relationship with his patient in spite of the highly variable settings to which he has to adapt himself; and (*b*) what changes may occur in an on-going treatment, changes which both doctor and patient think are caused either by illness or by the patient's personality, but which in fact are brought about by variations in the setting.

The first, the simpler of the two cases to be reported, will show what a general practitioner was able to do through an on-going psycho-

11

therapeutic relationship with the patient, and where and why his equally experienced colleague not interested in psychological problems came to a halt with the same patient. Our second case is more complicated. There on one occasion the doctor could make full use of her opportunities and help the patient considerably towards regaining his equilibrium, whereas on a subsequent occasion she failed to do so because she failed to understand the meaning of the patient's symptoms. This latter occasion will be an instructive example because its discussion in our seminar brought to light the variations in the doctor's personal involvement which unintentionally, but fundamentally, changed the setting and hindered her from using the opportunities offered to her.

CASE 1

Our first story, Case 1,[1] started more than nine years ago in February 1952, when Dr. M. decided to offer psychotherapy to Mrs. Q., aged twenty-three. Her presenting symptoms were attacks of trembling, pains in the right lower abdomen, alarming feelings of having appendicitis, obsessional thoughts about the dangers of the impending operation, fear of death and, above all, of pain, as well as other minor symptoms. Till late puberty she was a bed-wetter and a nail-biter. She spoke without embarrassment about her masturbation which had been going on ever since she could remember. She was, in fact, an immature woman; true, she got married, but after a very short period had to return with her husband to her mother's home, surrendering the whole running of her life to her mother to the extent of agreeing that her husband should pay the weekly household money to her mother who then gave Mrs. Q. 5s. a week pocket money.

After about two months she broke off treatment, saying she was much better, although the doctor was dissatisfied with the results. In the autumn she returned, and as Dr. M. was uncertain what his next step should be, in September 1952 he referred her to the Tavistock Clinic for a psychiatric assessment. As is customary in our research, she was seen independently by a psychologist and a psychiatrist who then reported their findings to the seminar. The case is of additional interest in that it is among the few instances in which the psychologist and the psychiatrist disagreed. On the basis of the Object Relations Test, the psychologist found no coherent personality, hardly any existing controls over her primitive urges, very poor contact with

[1] For further details see Case 21 in *The Doctor, His Patient and The Illness.*

reality, and very little capacity for change; according to him the prognosis was poor. We were so puzzled that we asked another psychologist to do a second projective test, this time a Rorschach; but the second test agreed completely with the first. In spite of these ominous findings the psychiatrist remained firm in his opinion, namely, that Mrs. Q. could be considerably helped by psychotherapy. In his opinion the difficulty was the woman's extreme fear of pain; pressing treatment upon her would mean exposing her to pain and she almost certainly would respond to this threat by interrupting the treatment. It was thought that the only way to get her co-operation was to put this problem frankly and repeatedly to her, patiently showing her that nothing could be done unless she asked for help. It should be noted in passing that this condition is more easily fulfilled by a general practitioner than by a consultant with his more rigid time-table. After all, a general practitioner is always available; always on tap, so to speak, whenever he is needed.

Dr. M. accepted these conditions and we heard very soon that an external event had come to his aid. Mrs. Q's maternal grandmother had suddenly died, which meant that the grandfather who was without support had to come to live in the mother's house, which in turn meant that Mrs. Q. had to leave and find a home for herself. Our expectations proved to be correct, and Mrs. Q. asked for help early in 1953.

The treatment was of course rather stormy, with many highly tense critical periods. Apart from her fear of pain the chief problems worked through were her uncommonly strong attachment to her mother and her intense jealousy of, and rivalry with, her sister and sister-in-law. By Christmas 1953 Mrs. Q. had matured considerably, was capable of going out to work, and early in 1954 she became pregnant. This was an enormous event as before the treatment the idea of babies and especially labour-pains was terrifying for her.

Psychotherapy was allowed gradually to fade out but the doctor-patient relationship remained fairly strong. Mrs. Q. insisted that Dr. M. should do the usual ante-natal examinations and also that he should help her at the delivery. Characteristically the delivery had to be arranged in the mother's house, not in Mrs. Q's. According to Dr. M. the delivery was one of the easiest he had seen for years; Mrs. Q. was co-operative, wanted to see the baby at once, and had done all the caring and planning for her baby in a truly maternal way.

Before going any further with our story we should call attention to two points. One concerns the many ways in which Dr. M. was able to be of help to his patient. He was her ordinary family doctor to whom she could come and complain about her abdominal pains; he examined her and diagnosed the pains correctly as functional. Then he turned into a psychotherapist and, in spite of considerable difficulties, did a good piece of work. After he finished this task he reverted to the role of family doctor, carried out the ante-natal examinations, and then ended as an obstetrician, being present when his patient was facing her greatest test, the pains of childbirth. This, however, is not everything. Dr. M. did not finish his job after delivering the baby, as an obstetrician would, but has remained till today not only the doctor but also the trusted friend of the whole family. We must stress most emphatically that to function in all these roles is absolutely impossible for any specialist. This versatility is, and will always remain, the characteristic of the general practitioner. Moreover, it is unquestionable that Dr. M. was considerably helped both in his psychotherapeutic venture and in his function as an obstetrician by his experiences and contacts with his patient in his other roles, and vice versa. Thus everything can be said for not only retaining these functions for the general practitioner, but if possible enlarging and extending them so that he should be able to perform minor, and at times even major, psychotherapeutic 'operations' in the course of his practice.

The other point is equally important. Being a general practitioner Dr. M. was always available without any formality whenever he was needed. The patient could come and go practically as she wanted or as prompted by her instinctual or neurotic impulses; but whenever she returned she found her doctor—the *same* doctor, we wish to stress —there waiting for her. In fact we know from Dr. M's reports that at least three times during the psychotherapy the patient emphatically broke off the treatment. Though all this annoyed and irritated the doctor, he could take it in his stride because his setting lent itself to this kind of work. This would, of course, be much more difficult for a consultant working to a rigid time-table. This rigidity would impose, both on him and on his patient, limitations that almost certainly would have disrupted the treatment.

In 1958 we were carrying out with a group of doctors a long-term follow-up of all the cases reported at our seminars in 1952, 53, and 54. Of course, Mrs. Q. came up for discussion and Dr. M. reported as follows:

You remember, the psychologist said, 'to penetrate the defences would be dangerous; far better to leave her as she is'. In spite of it we went very far and deep. She was frigid and afraid of having

14

babies. Her frigidity was greatly relieved and she had a baby. She is a bit of a slut, her place is always dirty and the baby is always dirty, and she is not particularly clean either; still, she has been coping quite well. I see her from time to time. Earlier this year she had pains in the breast; I found a little nodule in one of them and had it taken out. She is now twenty-eight. Recently my partner was called to see her on my day off and reported that she had flu.

A few days later we were called again and I went this time. She was lying in bed and said she never had flu; only when she tried to get up she could not walk. Eva, her sister, had had a peculiar illness—when she walked her legs suddenly collapsed under her. I sent Eva to a psychiatrist and then mother came and said, 'Eva is all right now; a wonderful man, the psychiatrist'. Mrs. Q. said to me, 'You know, it's the same with me as it is with Eva, my legs just give way.' We discussed her relationship to her sister and sister-in-law, and the old sibling rivalry. She then said, 'That's really what it is. It's my sister and sister-in-law being preferred by mother. Mother gives Ivy (sister-in-law) money because she cannot manage, and she doesn't give me a penny. She buys a frock for Ivy's baby, but not for mine.' She went on complaining bitterly about it. After we discussed it she said she felt much better now, got out of bed and walked. I said, 'Let's finish it, let's have one more chat'. A few days later she came for fifteen minutes. We discussed the sibling business, and for the first time she started to cry. She knows I am there, and she goes home and manages, and when she needs me she comes. She knows that whenever she has an organic illness she can diagnose it extremely well, but she cannot get to the cause of a psychological trouble; she needs me to help her to see what it's about, and then she is all right again.

We should add that we know Dr. M's partner to be a really good, conscientious, and painstaking doctor; still, he was of absolutely no help to Mrs. Q., although we are quite certain he made all the necessary examinations and prescribed the proper treatment for the illness he found—but he could not find the real illness. On the other hand, Dr. M. did not need to do any examinations. He just saw the patient and the two together took up the threads where they dropped them a few months, or perhaps a few years, before. Two short interviews, one in the patient's house and the other in the doctor's surgery, were enough to re-establish the balance and, as Dr. M. says, the patient can now carry on.

This follow-up shows again how important it is that in general practice the doctor-patient relationship should be stable and lasting. A new doctor, even though he might be as good a therapist as, or even better than, Dr. M., could not have achieved so much in so short a time and so easily, both for himself and the patient.

CASE 2

Our second story[1] is still longer. It started in 1949, when Mr. V., aged twenty-six, consulted the Psychiatric Department of a famous Teaching Hospital in London, complaining of anxiety states, especially in crowded places, of being afraid of being hurt, having bad dreams, disturbed sleep, sweats, and tremors.

He was called up during the war in 1942, was sent to the Middle East, and was captured there by the Germans. He had several bad experiences while in camp; after release he returned home, married in 1946, and had a daughter in 1947. His condition, however, deteriorated and he asked for help from the hospital. He was then referred to a Neurosis Centre in which he spent four months, was treated by abreaction, and on discharge the final diagnosis was 'anxiety state in an hysterical personality', and the prognosis, 'good for the present anxiety state, poor for the basic inadequacy'.

Since his discharge early in 1950 he has been seen on and off by the psychiatrist at the hospital, who did not, however, do very much except keep him going with sedatives.

In the spring of 1953, more than three years, that is, after his discharge, his wife complained to their doctor, Dr. H. (a woman), that her husband was moody, depressed, had pains all over his body, became often violent, and threw things at her. The wife was desperate to the extent that she was thinking of separation. Subsequently Dr. H. saw the husband and treatment started. This too was a very stormy affair, as could be expected after the diagnosis at the hospital and Neurosis Centre. It lasted for about a year. The work centred upon two main topics; one was the patient's compulsion to stand up against father figures, especially in order to protect his younger siblings—that is his subordinates—against unfair treatment; in his endeavour he often accepted the blame for things he had not done, and this usually led to a severe anxiety attack, amounting almost to a breakdown. The other topic was his compelling need to protect weak and ill-treated women, that is his mother, and to do everything in his power to satisfy them. His choice of profession was also determined by his problems: he became, like his father, a painter and

---

[1] For further details see Case 22 in *The Doctor, His Patient and The Illness*.

16

interior decorator in constant rivalry with him; symbolically what he did in his profession was making houses and rooms—i.e. his mother— better and more attractive.

In early November 1955, Dr. H. reported that Mr. V. was apparently all right. He had been working for more than a year as a foreman for a big firm of decorators, could keep up his job, and had not been off work at all. Occasionally, about once in three months or so, he came to the doctor with minor complaints; instead of giving him a prescription the doctor had a talk with him, which seemed to be enough. His wife was pregnant again; this was a planned pregnancy, and even his daughter, who had been enuretic when Mr. V's treatment started, was now giving no trouble.

A few weeks later, however, he again had to take the blame for something he had not done, became frightened, and gave up his job. This happened just before Christmas and he spent a most miserable holiday. After a severe struggle with himself he rang up the manager of his firm and asked to be taken back; to this the firm willingly assented. After he had rejoined his old firm he asked Dr. H. for an interview. When asked why he did not come earlier during the time of the upheaval, he answered, 'I didn't want to disappoint you'. Dr. H. could then show him again, as she had before, that he was transferring emotions which belonged to his childhood's conflicts with his father on to the manager of the firm, and at the same time using her as a representative of his mother. He came the following week to report that everything was all right now, after which the doctor did not see him for three months. Then in April 1956 he 'phoned up happily reporting that they had a baby; he added that he considered himself a very lucky man.

When our long-term follow-up research reached Mr. V's case in February 1958, Dr. H. reported as follows:

Mr. V. is amazingly well. He used to work as painter and decorator with a large firm; he met a man there; they left and started a business of their own at the beginning of 1957. He hardly ever comes to see me; nothing wrong with him. His wife told me he now employs other people, has a lot to do, and is well established. His wife is expecting their third child in March and they have moved to a bigger flat, which is very nicely furnished. Three months ago, in November 1957, he came with his wife complaining about her mother, who has recently moved to our district and who is severely disturbed with hysterical symptoms. They asked me to tell the mother that something was wrong with her, give a name to her complaints, and that would please her. I used the opportunity to have a chat with them about hysteria and I explained that what they suggested would not help. Since then I have not seen him.

Then Dr. H. added:

One thing is significant. Somehow the whole family is breaking away from me. Whenever there is anything wrong with the children they 'phone our partner at his home, and not at the practice which is in our house. True, Mrs. V. has been under our partner because he is a gynaecologist and she attended his ante-natal clinic. Now if there is anything wrong she calls him at his private address. So I am cut out.

The seminar has studied several similar cases when a patient or a whole family change, without any apparent reason, from one partner to the other in the practice. In every case studied we have found that the cause of the change was—without exception—some considerable, but not openly recognized, strain between patient and doctor. It is never an easy task to discover the extent and origin of these strains since the doctor himself is, as a rule, unaware of their existence; he is only conscious of their consequence, the *fait accompli* of the change. In this case, too, when the seminar asked about possible causes of the change, at first Dr. H. was rather puzzled and could not remember any. On the contrary, she told us that everything seemed to be going smoothly; no relapses like that at Christmas 1955. Moreover, though Mr. V's partner is a bossy kind of man, they are on excellent terms and work well together. In fact Mr. V. has far surpassed his father, who could never become an independent tradesman, which, in view of Mr. V's previous history, must be considered as an important improvement.

Still, we persisted, something must have taken place in the last few months, unrecognized by Dr. H., which had led to strains, and in consequence to a change of doctors. In fact, what we asked for was that Dr. H. should go over the events of the recent past and examine them honestly with new critical insight. After some pressing Dr. H. admitted that about six months ago, in summer 1957, soon after he started his own independent business and when his wife became pregnant, Mr. V. was apparently upset and 'phoned up Dr. H's partner privately and said he wanted to see that doctor because he did not feel well and Dr. H. would not give him any medicine. He was given an appointment but did not keep it; instead he turned up a week later to see Dr. H. He was somewhat depressed but one or two interviews helped him over it.

18

All of us were rather puzzled by this report and we pressed for further information. First, Dr. H. thought that the reason why Mr. V. tried to avoid her might have been his wife, who possibly resented her husband's intimate relationship with another woman. Then Dr. H. recalled that this last incident agreed with Mr. V's usual pattern; he showed some aggressiveness in rejecting her and wanting to consult the other doctor, but had to change his mind and eventually came and saw her.

During the interviews at that time the chief topic dealt with was Mr. V's preoccupation with his wife's wish to have the baby at home; that would mean that he would have to witness his wife's labour pains which in a way were caused by him. We also reminded ourselves that Mr. V. was an interior decorator and could not tolerate any mess inside a home, that is, a woman. The interviews ended by Mr. V. reporting to the doctor that he had consented to his wife having the baby at home on the condition that during that time he could go and live at his mother-in-law's. In fact, what he wanted was Dr. H's consent to this arrangement, and this was really the last intimate talk she had with him.

We were duly impressed by the intensity of his fear of his own aggressive emotions; whenever he was made to face their consequences he had to either run away or break down. Dr. H. added here that intentionally she did not interpret this to her patient at the time because she did not want to start another intense period of psychotherapy, that is, she had deliberately changed to an ordinary family doctor. By this, however, she changed the setting in which the treatment was carried out, though she did not realize the importance of what she did. A timetable of the relevant events will enable readers to follow more easily the discussion of this, somewhat complicated, case history:

1923   Born
1946   Married
1947   Daughter born
1949   Attended hospital as out-patient
Early 1950   In-patient in Neurosis Centre
1953-4   Intensive treatment. Dr. H. married and had a child.
Nov. 1955   Follow-up: few minor complaints; wife pregnant again, planned; daughter's enuresis cured.
Dec. 1955   Panic attack, flight from work.
Jan. 1956   Resumed work, further help from Dr. H.
April 1956   Second child born, 'a lucky man'.
Early 1957   Started own business. Decorated Dr. H's *new* house.

19

Summer 1957   Beginning of unplanned (third) pregnancy. Attempted to consult Dr. H's partner but eventually saw Dr. H. herself. Mr. V. decorated Dr. H's *partner's* house, Dr. H's *old* house.

Nov. 1957   Consulted Dr. H. about mother-in-law

March 1958   Third child born

During the years 1953-4, i.e. the period of intensive psychotherapy, the setting was structured to make an intimate doctor-patient-relationship possible. After the termination of the psychotherapy this intense two-person relationship was relaxed; when, however, Mr. V. encountered difficulties—as at Christmas 1955—he could turn to his doctor who was willing to revive the relationship at the same level of intensity as during the psychotherapy. After that Dr. H. withdrew from this kind of work, which meant that some aspects of their relationship, mainly those accompanied by deep and intense emotions, were overlooked or ignored by the doctor and certainly not understood by the patient. These are the inevitable implications of what Dr. H. described as the 'different level'. A list of problems faces us here. Was the introduction of the 'different level' good therapy? What prompted Dr. H. to introduce it? How far was the change in Mr. V's attitude a direct consequence of the 'different level' and how far was it brought about by his illness or his personality?

In our effort at our seminar to assess the situation we had to go over the whole ground again. Dr. H. reminded us that her practice had developed considerably since 1953; in addition she had a young baby, and in consequence she could give much less time, and perhaps much less libido, to her patients. Then we learned that Mr. V's last baby was the result of a slip-up in birth control, and that the culprit was his wife; Mr. V. was, so to speak, forced to accept the baby. We had known from the original case history that it was during the period of intensive psychotherapy that Dr. H. got married and became pregnant—almost certainly also against Mr. V's wishes. Moreover, Mr. V's treatment belonged to the period when our whole group of doctors went through a time of enthusiastic psychotherapy. Several of the participants had remarkable successes, Mr. V's case being one; and all the doctors agreed that now they were somewhat reluctant to reconsider the situation if one of their great successes came asking for further help. After all, if the doctor improves on his success, then his original success was not perhaps so great. Reluctantly we came to the conclusion that the ideal general practitioner would be one who is always willing to improve on his success, for whom no case is ever closed—but also that this is demanding rather a lot.

Further details then emerged. When Mr. V. started his independent firm, his first considerable commission was to decorate Dr. H's new house, to which she moved with husband and baby after the job was finished. Here again we find one of Mr. V's automatic patterns. After all, a house is symbolically a woman and what he did was to help Dr. H. to become more attractive, more comfortable. The dates are also interesting. Mr. V's second child was born in April 1956, he left his old firm ultimately early in 1957, started to decorate Dr. H's house in April 1957, certainly needing a few weeks to finish it, and the slip-up in birth control must have happened in June or July the same year. We learned also that there had been some friction between Dr. H's husband and Mr. V. about the job and Dr. H. had some difficulty in keeping the peace between them.

Thus, three incidents emerged after a re-examination of the doctor-patient relationship during the past two years. The first in January 1956, a few months before the birth of Mr. V's second child, when Dr. H. was able to continue her work and helped Mr. V. to readjust himself. The second in the summer of 1957 after his wife had become pregnant for the third time, when an interview was first sought with Dr. H's partner and a 'different level' of work was introduced. The third in November 1957 when Mr. V. came with his wife to consult Dr. H. about his mother-in-law; the patient and his doctor were not able to make any real contact and in consequence they could not recognize the patient's underlying needs.

On the first occasion Dr. H's treatment was unobjectionable. Without any hesitation she continued the therapeutic work and helped Mr. V. considerably to preserve his health. On the second occasion the situation changed somewhat; although some work was done, Dr. H. was rather unwilling to get involved again in a thera-peutic relationship—the different level. On the third occasion either she could not or was not willing to assess the situation properly and consequently no therapeutic work was possible. Admittedly the situation was much more complicated, especially by the presence of Mr. V's wife; it is by no means easy to point out what Dr. H. could have done in these circumstances in order to re-establish the thera-peutic relationship with Mr. V. This, however, is a technical problem. The main problem that faced us at the seminar was that on that occasion Dr. H. did not come to a proper evaluation of the patient's needs.

When we reached this point, Dr. H. with her customary frankness admitted that she simply did not realize that the mother-in-law should have been considered as a presenting symptom of Mr. V's

21

own condition.[1] She said, 'I must confess I only see it now that we are talking about it. When he came, I was really pleased because I knew recently they used to see my partner.' Then a pause followed and after overcoming some resistance she told us that about six months before this visit Mr. V. decorated Dr. H's partner's house, which in fact was Dr. H's old house, in which the treatment was carried out in 1953-4. She realized now that this must have been a disturbing experience to Mr. V. as he had to decorate the very room which was her surgery during the intensive period of his treatment.

The inference is that Dr. H. was able to give proper assistance to her patient as long as her own involvement was within limits acceptable to her. When her life changed and she felt that her patient might need more than she could afford to give without strain, she withdrew slightly; that happened at the second visit in the summer of 1957. Eventually she became an average general practitioner who just gave sound advice or some superficial understanding, as happened during Mr. V's last visit.

Now let us return to our thesis that the setting in which a general practitioner does his psychotherapeutic work is so different from that of a psychiatrist or a psycho-analyst that a wholesale transfer of their methods is unjustifiable. The two cases quoted amply prove that the setting in which the general practitioner works is incomparably more variable than that of any of his colleagues.

Taking Mrs. Q's case, it is highly unlikely that any doctor but a general practitioner would be called upon to act in so many and such diversified roles as Dr. M. did. Similarly it occurs but rarely that a patient brings his wife to his analytic session in order to discuss what to do with his troublesome mother-in-law; moreover, if he did so, his analyst would consider it as an 'acting-out' episode, would speedily get rid of the intruder, and continue the analytic work.

In general practice, as a rule, the patient's wife is not an intruder, but also a patient with equal rights, who cannot and must not be got rid of but must be treated with equal attention and application. Thus if husband and wife consult a doctor about what to do with a troublesome mother-in-law, as Mr. and Mrs. V. did, the doctor must consider whether this is the most important symptom that needs to be examined or whether, over and above it, other underlying problems connected either with the husband's or with the wife's previous

---

[1] This is a phrase often used in our seminars. In this case its real meaning was something like this: this time the patient presented overtly neurotic problems (i.e. of his mother-in-law's) implying that what was needed was not an ordinary general practitioner like Dr. H's partner, but someone who really understood them like Dr. H. used to do.

illnesses—or with their joint marital history—may need attention as well. This problem, who is the patient, who at this moment needs medical help most urgently, and to whom at this moment will it be profitable to offer it, has to be solved by a general practitioner several times a day; whereas we psycho-analysts, apart from a few knotty diagnostic interviews, hardly ever encounter it.

We would add that the two cases present a tiny sample of the very large collection of situations gathered during our research, which have not been studied and therefore are largely unknown to any specialist, including psychiatrists and psycho-analysts. Thus there is no justification for the unqualified claim that psychiatrists can teach general practitioners how to do psychotherapy; in its place there emerges something like an obligation, or even duty, for psychiatrists to study the specific psychotherapeutic methods determined by the nature of general practice.

On the other hand, everything can be said for a qualified claim. Psychiatrists and, in particular, psycho-analysts can contribute considerably to the understanding of *some* aspects of general practitioner psychotherapy. Thus, our first case shows convincingly the value of continuity and teaches us what this continuity means in psychological terms. There are several ways of describing it, and perhaps the one using intensity of the doctor-patient relationship as the operative term is to be preferred. Though the setting may vary—as we saw in Mrs. Q's case even considerably—and though, parallel with it, the ways may vary in which doctor and patient may express themselves, the intensity of their relationship must remain about the same. In Chapter 12, 'Variants of Psychotherapy', we shall have to formulate this thesis in more exact terms. This condition was fairly adequately honoured in the relationship between Mrs. Q. and Dr. M.

If, however, the intensity—or intimacy—of the doctor-patient relationship changes, a new factor enters the field, as happened in Mr. V's case. It is noteworthy that Dr. H. was fully aware of this change, in fact it was she who described it as the 'different level'; and yet she failed to realize how profoundly this new factor had influenced the patient. Mr. V. confidently expected that his doctor, whenever there was an emergency, would understand him in the same way, at the same intensity as during the period of intensive psychotherapy. The events around and after Christmas 1955, the successful treatment of the panic attack and the flight from work, certainly reinforced his confidence.

When, then, during the later part of 1956 and certainly in 1957, he was received, instead of with the expected degree of intensity, with the 'different level', he must have felt baffled, perhaps let down, and

23

certainly puzzled. We now understand better why he allowed his wife to steer towards Dr. H's partner, why he himself drifted in that direction, and also his curious vacillation between the two doctors in the summer of 1957. As he still did not get what he so badly needed, i.e. the 'different level' continued to prevail, he produced his troublesome mother-in-law as the presenting symptom of his own puzzled uncertainty.

This sequence of events is well known in analytic technique. If the analyst, no matter for what reason, cannot find the right answer (mostly in the form of an adequate interpretation) to the patient's communications, as a rule, the patient will be forced to produce new and more impressive 'offers', at times in the form of 'acting-out', to induce his analyst to make greater efforts. Our research into general practice showed that exactly the same happens between a patient not understood and his doctor; in certain cases the new 'offer' may even take the form of an alarming physical illness. This unexpected change in the patient's behaviour or symptomatology is almost always attributed to some extrinsic factor such as environmental changes, sudden infection, accident, the patient's well-known ingratitude, or unaccountable personality, etc.—but hardly ever to a change in the doctor-patient relationship.

It was exactly this that happened in our present case. Dr. H. thought of Mrs. V's jealousy, the naturally developing intimacy between the obstetrician and his patient, Mr. V's short-lived gratitude, etc. Of course this led to a false evaluation of the situation and thereby to a well-meant but ineffective therapeutic attitude. It was only the discussion at our seminar that opened Dr. H's eyes, but it must be pointed out that without the pressure of our systematic long-term follow-up she would not have felt the need to report about these events.

One more point. Perhaps the most instructive period in the history of an illness is the time before patient and doctor agree what the illness is about and then settle down to treat it. During the unsettled, 'unorganized', period it is not difficult to follow the various 'offers' by the patient and the corresponding 'responses' by the doctor. This interplay goes on till eventually an agreement can be reached. Mr. V. apparently had to go through a similar unsettled period in 1956 and 1957; let us hope our discussion will help Dr. H. to find an adequate answer, and that in consequence the pressure on Mr. V. will diminish, so that he will not be forced to present to his doctor a new, more impressive, illness than his mother-in-law's.

As mentioned, the lack of 'fit' between patient and doctor and its inevitable consequences were first studied in the psycho-analytic setting. This study, however, is a fairly delicate task, as the changes in the analyst's understanding are usually neither highly conspicuous nor easily demonstrable, and the changes in the patient rather complex and sophisticated. General practice offers a much easier field for this important study, because the changes in the patient, the various 'offers', are obvious, easily demonstrable, one might say spectacular. Similarly the doctor's responses are also more easily accessible than the analyst's. In addition the whole of general practice consists of nothing but—successful and unsuccessful—fits between 'offers' and 'responses', and so a study of this interplay will certainly prove rewarding.

We wish to add that in the specialist's diagnostic practice it is very difficult to get hold of these events, as the contact between patient and doctor is much too brief. On the other hand it is almost certain that this interplay at times may influence the diagnostic findings considerably and thus is well worth a searching study.

CHAPTER 3

The Specialist's Setting

Before starting out to survey the field of the specialist, we should point out that although, in principle, we could not be certain that our work with the general practitioners was able to cover all the data relevant to the doctor-patient relationship, we understood the full significance of practically every step taken by the doctors. This pretty complete understanding arose from several causes. One is occasioned by the setting of our seminars, which allows, and even demands, that every detail of the participants' work shall be meticulously scrutinized and dissected. The continuity of the doctor-patient relationship on the one hand, and of our conferences on the other, has enabled us to follow up the consequences of any one therapeutic intervention, in particular, whether it has led to the results intended or to some other results. In this way the various details of the therapeutic work as well as the whole atmosphere in which the work was carried out could be assessed fairly reliably.

The situation is utterly different in the other setting to which we are now turning—the characteristic work of the specialist-consultant. First, there is no continuity. The consultant sees his patient once, twice, or perhaps for a week; comes to an opinion; reports to his colleague, the general practitioner; and more often than not thereafter loses sight of the patient. This essentially ephemeral relationship is not changed in principle if a patient has to be admitted for a short stay—say for a few weeks—to a hospital or nursing home. The specialist will hardly ever learn what the patient felt about his diagnostic or therapeutic interventions; what long term results they achieved; or in what way they may have failed. The general practitioner learns from his patient something about these events, but his respectful relationship towards the consultant hinders rather than encourages a free discussion of the extent or limitations of the consultant's personal skill, tact, or idiosyncrasies in handling a patient. If there is a follow-up, it is carried out, as a rule, not by the consultant but by the general practitioner or by the consultant's

26

registrar or assistant, who may or may not fully understand—or agree with—the consultant's motives and therapeutic intentions, thus bringing an alien element into the doctor-patient relationship.

Another reason for the difference is the setting of our original research, which was centred upon the general practitioners. The participation of consultants in seeing patients was neither systematic nor planned; they were called in irregularly when a general practitioner felt that he needed help. This, of course, was a somewhat subjective indication; moreover it changed considerably and continuously with the development of the particular group of doctors. Furthermore, the consultant who was asked for help was either the psychiatrist-leader of the group or one of his colleagues. Though we have tried to live up to the principle that all of us are of equal status, the fact remains that the leader is the leader and the other participants are members of the group. Thus the leader's work does not receive quite the same impartial criticism that is given to the work of any of the other members: either it is respected too uncritically or subjected to a greater amount of ambivalent criticism. On the other hand, if the psychiatric interview was undertaken by one of his colleagues, the atmosphere was disturbed by the usual rivalry among parent figures. Even though we were aware of these complications, we could not altogether avoid them. All this has, therefore, to be borne in mind when we discuss the next cases. Here too we wish to report on two patients.

CASE 3

In September 1952 one doctor reported to our seminar about our Case 3, Miss I., a very attractive young woman of twenty-five, a telephonist. She had a multitude of complaints, among them a consciousness of Lesbian feelings; no overt activity, only a fear of, and a curiosity about, these matters. This situation arose at the age of twenty when she joined one of the Women's Services; a compulsion to masturbate practically every day resulted in severe struggles, guilt feelings, and fears of various illnesses, such as leprosy, tuberculosis, cancer; she also had fears of attacking her twelve years younger brother or any young boy on buses; in consequence she could hardly travel on buses, had to leave her home and went to live in a hostel. This move, however, reinforced her Lesbian urges; this then led to all sorts of depressive feelings, fear of dying, thoughts of suicide, and so on.

In March 1952 after some unsuccessful attempts at understanding his patient, the doctor referred her to a psychiatrist, who diagnosed

27

hysteria with some depression and offered her psychotherapy. Miss I. attended for a few sessions and then dropped out. Soon afterwards she returned to her doctor complaining of epigastric pains and nausea, which the doctor treated symptomatically. In September 1952 she appeared again reporting that her suicidal thoughts had become stronger; everything felt unreal, she was most depressed, was unable to get on with her work, and had been compelled to give it up. Now she cannot think that she will ever be able either to work or to enjoy anything again. As she was an attractive girl several men were interested in her. She became engaged a few times but after some months each engagement had to be broken off.

At this point—September 1952—the doctor felt that this patient was too difficult for him, that she really required expert opinion, and asked for an emergency consultation at our Clinic. As usual she was seen independently by a psychologist and a psychiatrist. The psychologist, in the same way as the doctor, found her very attractive. Although aware of the shallowness of her depression and of her need for gaining sympathy he could not help responding positively to her. In the Object Relations Test, of the thirteen stories given to the various cards, ten were depressive in character, and in the remaining three nothing whatever was allowed to happen. On the whole the parent figures of the stories were kept indistinct; where a mother figure was allowed to emerge she was seen as an idealized but powerless person, incapable of providing the love that the patient needed; father was thoroughly bad and in addition hostile to the idealized mother figure. Fantasies of destruction were fairly conspicuous in the stories, often in the form of self-destruction and annihilation. The psychologist's final diagnosis was hysteria associated with depression, the latter rather superficial, largely designed to gain sympathy, rather than indicating a danger of suicide. On the whole he considered her very ill, using various hysterical defences against deep depressive problems, having but few sources of strength in her personality.

The psychiatrist took a less sympathetic and more matter of fact line of approach. In consequence the patient broke down on several occasions during the interview, whereas in the test situation with the sympathetic psychologist she managed to keep her tears under control. During the interview Miss I. told the same stories as reported by her general practitioner and the psychiatrist was struck by the rigidity of the narrative; the patient used almost exactly the same phrases and words as contained in the doctor's report, which gave the impression that the whole thing had been carefully rehearsed and could now be repeated without feeling, almost parrot-like.

The patient's whole attitude suggested a shallow, hazy, fairy-tale-like pretence, put on in order to impress the world and to protect herself against the realization of her own true feelings, i.e. of being jealous, naughty, and catty; of having illicit sexual desires; of being unwilling to put up with real hard work, and so on. The psychiatrist tried to brush all this pretence to one side and to make her talk about her real problems, and in this he succeeded up to a point. His diagnosis agreed with that of the psychologist except for the severity of her illness. According to him there was no cause for alarm; true, Miss I. was suffering from slight hysteria with some depressive features, but the ultimate prognosis was fairly good. She either could be referred for psycho-analysis or could be treated by her general practitioner provided he was not taken in by the patient's shallow pretences.

The doctor saw her a few days after the psychiatric interview, since the patient wanted her chest x-rayed because of her fear of tuberculosis. On this occasion she complained that she had had a very unpleasant interview with the psychiatrist, who asked questions about all sorts of intimate details of her sexual life, which she strongly resented. On the whole she felt that she had been treated unsympathetically because her many impressive complaints—fear of the future, fear of dying, depression, feeling that she might attack young boys or her own brother, fear of tuberculosis and cancer—had not been taken seriously.

The doctor did not see her after this for about a year, that is till the autumn of 1953, when she reappeared complaining of a slight cough. In the meanwhile she had kept her job; in fact she had not missed a day because of illness. She volunteered that she had not thought much about her old troubles and seemed fairly well.

The next report is from February 1954; the doctor rarely saw the patient, who was cured apparently by the one interview at the Clinic; in fact, she who had earlier been away from work for more than six months had not lost a day for illness since. Moreover, she was happy and was engaged.

Our long-term follow-up research reached her case in November 1957, that is, almost exactly five years after the interview at the Clinic. The doctor reported that she was now a rather well-padded married woman who consulted him perhaps once a year about a cold, or something similar. Whenever she comes, she beams at him. He knows that she is happily married, both from the patient herself and from her sister, whom he sees more frequently. They have not had a child yet, but are now building a bungalow some distance from London and intend to start a family as soon as they have settled there. During her last visit she said to the doctor, 'Isn't it funny, all the strange thoughts one has. That's life; life has to work itself out. When I think of my peculiar funny thoughts of the past, it doesn't seem like me at all'. The doctor added, 'In fact, she has not looked back since the psychiatrist saw her'.

It is difficult to explain what caused this quite remarkable cure but it is a fact that the improvement started immediately after the psychiatric interview. Thus it is a case of consultant psychotherapy, although admittedly it was not intended to be. However, after this one interview, not only did her impressive collection of symptoms disappear, but this pretty girl, who attracted a number of boys and ran away from them as soon as they meant business, could settle down with a man, marry him, and, as in fairy tales, live happily ever after.

On every occasion that the general practitioner reported about this remarkable cure, we asked ourselves whether it would be a good idea to send her for psychiatric re-assessment. Each time after long discussion we came unanimously to the conclusion that she was better left alone. After all, she was well, happily married, intending to start a proper family life; there was no cogent reason why she should be exposed to an unnecessary risk or even merely to an unpleasant interview. On the other hand, the fact that we were so reluctant to accept this risk shows that somehow we did not feel confident that this woman's improvement was quite stable. A further important point is the change in her figure. The previously unhappy, but slim and very attractive girl became a buxom, smiling woman. Is this a normal development—a harassed girl turning into a satisfied married woman—or have we to consider it possibly as a case of overeating in order to stuff herself with good things, as many depressives do? Since, however, this happens quite often with newly married women, or for that matter with men too, should all normal marriage be considered as a defence against depression? As we cannot solve this problem, let us turn now to our next case; also a seemingly miraculous consultant psychotherapy.

CASE 4

In October 1953 one of our doctors mentioned a puzzling case. The patient, our Case 4, Mr. N., was thirty-four, in a responsible job, married for twelve and a half years, with a daughter of nine and a son of eight. All four of them were well known to the doctor and he thought of them as a very happy normal family. Although there had been some tension in his parental home, the father being placid and the mother domineering, Mr. N. got on well at school, was a success in the Army—in fact he became a Sergeant-Major—enjoyed all sorts of games, and still remained an active football player. He set very high standards both for himself and for everybody else, and was tidy and methodical at home and at his office. Although this caused some strain, especially in his son who had some difficulty at school, the family apparently could cope with the situation as they had been no trouble to the doctor.

Mr. N's complaint was of impotence which set in suddenly after he came back from holiday a year before. They spent the holiday, as they had done for many years, at a seaside resort, the home town of his wife, where they stayed with his wife's cousin and her husband. He enjoyed the holiday thoroughly, and could think of nothing that might have caused the trouble, except perhaps that recently he had been doing a lot of overtime. For a whole year he hesitated to come to the doctor, and even now he came only at his wife's instigation. Recently he had had a wet dream which upset him, and so accepted his wife's suggestion.

As the doctor could not make much headway with this well-defended patient he thought it would be a good idea to see the wife, and he asked her to visit him. He learned from her that the day Mr. N. went back to work after their holiday he came home very upset as he had had a row in the office with one of his subordinates. In consequence the man had to leave the office, which again upset Mr. N. considerably. As a matter of fact he disliked this junior, who reminded him of his father-in-law whom he hated because he was a scoundrel and led his family an awful life.

The doctor felt he had come to a full stop and could not see how he could get any further with this man. Although the seminar accepted that because of his excellent defences Mr. N. might be a difficult case to treat, it was pointed out that perhaps the main cause of the doctor's difficulty was his reluctance to change his favourable impression of this family. He always thought that they were a nice and happy lot of people and perhaps he was loath to recognize that things were not quite so satisfactory. The doctor promised to try again but reported a week later that he had made no progress at all; he saw the patient, who stood by his statement that everything in his married life was perfect and that there was no trouble whatever; so the doctor asked for permission to refer Mr. N. to our emergency service.

Since, through some administrative mishap, the psychological test had to be postponed, at first we had only the psychiatrist's report. On the whole it confirmed the doctor's original opinion but could

31

add a few interesting findings. First the psychiatrist emphasized the very severe rigidity of this man's obsessional character. As usual with these people, Mr. N. was sensible and co-operative so far as reality was concerned, but simply was not able to say anything about his internal emotional life. We learned that he had been rather late in his sexual development, and that he had never masturbated. When he joined the Army at the age of twenty-one he was practically ignorant of sex. He said he had never been 'keen on sex' and, as was to be expected, it took his wife more than a year to get 'proper satisfaction' in intercourse. Although very fond of each other they were embarrassed when undressing, and Mr. N. disliked knowing that his wife used contraceptives. Their sexual life brought no free, but only rather surreptitious, enjoyment; still, until the holiday they had had fairly satisfactory intercourse practically twice a week.

His impotence did not worry him very much although he admitted it was a very bad show, especially as his wife might interpret it as diminished affection for her, which was certainly untrue. It was in order to disprove this that he accepted his wife's suggestion to consult the doctor. In the past fourteen months or so he had made about six or seven attempts, about half of them proving failures.

For the past five or six years every summer they had stayed for the whole of the holiday with his wife's cousin. In 1952 there had been real tension between the cousin and her husband, which on several occasions had led to explosions. The cousin was rather cut up and had obviously fallen out with her husband. As the husband was one of his most intimate friends, Mr. N. felt very sorry for him, especially as he thought that the strain might have been aggravated by their presence. For this reason, in 1953 they had decided to spend only one week there. Another reason for this decision was that the house was rather small, and the four children, two of the N's and two of the cousin's, had to sleep in one room, which, according to Mr. N., was undesirable because of possible sexual excitement in the children. In the psychiatrist's opinion the holiday in 1952 had been actually traumatic because Mr. N. had to realize that there were homes in which rows were possible and that children might be sexually excited. Apparently this represented too great a threat to his own defences. This might explain the patient's questions at the end of the interview, when he enquired rather anxiously whether anything might be wrong with him physically or whether therapy might make his state worse.

When discussing these findings at our seminar, we were rather uncertain what to recommend for him, but the doctor reported that a few days after the psychiatric interview Mr. N. was very pleased with the attention he received at the Clinic; he felt that at long last something really had been done for him, and for him alone; he was looking forward to the test that was promised him. Although it was clear that he was rather afraid of being stirred up, in view of the doctor's report the seminar decided to proceed with the test.

He was given a Rorschach, and the gist of the report is as follows: Mr. N. has a well-defended obsessional character and until now has been able to control his aggressive impulses by rigid obsessional mechanisms. Something must have happened to him recently to upset the situation, either by stimulating his aggressiveness, especially against women, or by weakening his obsessional mechanisms. Now he was in an unbalanced state, and as a precaution was forced to create distances between himself and any woman. The psychologist did not see any danger of a psychotic breakdown, but he was rather uncertain whether Mr. N. could stand any further increase of tension, especially by psychological treatment which, in his opinion, might lead to a severe neurotic breakdown.

The seminar then went on to discuss what ought to be done in this case. Under the impact of the two reports, which had reinforced each other, our discussion was rather cautious, since all of us were afraid that any radical therapy might upset this man so much that a temporary breakdown might result. Nobody proposed that he should be taken over by the psychiatrist; some general practitioners suggested simple reassurance and some supportive therapy, whereas the most daring advised that the doctor should go on seeing Mr. N. and cautiously try to get him to speak a bit more freely. On the whole the discussion was rather subdued, desultory, almost defeatist.

We must add that both the psychologist's, and particularly the psychiatrist's, reports were not much better. Now, from a distance of several years, the psychologist's approach seems to have been orthodox but not very enterprising; the psychiatrist's definitely inhibited. There are a number of obvious cues in his report which apparently he had either failed to notice or simply disregarded. In addition, apart from this general inhibition, the psychiatrist did not try to provide any therapy. His only aim was diagnosis. Even this aim was approached in a rather indifferent way, and the achievement cannot be called outstanding. Moreover, because of the administrative mishaps already mentioned, we took rather a long time to achieve even that much. The patient was first mentioned in September 1953 and was tested only in mid-December, about three months later.

To our amazement we heard from the doctor in mid-February 1954, two months, that is, after the psychologist's interview, that Mr. N. was now a changed man. Although he had received no further psychotherapy he had apparently been given a jolt by the two

D   33

interviews, and he and his wife had had regular normal intercourse ever since and were apparently quite happy. This was surprising indeed and we did not think that the result would be lasting. Our scepticism was, however, quite unfounded. The next report came in March 1956, more than two years, that is, after the apparently miraculous cure; the doctor had not seen the husband but his wife reported that everything was fine: Mr. N. was once again his old self and their sexual relations were normal. The doctor added that he could take no credit for this change as he had not given any psychotherapy. Somehow something had happened in the interviews at the Clinic that had made all this difference.

We reached this case in our long-term follow-up research in December 1957, four years after the interviews. The doctor was still in very close contact with the family and reported that Mr. N. was doing very well indeed. There was no trouble whatsoever, the two children had developed very well, and even the boy had somewhat overcome his inhibitions and lack of confidence. The only detail that did not fit into this rosy picture was a passing depression with headaches and sleeplessness in the wife. She came complaining about these symptoms in May 1957 and asked the doctor to send her away for a week's leave. After the week she signed off and went back to work, and no further trouble was reported.

It is perhaps advisable to state at this point that we do not suggest that Mr. N's neurosis had been cured. On the contrary, his wife's passing depression must be considered as a sign of the continuing tension in this marriage. Having said that, however, the fact remains that his impotence, that had lasted for about fifteen months, was cured by a single interview and, as the follow-up shows, the cure was maintained for more than four years, and there was no indication that a relapse was imminent.

Thus these two cases—the young telephonist and Mr. N.—must be accepted as therapeutic successes, limited but irrefutable. In both cases the cure was brought about as the result apparently of a single interview. A further surprising fact is that in both cases the aim of the interviews was purely diagnostic. In Mr. N's case the psychiatrist restricted himself to obtaining sufficient information from the patient for a well-founded diagnosis; with the telephonist he was somewhat more ambitious and deliberately tried, and in fact succeeded in, breaking down her defences, but this was not done with any therapeutic aim in mind.

This is entirely different from the general practitioner's work. A general practitioner never limits his aim to diagnosis only; he is always, and above all, a therapist. In contrast, the specialist is often called upon to do no more than examine the patient and then return him with a diagnosis and some therapeutic recommendations which will be carried out by the general practitioner referring the case. In spite of this fundamental difference, as our two cases demonstrate, occasionally quite remarkable success can be achieved.

A psycho-analyst can add a few ideas, or hunches, to the explanation of these two cures. As the transference relationship is only scantily adumbrated, but not properly described, in Mr. N's interview, all one can do is to resort to some generalizations. Consultant interviews, in the same way as psychological tests, are abrupt, and therefore more likely to be traumatic than an on-going treatment usually is. The shock caused by the interview may have a therapeutic effect, especially if it occurs in a sincere and honest relationship created by the interviewer and accepted by the patient; in such circumstances the patient may have a real experience of being understood, i.e. he can see for himself that at least some of his various problems, hitherto inexplicable to him, make sense in the light that the specialist can throw on them. Stated thus briefly, this explanation may sound too simple, too rosy, perhaps even sloppy. It will come up for a more detailed discussion in Chapters 10 and 11.

In Miss I's case we are on a somewhat firmer basis, as we know something about the developments during the interview. The psychiatrist saw something of the patient's problems behind her defences, and induced her—despite her resistance—to listen to his version of her situation. Thus his work amounted to a kind of direct hit, not merely an accidental score, as happened possibly in Mr. N's case. It is rather uncertain whether this kind of technique would work in an on-going treatment. Here Miss I. was not compelled to face the consultant again and could, therefore, hate and denigrate him freely and without feeling guilty about it; in this way she could—after some time had elapsed—accept and use what the consultant had shown her without humiliation or loss of face; moreover it is highly probable that, temporarily at least, she simply forgot, or suppressed, that it was the hated consultant who gave her the new insight. If in an on-going treatment the therapist were to adopt the same technique, he would plunge his patient into a serious conflict; her hatred, originating from the pain when the new insight was forced upon her, would either tend to make her reject and destroy everything connected with the therapist or, if she were to accept the new insight as valid and beneficial, it would demand that she should fight down her indignation and bitter resentment. This difficult process—various aspects of which are described in psycho-analytic literature as working-through, acceptance of unpleasure, and acceptance of a depression—requires

35

considerable time and energy in an on-going psychotherapy. Our two cases suggest that some of it apparently may be done by the patient on his own.

A further difference is that in a diagnostic interview, as distinct from the psychotherapeutic setting, the patient is much less protected. A therapist, as a rule, weighs up carefully when he should confront his patient with a new piece of insight—how and in what dosage— all of which is called the technique of interpretation. In a diagnostic contact the patient is not 'treated' but 'examined'; the protective—or even over-protective—therapeutic atmosphere is largely absent. This may help the patient to discover that shedding some of his defences is not necessarily a delicate process, but one needing a good deal of consideration and protection; though harsh and somewhat painful, it is not necessarily disastrous.

All these explanations and many more that could be added are mere speculations, especially if one compares them with the detailed analysis in the previous chapter of the techniques used by general practitioners. One reason for this state of affairs is the fundamental difference between the inevitably diagnostic approach of the specialist and the invariably therapeutic approach of the general practitioner. There is, however, a further difference. The friendly atmosphere of our research seminars has enabled the participants to overcome their natural resistance to the disclosure of their personal contribu- tions to the therapeutic processes. Thus, these personal details, which are rarely mentioned in professional publications, were changed by our research method into proper scientific observations, on the basis of which we gained remarkable insight into the complex inter- play between doctor and patient that is called medical treatment. One might say that the doctor's surgery, with its jealously guarded inti- macies, has been turned by our methodical research into a scientific laboratory, in which properly observed psychological experiments can be carried out. This is not yet true of the specialist's consulting room. For the time being it remains the sanctum in which occasional miracles, like the two reported here, do happen.

We saw this state of affairs as a tempting challenge. If miracles, such as the two documented here, can happen, then why not aim at them deliberately? What is needed is to create conditions for specialists similar to those we have created for general practitioners. Under such conditions it may be hoped that the specialists will be able—in the same way as the general practitioners—to overcome their natural resistance against disclosing their contributions to the therapeutic processes that take place in their consulting rooms.

This, however, demands that the specialists—in the same way

as the general practitioners—should be willing to discuss frankly the intimate details of their daily work and accept the criticisms of their colleagues. This is not an easy task but neither is it impossible. For about five years we have been conducting a research workshop on these lines for qualified psycho-analysts, and recently we have succeeded in organizing a workshop that comprises within it practically all the specialists in medicine: paediatrics, gynaecology, physical medicine, dermatology, and, above all, general medicine. It is perhaps not without significance that the last specialist to join in our research was the surgeon.

CHAPTER 4

Evaluation

We have surveyed in some detail two medical worlds—the general practitioner's and the specialist's—each fundamentally different from the other. In both of these irrefutable psychotherapeutic results may be achieved. We then compared them with the world of the psycho-analyst and found that the techniques used, and perhaps also the results arrived at, were significantly different.

The next question that immediately arises is this: are the therapeutic results comparable at all? Before embarking on this very difficult problem of evaluation, we may perhaps quote an old joke to illustrate the difficulties confronting us. It is about an apprehensive man who broke his leg and about his doctor who put it in plaster of paris. The man, being apprehensive, could not help pestering his doctor with questions about whether his leg would be all right; how long would it take; whether he would be able to walk, to run, and so on. In the end the doctor lost his patience and said in despair, 'In six weeks time you will be able not only to walk and to run but also to dance.' The man then turned round, 'You must be quite a marvellous doctor because all my life I have tried to learn to dance but have never managed it'.

Surprisingly, this story is a fair illustration of the standards required for an ideal analytic treatment, and of those that analysts use when judging any other psychotherapy. If, after treatment, any one of our patients remained so inhibited that he could not manage to dance, this fact would automatically stamp the treatment as, at best, only partly successful. Of course, no orthopaedic surgeon would bother about his patient's ability to dance; his standard is simply whether he has been able to restore the function of the limb to what it used to be before the illness or the accident.

For the sake of argument, let us accept these exalted standards and ask which of the four patients described in the two previous chapters have learned to dance. The answer is, none—with the possible exception of the young telephonist. Quoting her doctor's description, Mrs. Q. will always remain a 'slut' and, we must add, almost certainly will need help from time to time. However, it is equally true that from a useless woman, just a nuisance and a misery to herself and to every member of her family, she was helped by the treatment to develop into a companion to her husband and a mother to her child.

The balance is still more favourable with Mr. V. When the treatment started he was inadequate and was barely able to keep up with his work; his wife was on the point of deserting him; his child was enuretic; and he himself was a nervous wreck. Now he has a flourishing business, a satisfied wife, and three children who are apparently developing well; he himself is a very infrequent visitor to the doctor, perhaps two or three times in a year. His ambivalence to a superior, bossy type of man has so diminished as to cause him no more trouble. It is only when he is forcibly confronted with the results of his own aggressiveness that he has some difficulty and needs further help. Thus, though he definitely cannot dance an aggressive dance, shall we dismiss his case as a failure?

Unquestionably Mr. N., our third case, remained the same obsessional man as he was from childhood. The strain on his family caused by his neurotic, over-exacting behaviour, though somewhat diminished, is very probably still considerable, as is suggested by his wife's subsequent slight depression and sleeplessness. Still he is carrying on; his potency is fairly adequate, though perhaps not quite ideal, and as far as we know there are no signs that any deterioration in his state might be threatening.

Perhaps the best therapeutic results have been achieved with the young telephonist, the former Miss I. This seriously neurotic girl was helped to develop into an apparently normal woman who is, as far as we know, happily married, preparing to settle down in her own house, and looking forward to having children. Thus, it is not quite impossible that she might have learned how to dance the dance of a normal woman.

A further important point in favour of these four cases is our long follow-up extending in every instance for five to six years. This fact must be stressed in order to prevent the emergence of the usual criticism that all this only amounts to a short-lived transference improvement. Unquestionably these are durable therapeutic results, not, perhaps, lasting for ever; needing, possibly, some patching up here and there; but certainly perennial. And here we should observe that even Freud considered that certain patients who had received analytic treatment might need re-analysis, say, every five years. The four patients quoted are in no need of this. Thus the results achieved seem to be fairly stable if measured by this yard-stick.

Moreover, if we put against these limited, though unquestionable, results the cost in time, money, and, above all, mental effort that was required to achieve them, the comparison with psycho-analytic therapy becomes still more favourable. True, under proper analysis the treatment would have gone further and deeper; the patients could have had better opportunities to develop their personalities, and thus the results would probably have been better and more safely founded, but the 'price' to be paid for all that would also have been considerably higher.

Though the 'price' involved is lower, on the whole the same picture will emerge if we compare these four results with those obtainable by any sort of group therapy.

This consideration of 'price' now makes the task for us, who set out to evaluate the results of the various forms of psychotherapy studied by us, still more difficult. It will not now be sufficient to show that definite therapeutic results have been achieved; we must assess them against the 'price' that patient and doctor (and perhaps the National Health Service) had to pay for them.

This is a much too formidable task, so let us start with an old story about a Jew who went to Rothschild to ask for a 'loan' because he had to go to Carlsbad for a very expensive cure. When the Baron remonstrated that there might be found cheaper places, the Jew replied with indignation: 'But Herr Baron, for *my* health nothing is too expensive.' This may be true as long as someone else will defray the expense, but will it be true if we ourselves have to bear it? Shall we then find also that nothing is too expensive for our health? The idea that health is not something absolute but a kind of commodity which has a 'price' will be likely to create an unpleasant and uneasy atmosphere.[1]

This uneasy atmosphere makes the dispassionate discussion of this topic well-nigh impossible. We all have a cherished fantasy about perfect health and absolute normality which ought to be our share, and it is difficult to accept that both health and normality are only relative and that, however healthy and normal we may be, their absolute value is on the whole inversely proportionate to our age. It seems like adding insult to injury when we are made to realize that

[1] It is worth remembering that at the inception of the National Health Service in Great Britain it was promised officially to provide the best available treatment for every patient, irrespective of cost. It would be unfair to say that this remained a paper promise only, as to a very large extent it has been fulfilled; but it must be pointed out that the National Health Service has found it impossible to include psycho-analysis among the treatments provided. One reason, and possibly the most important, is the one illustrated by the Rothschild story just quoted.

part of this health and normality is a kind of commodity that might be paid for by time, money, and serious mental effort. Unfortunately, whatever our feelings, this bitter fact must be accepted. That means that in assessing therapeutic results we must ask how much health for what 'price'?

As the two authors of this book are practising psycho-analysts, it may be expected that their view is that psycho-analysis offers most patients the best possibility of gaining health and normality at a reasonable 'price'. It must be stressed that this statement contains the qualification, 'most patients', and that the 'price' required by analysis, though not unreasonable, is definitely high. In this connection we do not think so much of the financial costs, usually highlighted by our opponents, but of the time and mental effort that a psycho-analytic treatment inevitably entails. There are many people, in need of real psychotherapeutic help, who can muster only a limited amount of time and mental effort—certainly insufficient for a full analysis.

Moreover, as has been stated on numerous occasions, the number of properly trained practising psycho-analysts in Great Britain is at present about two hundred. In spite of the great efforts put into training, the yearly rate of increase is about 5% to 10%, and it is highly unlikely that this rate could be increased in the next ten to fifteen years. (For comparison: there were in 1957 about 90,000 doctors on the Register of the General Medical Council and the number of newly registered doctors in the same year was 3,226, roughly $3\frac{1}{2}$%). Thus, even if one were convinced, as many of our analytic colleagues are, that psycho-analytic treatment should be the chosen method whenever a patient is in need of psychotherapy, one must realize, in the light of the figures quoted, that this conviction cannot lead to a realistic policy.

We have felt obliged to stress this state of affairs as many analysts feel that the demands of our own science are so pressing and every advance in our field so valuable as to eclipse any other claim. In their endeavour to keep all effort concentrated for the advancement of pure psycho-analysis, they tend to treat everything beyond the confines of pure psycho-analysis as unworthy of attention, and any attempt to enlist analysts' interests in those other fields almost as high treason or, at the least, as subversive activity. Since, in our view, the participation of well-trained analysts in the medical field of psychotherapy is highly desirable, we have thought it necessary to demonstrate that the therapeutic results that can be achieved merit attention.

Having done so, we turn to our next two questions. The first is about indication, a most complex subject bristling with misconceptions, most not stated explicitly. One of them, met with most frequently, runs approximately thus: once a neurosis, an emotional problem, a psychological disturbance or a complication has been diagnostically established, it constitutes an absolute indication for the type of psychotherapy practised by the doctor making the diagnosis—adapted, of course, to the patient's illness and personality. In some cases this is modified to the assertion that the particular type is the method of choice and that anything else is merely an inferior second best. Once stated explicitly, the fallacy in this attitude about indication is evident; its only justification is the unfortunate atmosphere of mistrust and suspicion that turns every psychotherapist into a partisan fighter for a noble cause—a most dangerous specimen in any scientific field.

It is this atmosphere that has made the study of proper indications for the various forms of psychotherapy well-nigh impossible; any attempt at inquiry into the possible limitations of one form will be felt by its adherents as an attack and by its opponents as a gain, and, on the other hand, if the result of the study should show that one form of psychotherapy had certain advantages for some conditions, psychotherapists belonging to all the other schools would regard it as an unfair denigration of their profession.

Our experience strongly suggests that various illnesses, personality structures, emotional problems, etc. respond differently to the various psychotherapeutic approaches studied. These variations are great enough to make certain approaches contra-indicated for certain conditions, whereas other forms of psychotherapy may have at least a fair chance of success in the same conditions. We feel that the answer may here be found for the highly embarrassing observation, reported from all over the psychiatric world, that a very high percentage of patients who are in bad need of help drop out from their treatment— apparently without good reason—in the early stages. This is especially true for group treatment.

Although, on the basis of our experience, we have no doubt about the paramount importance of proper indications—and we have kept this constantly in mind during our work—we have not yet been able to establish sufficiently firm criteria. One aim of this lengthy digression is to state this problem and enlist other workers' interest in it. In our opinion, psycho-analysts could contribute valuable material, if only they would come out of what we might call their ivory towers, and undertake a comparative study of the various forms and settings of psychotherapy.

Our last question is concerned with technique. Even if we accept that results may be achieved on the one hand by non-psychiatrists or non-analysts, and on the other hand by analysts using techniques which, though based on analytic ideas, are not purely analytic, what are these techniques; who knows anything systematic about them; and—most important for practising doctors—how can they be acquired?

May we repeat: a wholesale transfer of psycho-analytic techniques into these other medical fields is unrealistic, undesirable, and may even result in disaster. Still, a number of analysts, and especially para-analysts, are tempted to essay this tranfser, ending, as a rule, with a watered-down form of analysis, equally disappointing for patient and doctor. What we plead for is the recognition of these diverse techniques, each characterized by its own setting, as varieties or even species in their own right, each of them meriting proper study.

Our first aim was to establish this fact. We hope we have done so in this part of the book. In the following three parts we shall try to work out some general characteristics valid for every kind of psychotherapy belonging to the family of dynamic psychotherapies.

We confidently believe that this task can and should be undertaken by psycho-analysts. An analyst, by his training and professional experience, is better equipped to evaluate the subtle mental processes that constitute the material of every form of psychotherapy than are any of his colleagues. In particular, his constant preoccupation with the phenomena of transference qualifies him exceptionally to study the intricacies of the doctor-patient relationship which is the vehicle, if not the essence, of all therapeutic intervention. Of course, he must first abandon the time-worn air of superiority and accept some other—though not all—forms of psychotherapy as warrantable alternatives to his own.

In this comparative study an important variable to be watched will be what we call the 'setting' in which the psychotherapy is carried out. We hope it will be evident from the previous chapters that by 'setting' we mean much more than the arrangement of the therapist's room, that is, the physical situation during the treatment: the patient either sitting face to face with the therapist, or lying on a couch with the therapist out of his line of vision; the length or frequency of sessions, and so on. Admittedly all these details have an important bearing on the therapeutic processes, and their effect must be assessed; but what we have in mind is largely independent of the details just mentioned. By 'setting' we mean the sum total of the fairly constant conditions, created by the doctor's individual way of practising medicine, which the patient may make use of *and* must accept. In

43

other words, it is the therapeutic atmosphere 'offered' to the patient to get on with in his endeavour to obtain professional help.

We discussed in this part of our book four such settings—classical psycho-analysis, group therapy on analytic lines, specialist psychotherapy, and that offered by a general practitioner; of course there are many more, such as remedial teaching, probation service, pastoral psychology, and the innumerable varieties of psychiatric and other forms of social work. Certainly a rich field for research, which should be undertaken in a joint venture between analysts and the therapists working in that particular field, in our own case, general practitioners and specialists.

As mentioned in the Introduction, this volume is a kind of second progress report on one such joint venture, the first report having been published by one of us (M.B.) in 1957 under the title: *The Doctor, His Patient and The Illness.*

PART II

SOME COMMON PROBLEMS IN PSYCHOTHERAPY

CHAPTER 5

Examination by the Patient

Psychotherapy is essentially an interaction between two people. One of them, the therapist, creates and maintains by his professional skill an atmosphere in which the patient can reveal and recognize himself. Prompted by his symptoms and sufferings, and in response to the setting provided by the therapist, the patient becomes willing to let emerge to the light certain parts of his personality, his character, his past history.

We saw in the previous chapters that what the patient reveals of himself is determined also by the nature of the setting provided by the therapist, and it is in this respect that the structure of the psychiatric interview differs considerably from the far better-known structure of the medical examination. This latter belongs—as we shall discuss in more detail in Part IV—to the field of one-person biology or psychology, whereas the former belongs to that of two-person psychology. A further fundamental difference between the two examinations is that every successful psychiatric interview, no matter whether diagnostic or therapeutic in intention, contains some element of therapy; one of the chief aims of every diagnostic interview is, if at all possible, to enable the patient to decide for himself what his next step should be—a decision which, as a rule, he has been unable to take before the interview. True, in a number of cases this 'therapeutic' change is minimal, or it may even happen that the patient has come to the interview with this decision already made; still, the psychiatric examination definitely has this therapeutic bias, and in this way it is hardly ever as purely diagnostic, that is scientific, as a physical examination.

It follows, then, that the technical problems to be solved in a diagnostic interview and in the early phases of psychotherapy are similar, or even partly identical. This fact explains why the skills needed for tackling these problems are so important for every doctor. At present hardly any real training in psychotherapeutic skills is offered by the teaching hospitals, and most doctors when entering

47

practice must rely on the hope—either implied or explicitly stated—that it will not be too difficult to pick up some skill in psychotherapy as they go along. Perhaps all that will be needed is sincere interest in this field, sound common sense, and human sympathy; it is often maintained that, as a rule, it will be enough if the doctor can give the patient some encouraging reassurance and show by his whole behaviour that he is honestly interested; some people even recommend giving generously to the patient the attention and affection that most of us so sorely need. A simple, alternative technique, somewhat in contradiction to that just mentioned, requires that the patient should be firmly confronted with an undisturbed picture of the reality which his neurosis has prevented him seeing correctly.

Unfortunately both these recommendations are mainly, though not entirely, incorrect; consequently their discussion is rather difficult. Let us start by stating that psychotherapy, whether done by expert specialists or by any other doctor, requires a certain amount of skill which must be learned; that the learning process demands considerable application and a never-relaxing self-criticism; that—contrary to general belief—common sense, sympathy, and confronting the patient with reality, are not by a long way the most important techniques; and lastly, that encouraging reassurance—perhaps the method most frequently used—proves almost always utterly futile in the long run and is better not used at all. We are prepared for a number of our readers to ask in despair: if not these time-honoured methods, then what?

Let us quote an example that was recently reported by a psychiatrist to an audience of general practitioners. It was about a woman patient who was referred to him with a devastating letter from her doctor. In it she was described as an insincere horror, an unscrupulous egotist, who had driven her husband almost to suicide but mercifully left him just in time, and the psychiatrist was fervently urged not to do anything that might move her to return to her husband. As the patient entered the consulting room she said to the doctor, 'I hope you will not think me an awful fraud'.

Now that is a clear challenge to the doctor, an unmistakable opening gambit. How should he respond? Obviously it would be useless to agree with the patient in the manner shown by the general practitioner's letter. This would create between doctor and patient an extremely strained relationship, anything but favourable for any attempt at psychotherapy. The only value of such an agreement would be that it might reinforce the doctor's defences, which—in the case of the general practitioner—possibly have been sorely tried in the past.

Another possibility would be to reject any idea of the patient being a fraud, to 'reassure' her about this, for instance, by arguing with her, 'No, you are not a fraud, I don't believe it at all', and to reinforce this statement by sincere interest in her problems. This policy might ease the situation temporarily, but it may engender an insincere relationship and sooner or later the strain will be too much, either for the patient or for the doctor, and one of them will not be able to stand it any longer.

A third possibility might be to disregard this statement, as if it had *not* been made at all, or side-step it by changing the subject. This policy, too, may help temporarily; even this, however, is not certain at all since it is bound to increase the patient's anxieties. Her question shows that she feels awful about herself, and in her distress the first thing she must convey to the new doctor is this horrible feeling; if the doctor now side-steps this communication, the patient might take it to mean that he was really thinking that she was so awful that the only helpful thing he could do was to pretend not to have noticed this fact.

If none of these methods are to be applied, what can be done then? The point that we wish to make here, and to make emphatically, is that *in psychological medicine, exactly in the same way as in physical medicine, every symptom must be taken seriously*. If, for instance, a patient complains of abdominal pain, the doctor will not say, 'How awful, I can't stand you with these pains, go away to another doctor'; neither will he reassure the patient, 'Never mind, it is not so bad and, in any case, I still have sympathy and affection for you'; still less will he side-step or disregard the symptom. What he will do is to accept it and to examine it as well as he is able to. To apply this maxim to our case, as a response to the patient's communication, the doctor could ask, cautiously, 'Why should I think so?'; daringly, 'Why do you feel such an awful fraud?'; or simply, 'Are you?' If he is a sophisticated psychotherapist he might even try to lead the conversation round so that he might ask in due course, 'What made you start our interview with this appeal?'

Any one of these responses will start the process of examination. However, here we encounter an important difference between psychological and physical medicine. In physical medicine the examination is done almost entirely by the doctor; what is required from the patient is to agree to it and in a very minor way to co-operate with his doctor. True, in psychological medicine too, it is the doctor who examines the symptom but he conducts the examination *together with the patient;* and if it can be done at all, he ought to aim at having the symptoms examined *by the patient*.

Let us quote an example in which the examination was done entirely by the doctor. This instructive case will show us—among many other important points—how far the doctor was able to clarify the problem and at what point his examination came to a halt because he did not succeed in inducing his patient to take part in it.

Recently at one of our case conferences Dr. A. reported on Mrs. L., aged forty-two, who had been on his list for more than ten years. It was conspicuous that the doctor, who had been attending our case seminars for more than a year and knew our customs very well, took out his notes and practically read them to us. This is something almost unheard of in our work, as we lay great emphasis on the spontaneity of the report. With a prepared manuscript one may confidently expect to get all the facts of the case in proper order, but unfortunately, more often than not, one would miss completely the doctor's psychological involvement in his case which, we have found, is essential for the understanding of the problems underlying the illness. That is why we insist in our conferences that every contribution must be made without any prepared notes. Still, on this occasion the doctor tried to read his notes, and when he was challenged he replied that he must do so because, though he had spent some considerable time now with this woman and had got all the data, they did not add up to anything, and he felt completely lost.

What to do now? Should one insist on the doctor discarding his notes, or should one tolerate him using them? Evidently we have come up against the same sort of gambit which was used by the woman patient just quoted. The correct response to this gambit is always to accept it and then to enquire what made him behave in this way, what happened to him. However, we must realize that by this approach we enter dangerous ground. The aim of this book is to discuss psychotherapy *by* the doctor, here we are about to embark on a psychotherapy *of* the doctor. Is this a fair and sensible step? What can be expected from it? These questions will be discussed in the next chapter, so let us follow our colleague who, with good humour, accepted the implied rebuke and continued his report without notes. The gist of the report, presented in 1955, is as follows:

CASE 5

Mrs. L. aged forty-two, married for nineteen years, one son aged nine and a half. For about four months complaints of panic in trains and buses when travelling alone.

Husband: in show business, getting on very well. Married for three years before the war, then away in Army for five years. Son born eighteen months after his return. 'Difficult baby for first six months.' 'Patient got in a state over him.' No further children by choice—small flat, etc. Mrs. L. worked until ten years ago as typist, enjoyed it, was highly competent, practically ran the office by herself at the end. 'Alone a lot since then,' especially since boy at school; no particular friends, lots of spare time. Not very keen on housework as only interest. Cannot face cinema alone.

Has been seen only occasionally after the early difficulties with her baby had been overcome; more frequently during past six years for numerous psychosomatic complaints, including indigestion, palpitations, etc., but treated first symptomatically, then sent to various specialists for examination re heart, abdomen, etc.

Father died two years ago at the age of seventy-two. Mother well—sixty-nine. Patient has a younger brother and a much younger sister. Father described as a placid easy-going man, nagged a great deal by mother who is quick tempered, temperamental, and difficult to live with. Patient scared of mother's tempers. 'Mother didn't like her,' was unable to show affection; 'father loved her' (tears whilst talking about father: 'doesn't want to talk about him'). Keeps referring to being alone as giving her time to brood about her health and suggesting this is why she gets worried and scared. 'Would like to do a job but part-time work difficult,' anyway has to be at home when son comes home from school.

We must agree, Dr. A's initial remarks were justified. The case really did not make sense, and not only he, but most of us in the seminar who listened to him, were lost and could not understand why Mrs. L. had developed her phobia and still less what was to be done to help her.

The situation changed as soon as we realized that the whole examination, as reported by the doctor, was carried out entirely by himself. Though the patient co-operated to that extent willingly, her co-operation went about as far as would be required for a physical examination; in other words, Mrs. L. was merely a passive object but not an active partner in it. We should point out, by the way, that the average report, no matter whether given by a general practitioner in his referral or by a number of psychiatrists in their reply to the referring doctor, does not go further than this. This limitation is one of the commonest reasons why so many psychiatric reports are rather unhelpful to general practitioners.

We must interrupt here the discussion of the case of Mrs. L. and her frustrated doctor, but we shall return to them in the next chapter to see whether we can discover what really happened between the two, why the patient remained an accommodating but uninvolved passive observer during the examination, what the obstacle was that prevented Dr. A. from understanding his patient's real problems, and what could have been done to create a more favourable situation.

We quote now two further cases in which the patients took part in the examination. The intensity of the participation was lower in the first, higher in the second.

CASE 6

The first, Case 6, was reported by a Medical Registrar of a Teaching Hospital who, at the time of his report, had been attending our seminars for less than a year. The patient, Mrs. X., was a married woman of thirty-six with three children of ten, seven, and two years old. She was first seen as an outpatient by the Registrar's predecessor at the beginning of October 1958 and the clinical notes ran as follows: 'Vomiting once or twice a day for three weeks intermittently. Epigastric pain for three weeks, pain across the lumbar region of the back. Medicine no help. Not on a diet. Nothing found on physical examination. Barium meal ? D.U. Gastric 3 diet.' It has to be added that a previous x-ray at another hospital, done about two years before, suggested the presence of a small pyloric ulcer. At this point the predecessor disappeared from the service and our Registrar took over. He saw the patient on October 29th and he noted down 'No pain, no sickness for five days, no obvious stress'. He asked her to come back after six weeks, but in fact she did not return until the 28th January 1959, that is, three months later.

At that time she complained of renewed pain, sharp and drawing, on the right side of the abdomen, which waxed and waned and went on for about ten minutes. In addition she had fairly strong nausea and some lower back pains which came on after several days of constipation. Physical examination produced no convincing signs and a tentative diagnosis of spastic colon was made. As the husband accompanied her and both of them appeared to be rather anxious and worried, the Registrar had a talk with each of them separately and then with both of them jointly in order to reassure them. The patient responded well and seemed to improve rapidly on a diet and some alkalis. A letter was written to the general practitioner reporting that the patient's pains had disappeared and that she seemed to be reassured. Two months later a further letter was written closing the case for the time being but offering to see the patient whenever she or the general practitioner felt it necessary.

Before going further, let us summarize the developments up to this point. It is somewhat uncertain whether in fact there was or was not a duodenal or pyloric ulcer present. One film was highly suggestive, another film taken two years later, rather uncertain. This, as we all know, is not unusual. The pains were not very characteristic either; on the other hand, the patient responded well to a rational diet and alkalis. The syndrome of 'spastic colon' is a not unusual concomitant of peptic ulcers. Anxiousness and the transitory good effect of reassurance fit also well into this picture. We may also add the favourable follow-up; nothing was heard of the patient or of her doctor till the end of January 1960, that is, for almost a year. All this seems to suggest that our Registrar did the right thing. Now let us return to the story.

The patient was referred again by her doctor, this time for coughs and pains in her chest. She was seen on the 3rd February 1960. The Registrar described this interview as his retribution. His chief reason for using this phrase was that in the meantime he had joined our seminars and had become familiar with a different approach to what we call the patient's 'offers'. We shall quote his report verbatim from the transcript of our discussion:

When she coughs it comes up in a lump and when she massages it it clicks and goes down; the cough was worse lately but had been present for years. On examination she had a localized tenderness over the right costal margin, exactly where she got her pain, and this was reproduced by moving her costal margin; this seemed to me to fit in with the 'clicking rib syndrome' which has been described but not explained by Wright. She also told me that she smoked fifteen cigarettes a day and I said the cure was to cut her smoking down. She said this would not be easy as she was always rather tense.

I had now seen her on three occasions with three different symptoms and I realized that she had been tense and rather depressed for the last two years, that is, since her last child. It was not planned, it was an accident, and she was very upset about it. On this particular occasion her husband came home drunk, refused to use a contraceptive and so she became pregnant. Since the last child they have had no sexual relationship because she was terrified of getting pregnant again. Before that I think he used a sheath as she did not want to use a cap because she had a strong distaste for it. I concluded that I thought this was probably why she had got so irritable and depressed lately. She agreed and added that she would not refuse to get advice on contraception for herself.

53

At this point the Registrar terminated the interview by referring the patient to a gynaecologist who, he knew, would not only fit the patient with a contraceptive cap but also ascertain the reasons why she had been reluctant to use it until now and, if necessary, treat her for them. The Registrar then told us that he was fully aware that the case had not been completely clarified but that he thought that the further examination and especially the further treatment of the case were not his duty any more.

There are a number of interesting features in this report. For our topic the most important is that it is clearly about two periods. In the first, all the examinations were done entirely and exclusively by the doctor. Mrs. X's participation was at about the same level as Mrs. L's in the previous case. The results were also similar. Every physical symptom that the patient 'offered' was dealt with promptly and efficiently; in response to this treatment one physical symptom after the other disappeared only to give way to another. In addition, the doctor went out of his way to give his patient 'reassurance' on a generous scale, seeing husband and wife first separately and then jointly. His efforts were apparently successful, the patient got 'reassured', which is far better than the usual response, but after a time she returned with a new symptom.

Thus her journey along the road of 'medical history' progressed in much the same way as did Mrs. L's. Then the doctor changed his approach. Instead of starting off on a new series of examinations, such as gastroscopy, a new barium meal and follow through, x-rays of the chest or ribs, possibly of the spine, etc., he tried to create an atmosphere in which the patient was enabled to have another look at herself, that is, to take part in the medical examination. The result was the discovery of new, hitherto unrecognized, causal connections which enabled both patient and doctor to have a more comprehensive picture of the patient's illness in relation to her whole life, especially to her marital problems.

It is an old maxim of medicine that the more signs and symptoms can be understood on the basis of the same pathological cause, the more probable it is that the diagnosis will be correct. This is exactly what happened in this case. A number of 'symptoms' which had hitherto seemed to be utterly unconnected have become well-fitting parts of the same picture; they comprise, apart from her gastric, intestinal, and thoracic symptoms, also the birth of her child two years ago and the events leading to it, her strained relationship to her husband, her smoking, and perhaps also her husband's periodic drunkenness which, at any rate partly, must have been conditioned by the sexual dissatisfaction in this marriage.

It is almost certain that if the doctor had continued to conduct the examination of this patient solely by himself, none of these connections would have emerged. Moreover, even if the doctor—by some lucky hit—had been able to get hold of these causal connections, and on the basis of his findings could have advised Mrs. X. to seek contraceptive advice, it is not very likely that she would have accepted it.

Our third case, Case 7, is still more interesting. The two periods and the abrupt change in the doctor's approach will appear still more clearly; over and above it we shall be able to see that in the second phase the patient was at times a few steps ahead of the doctor in the examination and the doctor needed some help to catch up with the events. The first period, in which all the examinations were done by the doctor and his specialist colleagues, lasted for several years; it included the whole time during which the patient was attended by the doctor's predecessor and six and a half years while he was looked after by our colleague and his partner. The second period started in November 1958.

The circumstances under which this abrupt change happened are also interesting. One day we discussed one of our findings, namely, that in a number of cases, in particular if the patient presented or 'offered' several illnesses, his family doctor had a much better chance to get hold of and to understand the real problem than any specialist. This is always hard to believe; it is invariably argued that specialists know so much more, that they have all the refined methods of examination at their disposal and that, after all, they are, or at any rate ought to be, better doctors. To prove that this is not necessarily so, we asked one of the members of our group to pick out one of his patients who had had many hospital and specialist examinations and treatments and offer him a proper psychological examination lasting for about an hour. What follows is an extract of the report as presented in December 1958.

Case 7

Mr. G., aged fifty-three, is a clerk in a big firm, is married and has a son of about twenty. He changed to the partner of our colleague in 1952 by giving notice to his previous doctor, a rather characteristic symptom. The immediate reason, according to the patient, was that his doctor told him that he could not do anything more for him. Something of this sort must have happened as words to this effect were found in the doctor's handwriting on the patient's card. The change actually happened while Mr. G. was recovering from a perforated duodenal ulcer. In 1954 his ulcer pains exacerbated and a partial gastrectomy was performed which, however, had no lasting effect. The pains were so bad in spite of constant antacid medication and diet that the doctors were frequently called out during both day and night and Mr. G. had to be admitted twice to hospitals as an emergency case.

In 1955 he was operated on for anal fissure. In addition he had various minor illnesses and in the six and a half years, that is, from joining the practice until December 1958, he was away from work for a total of over 400 days, and in hospital five times for a total of twelve weeks. He has had x-rays of his stomach, his colon, his chest, his gall-bladder, and his spine. His file contains thirty-four reports from specialists. Recently a gastroscopy was performed when the specialist found a small gastric ulcer. In the summer of 1958 he was brought home from holiday by an ambulance because he was seized with sudden pain in his back while pulling at a try-your-strength machine at a seaside resort. Eventually the pain was recognized as due to a crush fracture of his first lumbar vertebra. In addition to all this array of serious and verifiable illnesses, he has a curious symptom—a clinical entity well known to neurologists—sudden leg jerks during the night.

Every specialist who saw him diagnosed properly that he was a neurotic man but then went on treating the organic illness which was found during the 'examination by the doctor'. The result is this museum piece of medical efficiency and rigorousness which used to be called in the practice 'that man G'. It was this patient that our somewhat doubting doctor selected for testing out our ideas. Out of the blue he rang up Mr. G. and asked him to come for a long interview.

They were together for an hour, and we have again to condense the examination and the treatment that took place. Mr. G. proved to be a man with a chip on his shoulder, everything and everybody around him was bad; doctors no good, hospitals no good, colleagues at work no good, nothing in fact was any good. Mr. G's remarks were bitter, devastating, and uncontradictable. This took up a large part of the hour, but the doctor learnt also that Mr. G. started his working life as a clerk but did not like his job and changed it to become a private chauffeur for twenty years. He was quite healthy till his employer retired and as a parting gift procured him the present job where Mr. G. works as an anonymous clerk in a large office. Doctor and patient reached an understanding that in future they could relate his ill-health to his feelings about his work and the rest of the world.

At the end of the interview the doctor thought that all this sounded rather promising and offered a second session. He did not reckon, however, with his specialists. The orthopaedic surgeon who was looking after Mr. G's back decided that Mr. G. needed hospital treatment and whisked him away, but Mr. G. sent his doctor a Christmas card with the quotation 'For he that is mighty hath done to me great things; and holy is his name', Luke 1:49.

The doctor did not realize at the time the significance of this Christmas card. His reaction was mixed feelings of flattery and embarrassment at this rather exaggerated vote of thanks. In any case, perhaps not deliberately, he interpreted the exaggeration as a warning signal and not as an encouragement. In due course Mr. G. was discharged from hospital and resumed his regular attendance in the surgery to collect his prescriptions for antacids against his stomach pains and for Nembutal against his jerky legs. But contrary to his previous habits, during the whole of 1959 he did not pester his doctor with complaints, did not lose one day off work for illness, and there were no night calls. Imperceptibly, nobody knows when, he ceased to be called in the practice 'that man G.'

The discussions in our seminars are based on spontaneous participation. We had so many interesting things to discuss during 1959 that Mr. G's case was completely forgotten. At the beginning of 1960 we decided to study the various methods that patients adopt when approaching their doctor with their complaints. To have sufficiently contrasting material we chose patients suffering from peptic ulcer, ulcerative colitis, and asthma; and in order to have some control, it was agreed that every patient having one of these illnesses must be mentioned.

Thus it happened that in February 1960 our colleague reported that Mr. G. came to see him and we learned the results of that one interview in November 1958. Moreover on this occasion the therapy of the case was carried one step further. Mr. G. reported that recently his stomach pains had become worse. The doctor reminded him of what they had discovered at their interview more than a year before and asked him whether anything in his life had become more difficult. First Mr. G. denied any knowledge of such a change, but after some hesitation and puzzlement added that it might be connected with the impending change in his office to automation; the office would be still more impersonal than ever. Over the past few weeks they had had experts studying everybody's job in order to devise the new machines. The puzzlement disappeared from Mr. G's face, he collected his prescriptions and departed.

It was only in the ensuing discussion that the doctor realized that apparently what mattered most to Mr. G. was to be in personal relationship to someone (like his former employer) who appreciated his work. Mr. G. was healthy as long as this relationship lasted and started his impressive array of illnesses as soon as the personal relationship had to be terminated and he became an impersonal clerk. The recent exacerbation was now explicable as due to the threat of automation, that is, a further loss of personal relationship. Of course, we shall need further follow-ups to confirm this idea, but it undoubtedly fits the facts of his case.

There cannot be any doubt that while in the first period all the examinations were done by the two doctors and their specialist advisers, in the second period, that is, since November 1958, the patient himself took a very important part in them. The effect of the changed régime is striking. To take one difference as a sample: during the six and a half years before November 1958 the patient lost more than 400 days because of illness, that is, roughly one in six. Since November 1958, apart from the one instance when he went to hospital because his orthopaedic surgeon asked him to do so, not because he felt ill, Mr. G. has not lost one day for illness. We shall have to return in a later chapter to this case to discuss the nature and effectiveness of this kind of therapy, but we would point out that it would be as incorrect to say that the doctor gave Mr. G. this therapy, as that Mr. G. got this therapy for himself. Here we have to stick to the diagnostic aspect of the case.

During the second period the patient was examined on two occasions, first in November 1958 and again in February 1960. With some simplification one could say that on both occasions the examination was carried out jointly by the patient and the doctor. This is one of the reasons why the result of the examination, the 'diagnosis', is so vague. Roughly it runs: Mr. G's ill-health is connected with his feelings about his work and about the rest of the world around him.

In fact, our description is somewhat incorrect because Mr. G. on both occasions was a few steps ahead of his doctor in understanding his own case. True, he was not able to formulate his diagnosis in words—that is, his understanding—but his behaviour showed not only that he knew it but that his knowledge had a therapeutic effect on him.

In the winter 1958/59, although highly impressed by the result of the one interview, the doctor was still uncertain and full of doubts, while Mr. G. unhesitatingly chose and sent his Christmas card announcing the important change in him. It took quite a few months for the doctor to realize the full extent of what had happened in that interview.

Something similar took place in February 1960. Mr. G. came to his doctor complaining about the recrudescence of his indigestion. That was—to use an analogy—the court dress that he needed to obtain an audience from his doctor. Then the doctor reminded him of their findings more than a year before which had enabled Mr. G. to discard the conventional complaining and do a further piece of work. What the doctor did not recognize, however, was the importance for Mr. G. of a personal relationship in which he was appreciated and valued. It was only in our discussion, that is, several days later than Mr. G., that the doctor realized how potent this therapy had been.

The fact that the doctor and his patient were somewhat out of step, leap-frogging with each other in their joint work, makes it possible to demonstrate one more important point, namely, what sort of work was done by each of them. The first step was taken by the doctor in creating an atmosphere in which Mr. G. could discard his highly critical but well mannered, conventional behaviour, which he acquired during his long training in the first period. When he satisfied himself that the doctor would tolerate his criticisms and would not rebuff him, Mr. G. became free enough to reveal important parts of his emotional attitude towards the world. The next step was again the doctor's. It was his task to translate the revealed emotional attitudes into fairly concise words: that in future Mr. G's ill-health could be related to his feelings towards his work and the world around him. The next step was taken by Mr. G. Both by his Christmas card and by his whole behaviour during 1959 he tried to convey to his doctor:'You have done a very good piece of therapy, please go on'. The doctor's response was rather half-hearted. Though he could not see how to go on, he continued to show his personal interest in Mr. G. Thus the improvement was maintained but no further progress could be made.

The impending change in his working conditions then forced Mr. G. to demand more treatment from his doctor. The doctor, realizing that something had to be done, abandoned his half-hearted participation and the two together went one step further, but then, as the doctor failed to translate into words what they found together, Mr. G. had to go ahead on his own. The discussion in the seminar enabled the doctor to catch up with his patient by understanding better what had happened between them. If he is now able to use his understanding to translate into useful words what he understood of Mr. G's response to the treatment, we may confidently predict a further peaceful period, or even some improvement.

The interplay just described between doctor and patient is a good illustration of what should happen in every psycho-diagnostic or psychotherapeutic interview. In later chapters, particularly in Parts III and IV, we intend to examine in more detail what sort of contributions each of them could and should make to this joint work. On the whole the doctor's contributions have the effect of creating an atmosphere in which the patient can reveal and recognize himself; of understanding what the patient tries to convey to him; and of expressing his understanding in useful words which will help the patient to understand himself better, to reveal more of himself, and finally to change.

If we want to describe the patient's contributions, we have to describe the same events from his angle. In response to finding an understanding atmosphere he may reveal parts of himself of which he has not been consciously aware; this experience, reinforced by the doctor's interpretations, which convey to the patient his understanding of the revealed material, helps the patient to understand himself better, and this in turn may lead to a change in the direction of better adjustment. While the patient's contributions are determined by his illness, personality, and character, the effectiveness of the doctor's contributions is determined chiefly by two factors, on the one hand, his knowledge and skill, and, on the other, his ability to respond constructively to his patient's revelations. This latter depends on the doctor's personality. The freer, the better integrated, the more flexible it is, the more easily will he find the adequate constructive responses. Apart from these individual factors, there are, however, a number of difficulties that are very common. In the remaining chapters of this part we shall discuss a few of them, showing how far they limit the development of useful working conditions.

CHAPTER 6

The Doctor's Emotions

Perhaps the commonest difficulty that doctors encounter in their psychotherapeutic work is caused by their own emotions, which may seriously interfere with the development of the constructive inter- action described in the previous chapter. Doctors are therefore enjoined to be on their guard, to control their emotions, and to preserve an imperturbably objective and understanding attitude. This sounds very sensible; unfortunately—apart from recommending a thorough-going personal analysis as the most important preparation for any such psychotherapeutic work—the literature is rather silent about the ways in which this can be achieved.

Of course we have not found *the* general solution of these most tricky technical problems; but we have found *one* solution that has worked fairly well under the conditions inherent in the setting of our on-going discussion seminars.

We found that *if any feelings or emotions are engendered in the doctor while treating the patient, these must be evaluated also as an important symptom of the patient's illness, but on no account be acted upon.* To achieve this evaluation, and at the same time to resist the temptation of acting upon one's feelings, is a rather difficult task and one that can be mastered only through considerable training. Of course, the evaluation can be done more easily by a third, unin- volved, person who listens to the doctor's spontaneous report, than by the involved doctor himself. One of the most important functions of the on-going case seminars, which are the mainstay of the Tavistock scheme for training doctors—general practitioners as well as special- ists—in psychotherapy, is to create an atmosphere in which the doctor is secure enough to report spontaneously, revealing his emotional involvement, and the audience sympathetic enough to treat his report in a critical but friendly and constructive way.

The case we shall quote first is a good illustration of the candid atmosphere of the case seminars. The doctor in question did not try to disguise the truth that he could not control his bad temper and, so to speak, let the patient have it. True, the unmistakably good result of his 'treatment' may have helped him in his sincerity.

CASE 8

When I saw this patient I was in a filthy temper owing to a series of disasters—my car had been stolen, and though I had broken my toe I had to walk to the hospital for my outpatients' session; of course I was late and was in a hurry, but, before starting my normal list, I had first to see an extra patient who couldn't speak English and took an awfully long time. The next patient was Mrs. C. who brought an unusually long doctor's letter—absolute sob stuff. It said how unfortunate it was that this couple, who would be ideal parents, had not succeeded in either having a child or adopting one. They had taken a child of five a year ago for a few months without legal formalities, but then the mother had taken it away. Mrs. C. was twenty-eight, husband thirty-one, married nine years. Husband was a butcher; most considerate and pleasant, said the doctor. About eighteen months after marriage Mrs. C. was referred to a Gynaecological Department, where she would not allow the doctor to examine her and subsequently did not keep an appointment for examination under anaesthetic. At another teaching hospital she was examined but was so terrified that she did not keep the appointment for post-coital test. Her complaints were of severe pain in intercourse. The doctor added that he had put her in touch with an adoption society, who, however, would not pass her home accommodation as suitable for a child. In addition, according to Mrs. C., neighbours and relatives were accusing her of being a freak or of finding an infallible method of contraception. According to the doctor she was a poor, persecuted girl, badly treated all round. Immediately I could hear Dr. Balint: 'Be on your guard if a woman is described as an angel!' The doctor added at the end of his letter, 'If she can't be helped to have a baby I will get in touch with the adoption society myself to see if I can help'.

My first remark was, 'Is your house really unsuitable for a child?' She said it was overcrowded; only a few rooms and they had two lodgers, brothers (to each other, not to this couple). I said 'If that is so, is it going to be suitable for your own baby?' She said they were going to move. I asked why she had lodgers if she was overcrowded—was it the money? She denied it. Then she said they had intercourse about once in two months—'it hurts'. I did not believe anything she told me and said that for nine years she had wanted a baby but refused to have intercourse. Then I added in a rather cross voice,

'You don't really want a baby, do you?' She burst into tears: 'It's horrible, degrading—having intercourse and not having a baby'. She loathed it, fought against it, and wished the baby could be ready made. I asked if she had ever really had intercourse. This time she admitted that she did not think so. I said in a sarcastic voice, 'Then you don't want a baby. I suppose you know that intercourse is necessary'. She said she was so angry with me she could not speak to me. I retorted, 'Angry with me and who else—the adoption society, everybody?' I told her to get undressed in a cubicle just outside my room and added she had a wonderful opportunity to walk out of this hospital too—this time fully justified because I had been nasty to her.

To my surprise she stayed to be examined but had a bad adductor spasm. I said in a matter-of-fact way that she would have to separate her legs. She did and there was a severe vaginismus. I said 'Is this the usual thing?' She said 'Yes—it's all so horrible. I suppose it's because of my parents who did this awful thing. We could hear it though they used to shut the door.' She has a brother two years older and a sister ten years younger. She said she was very angry with her parents.

I could not follow the matter further at that interview, because I simply did not have the time, so I said we ought to talk about it more, but I did not suppose she would come back as she did not really want a baby. She said she did, if only she did not have to have intercourse. By that time I had become a bit friendlier and explained a post-coital test. She said the other hospital had wanted to do it, but it was in front of students and nurses and she could not bear to hear them talk about it. I gave her an appointment and she went out. Outside she told Sister she would be coming back for the appointment, on condition she saw me and nobody else. I was astounded when I heard about it, and out of interest I booked her for myself, but I said she would not come as I had never lost my temper so violently. She was a thin, rather shy, quiet sort of girl.

She did not keep her appointment, but I found her a week later in the waiting room crying and agitated. On her arrival she was told by the nurse—Sister was not there—that she must see, as everybody else, my colleague. She protested crying that she must see me. She could hardly wait to tell me that she had started a period a day after the last visit; the period lasted 12 days and so she came for the post-coital test after three weeks instead of two. She said 'I have been longing to come and tell you.' They had intercourse twice; the first time just after the period, and she was sick afterwards. Last night it was all right and her husband was terribly happy. It was the first time she had mentioned him. I asked her—I don't know if this was wrong—

63

if she had done it because she had to come today and wanted it to be all right for me. She had a magnificent post-coital test only the count was somewhat low. Both of us were cheerful and friendly now. Then she said, 'I have got to tell you how much I hated my parents'. They used to go into the bedroom in the afternoon, at week-ends. It was always preceded by violent quarrelling—they were always quarrelling. They would shut the door, and the youngest child, about two, would want to go in. Father would emerge and give the patient money to keep the child out. She could not see why they could not go in though she was about twelve at the time. She asked her brother to explain; she could not remember what he told her, she said, covering her face, but it was horrible. She went away saying she felt different now and that her husband felt much happier.

We learned then that at the second examination there was no adductor spasm and no vaginismus. In fact there was no difficulty whatsoever. Unquestionably Mrs. C. was eager and proud of her achievement. The doctor thought that on the one hand Mrs. C. wanted to please him and, on the other, to prove him wrong in his accusation that she did not really want a baby.

In this case there is no question that when examining his patient the doctor felt a strong emotion of anger but he did not stop to examine it, instead acted upon it. Does it mean that our impressive advice underlined in the beginning of this chapter has already been proved false? Not in the least; what happened was that in this case the doctor's emotions and the patient's needs happened to fit each other. This, however, is a very rare event and it would be utterly foolish to bank on such a rare coincidence.

Let us examine, then, how this fit has come about. First, we have to deal with a possible counter argument which would say that the doctor's 'flaming anger' had nothing to do with the patient, it was caused by external events. The external events were there all right, but there were causes for the anger in the patient herself. First there was the irritatingly over-protective and over-sympathetic letter by her general practitioner which, in addition, accused the doctor's hospital —together with the other hospital—of being unnecessarily harsh with this poor patient; and then there was the patient's overt insincerity, her clumsy attempts at minimizing her part, and blaming everyone else—husband, neighbours, relatives, hospital doctors, and so on.

The next argument is of an entirely different kind. Many doctors might say that in spite of these irritating facts Mrs. C. ought to have been treated with 'understanding' and 'kind sympathy'; moreover, any doctor who wanted to help her ought to approach her in a 'permissive motherly attitude'. It is not too difficult to see that this kind of approach may easily lead to an insincere, over-protective attitude, like that of her general practitioner. No doubt that doctor and patient had understood each other excellently, they were having the most friendly relationship, yet all this had not been therapeutic. Mrs. C. had remained as ill as ever in spite of the sympathetic treatment by her understanding general practitioner.

This was an additional reason why we included Mrs. C's case in this book. We wanted to show that kindness and sympathy alone, even if they lead to an almost complete acceptance of the patient's picture of the external world as real, are not necessarily helpful. We would like to add that this sympathetic attitude, treating the patient as 'you poor thing', is also based on the doctor's emotion, only this emotion is the generally recommended, the standardized one, whereas in our case the doctor's action was prompted by his emotion of the particular day.

It is perhaps important to add here that though this doctor did respond with anger to the patient, he knew all the time what he was doing. He was able to follow the changes his anger produced in the patient and did not resort to the usual reactions which therapists fall back on if they become aware of any strong emotions stirring in them. Some of these reactions are: trying to control the emotions, pretending that they are not angry, counteracting their anger by becoming soothing in the hope of counter-balancing the changes produced in the patient, etc., in order to have, after a stormy start, an emotion-free aseptic period of interview in the end. This procedure may alleviate the therapist's uneasiness or guilty feelings but its therapeutic value is questionable.

One could add that anger of the kind described in this report, though fairly intense, was not entirely uncontrolled as it was conscious. In this case the situation is less precarious and, on the whole, the same holds true for all sorts of emotions, not only for anger; of course, it is much more dangerous for the therapeutic situation if the doctor remains unaware of his feelings; in this case he may not even realize what he is doing to his patient either as a direct result of them, or indirectly by trying to over-compensate for his unconscious guilt feelings about them.

Then what did help in this case? First the doctor's anger, though exaggerated by external factors, was an honest and real response to the patient; neither over-sympathetic, as that of the referring doctor, nor hostile, as that of her neighbours. Our doctor's attitude, though angry, meant something like this: no adolescent nonsense, please, about sex; if you want a baby, however much you loathe, or are frightened by, intercourse, it must be accepted as a fact of nature.

This inexorably realistic policy enabled Mrs. C. to verbalize, possibly for the first time in her life, her first, most painful conscious experience with sex, namely, that she was excluded from it; that she was bribed to keep a curious young sister, who certainly represented her rebellious self, quiet all the time; that she had to discuss these things with her brother, which discussion was undoubtedly highly exciting, and at the same time distasteful, horrifying, and frustrating.

We do not know what sort of fantasies were luxuriating in the young girl's mind about what happened behind the locked doors, whether she identified herself in them with the managing and unscrupulous father, or found the weak protests and subsequent surrender of her mother both despicable and exciting, and so on. We only know that the doctor's honest, though exaggerated, anger helped Mrs. C. realize how angry she had been ever since her childhood towards everybody, that her anger, as well as the doctor's, could be accepted, worked through, and lived with, that no sympathy and kindness will change the reality that you cannot have babies if you do not accept intercourse as an unalterable fact.

Using what we have learned here, let us now return to the case (number 5) of Mrs. L. and her frustrated doctor, which we followed up to a point in the previous chapter. We broke off the narrative when we had to agree with the doctor that, in spite of his painstaking efforts, the ample material that he obtained from his patient did not seem to make sense. We found one answer for this unsatisfactory result in the fact that the whole examination had been carried out by the doctor exclusively; the patient herself did not take any part in it. This, however, is not the whole answer.

As we have said, the case was reported to a fairly experienced seminar, whose members were soon able to point out that the feelings of futility, of emptiness, and of being lost—or, to express it in somewhat poetic terms, the feeling of wandering aimlessly in the wilderness— were not only dominant in the doctor, but also an important symptom of the patient's illness, and possibly the most important communication addressed to him. The doctor, however, was not able to evaluate these feelings in this sense and still less could he induce his patient to accept them and examine them with him.

We then went on in our discussion by taking seriously the feeling of emptiness and futility created in the doctor. Dr. A. realized that for many years back he had had this feeling whenever he was attending Mrs. L., namely, that her world was empty; but he could not understand why it had to be so, since the family circumstances were developing well, both financially and socially. Mr. L. was successful in his profession, earned well; they were able to buy a nice house, and she had no need to go out to work. At this point of the discussion it was pointed out that perhaps this was exactly what she could not tolerate; Mrs. L. belonged possibly to that group of women who can take everything in their stride as long as they feel independent of, and equal to, their male partners; as soon as the man has successes and the woman becomes dependent on him, neurotic or psychosomatic troubles appear.

The case history began now to make sense, both to the doctor and to the seminar. Mrs. L. had been fairly healthy as long as she was working. When her baby was due to arrive she gave up work and promptly she had some difficulties with her child. We categorized this very frequent occurrence in terms of the baby as the presenting symptom of the mother's illness. As her illness was neither recognized nor treated, in her need for help she 'offered' various psychosomatic illnesses to her doctor, to which he responded with symptomatic treatments and, when these did not help, with specialist examinations —a well established pattern in medical practice. As a last resource she developed her phobia and then the doctor realized that something ought to be done.

There are many points in this instructive case history that are still unclear; among them are the answers to such questions as: What was the last drop that brought about the development of the phobia? Why was travelling alone chosen to be the focus of her illness? What was the connection between her symptomatology and her sexual life? And so on. Her effect on the doctor suggests a similar pattern in her marital life: she appears as a helpless, attractive woman, badly in need of support, which appearance almost certainly masks a deep dissatisfaction with men in general, and possibly considerable envy of and hostility towards the successful man. If our reading of her illness and character is true, it explains why she has been left alone so much (the husband sensibly avoids her) and why she dreads loneliness (she is afraid of facing the result of her hostility) and why her doctor felt so helpless (this was exactly what she—unconsciously —aimed at).

As we see, the understanding of this case hinged on the reassessment of the developing doctor-patient relationship so that it, together with all the other symptoms of the patient, should make sense. The steps in the process were: (*a*) the patient created a hopeless feeling of futility in her doctor, (*b*) the doctor handed this feeling to us because by himself he could not recognize it as a symptom of the patient's illness, (*c*) we were able to show him the meaning of these dynamic processes in a way that made sense to him, and (*d*) this enabled him to understand better the problems facing him. Had we reacted in the way he did, both he and we would have failed to understand the patient's real problem.

Unfortunately soon after this discussion the couple bought a new house in a different part of the London area and left the doctor's practice. In consequence this case could not be followed up and so we have no proof, unlike the other cases reported in this book, whether our ideas were correct. By the way, we have to admit that the follow-up of the cases reported in this chapter will be, on the whole, less satisfactory than that in the others. Once the doctor has for some considerable time allowed his feelings to determine his handling of the case, the relationship between himself and his patient becomes so involved that he will find it very hard to extricate himself, that is, to change his responses to his patient, and still harder to achieve any change in his patient. So it happens, as it did with the family L, that eventually external circumstances intervene and the patient leaves the practice.[1] But even if the patient does not leave the practice, either he fades out or the relationship with his doctor remains strained and unproductive. As we shall see, it is only seldom that the doctor can retrieve the situation.

Our next case will show some of the difficulties that may obstruct the doctor in trying to cope with this task. As a rule it is not easy to recognize these difficulties, and still less to demonstrate them clearly. That we can do so in this case is owing to an unintended side effect of an experiment. In one of our more advanced groups we experimented with a record form specially designed to focus the doctor's attention, among other things, on the interplay of emotions between himself and his patient. The form itself has a long history. Originally it was devised by us for use in the Family Discussion Bureau for recording marital problem cases; was then taken over by a group of psycho-analysts who studied the possibilities of planned short-term therapy—called by us 'focal therapy', and naturally has undergone many modifications in its development. This particular group of general practitioners decided to use it for some time in order to improve the reporting techniques of its members. To prevent a possible criticism, we wish to state that this form is meant to be used only for patients whose physical condition has been fully examined by the doctor.

As the form was completed after the first decisive interview, one can clearly discern Dr. O's emotions both during the interview and somewhat later while completing the form. Since he saw the patient on three more occasions, we can follow him in his efforts to disentangle

---

[1] In a study of 1,000 patients who left their doctors the process described here was found to be active in a number of cases which were coded 'R'—moving to another district—or 'X'—moving to another address in the same district.

himself from the effects of his emotions and can assess in which way
he succeeded and in which he failed.

CASE 9

Mrs. P. aged fifty-six. Mother of family of three children. Interview
on Easter Tuesday.

A. Antecedents. Emergency call last night for asthma. Seen by me the
following afternoon after another morning call.

B. (1) Appearance and manner of patient. Calm, relaxed, and comfortable in bed. No dypsnoea. Semi-defensive attitude about night call
and present position.

B. (2) Complaints. Concentrated on details of tablets and medicine,
dosage, etc. Her asthma seemed to be something external to herself.

B. (3) What seems to bring patient now. Acute asthmatic attack previous night.

C. Factual material. Attacks began after birth of her first baby.
Asthma has become much worse since Christmas, since her son was
discharged from the Army. He wishes to be independent, comes home
late and father is very angry about it. Quarrels occur; she is afraid of
rowdy arguments because of the neighbours. This family is Roman
Catholic and they have to set a good example. Son is courting a nice
acceptable girl. A married older daughter and a younger unmarried
daughter. Husband a semi-skilled artisan. Live in an old-fashioned
London County Council Estate. They are not poor but the house is
always untidy and unkempt.

D. (1) Patient's conception of herself. A good mother, eminently
reasonable and understanding. Unfortunately martyred by her
asthma and therefore unable to do as much as she would wish.

D. (2) Patient's conception of other important people.
Husband: Strict and, though reasonable, impatient with family.
Son: Wonderful. Few faults except a little inconsiderate. *Mother:*
Wonderful. *Father:* Very strict and imposing. Feared and respected
but secretly mocked. Father was a strict policeman and mother
used to help her secretly against his discipline. *Daughters:* Barely
mentioned.

E. Developing doctor-patient relationship.

(1) How patient treated doctor. At first, as usual, rather defensive,

69

but as interview developed became coy, almost flirtatious, and appeared a much more handsome woman.

(2) *How doctor treated patient.* (At this point whilst writing up the report, I stopped to make a cup of coffee!!). At first I was grumpy and cross at the nuisance value of this patient. I do not recall at what point I became interested. I had at that time completely forgotten about this interview report. I had concentrated on why the attack last night had occurred.

Change occurred when patient denied any cause for worry the previous night although her children had gone to Brighton for the day by car on Bank Holiday Monday (Aside: It was the day that a lot of fuss was made about accidents on the road. I had no doubt mother was very worried). I became much more interested at this point and took careful note of the various relationships when the father-son hostility emerged.

F. Important moments in interview.

1. Denial of anxiety about danger of road accidents.
2. Admission of concern about father-son quarrels.
3. Concern about the neighbours and her good home.
4. Similarity between her playing off son against father and her mother against her father.
5. Recollection of how she had fallen in love with her husband when going out with his best friend and how the latter had given up with a good grace.

G. Summary.

Ways in which disturbance is shown in patient's life

1. Asthmatic attacks.
2. Slovenly interior.
3. Defensive attitude towards the outside world.
4. Secret hostility towards men covered by an apparently respectful attitude.[1]

We are fairly certain that a number of people will think that this report, as well as the examination upon which it is based, is certainly adequate, if not very good. This is true up to a point. The doctor undoubtedly got hold of a number of important facts which considerably contribute to the understanding of the whole case. However, on the top right-hand corner of the form there is printed in bold

---

[1] When reading this account of his report, Dr. O. added that he had forgotten to emphasize the intensity of Mrs. P's fear of being left alone; there had been occasions when her husband or her son had to stay at home as she could not bear to be alone.

capital letters and underlined: NEGATIVE FINDINGS MUST BE EXPLICITLY STATED. Although this instruction sounds rather superfluous, a kind of statement of the obvious, experience has taught us that it is almost impossible to observe it to its full extent. Because of his emotional entanglement the doctor does not notice that he has missed one or the other of the important points either during the examination or during the write-up, while a trained third person finds it easy to put his finger exactly on these missed details.

This was how the discussion of this case started in our seminar. After agreeing that this patient's relationships seem to conform with what Freud described as the principle of the damaged third partner, Dr. O. added as an afterthought that during the whole interview there was no mention of sex at all. He seemed to think that he must excuse himself for this omission and pointed out that it would have been awkward to broach the subject in the patient's bedroom, and that anyhow he had spent too much time with her. The seminar's emotions were apparently also involved here because we agreed with the doctor that sex should have been discussed at the first interview and even linked this omission with the doctor's need to make himself a cup of coffee at the moment when he was trying to give an account of his developing emotions during the interview.

First we dealt with some fairly obvious inferences which were not explicitly stated in the report. The asthmatic attack started after the children returned home, that is, when there was no longer any cause for worry. It was suggested that perhaps her attack was an expression of her resentment at being left alone during the Bank Holiday. The fact that Mrs. P. cheered up as the interview proceeded, that is, at receiving ample attention from her doctor, appeared to be in good agreement with this suggestion. We concluded that possibly Mrs. P. must attract attention, especially from men, makes therefore great efforts to be attractive and flirtatious, but for some reason or other must keep them unsatisfied. In other words, she promises a lot by her behaviour but never delivers the goods.

Dr. O. then told us that before the second interview he realized the absence of any sexual material in the first and decided to remedy this slight omission in a routine way. The second interview took place in the doctor's surgery about ten days after the home visit. The doctor learned that Mrs. P's marriage started indifferently but she became gradually more and more frigid and, parallel with it, the husband depressed and difficult to handle. It was only during the discussion that he realized that no other topic was dealt with, for instance: the slovenly house or her defensive attitude.

He was not very satisfied with the result but, instead of trying to

71

find out what had gone wrong, decided to press further in the same direction in the third interview. Mrs. P. admitted that she was completely uninterested and often refused intercourse with her husband. The doctor succeeded in enabling Mrs. P. to see the connection between her refusal and her husband's increasing awkwardness. We quote verbatim from the write-up of our discussion:

> After we discussed this she suddenly asked me, 'Do you think that is why he has become more irritable and difficult? He is always ill now.' I said, 'What do you think?' She said, 'I suppose it is. I see that now. What should I do?' I didn't tell her what to do, I asked her what she thought would be better. Was it difficult for her to have intercourse, was it unpleasant? She said no; she was just tired. I said, 'What would you gain by having intercourse more?' She said, 'I suppose he would be much better.'

The doctor's technique received at this point the somewhat harsh comment: 'You ask questions so that the patient's answers must prove you correct'. Dr. O. continued:

> Little else came out. I did see her again a week or so later. All that amounted to was that she told me how much better she felt, things were much better, everything going wonderfully well, more wonderfully well than they should have gone. She had been thinking about it, and the Church Circle, and she was going to join that and . . .

As the write-up shows, Dr. O. was not allowed to finish his sentence. Various members of the group interrupted him to show how insincere Mrs. P. was, that her description of the 'wonderful' improvement was not to be trusted, that she was willing to do more for the Church Circle but not for her husband, that she gave promises but nothing else, and so on. Only one of the doctors in the seminar thought that pushing Mrs. P. to have intercourse more often would be 'a kind of therapeutic copulation—"If you had intercourse more, he would be happier". Extraordinary! "If you are happier you might have intercourse more"—that might be true'. The seminar as a whole, however, were so engrossed in their indignation against Mrs. P. that they brushed this on one side and hot on the chase rebuked Dr. O. for not having pointed out to his patient that she was only joining the Church Circle in order to avoid doing more for her husband.

Dr. O. tried to defend his patient by saying that going to the

72

Church Circle might be the proper remedy against the feeling of loneliness which was so unbearable to Mrs. P. In order to convince us how sincerely co-operative Mrs. P. was, Dr. O. reported a further detail from the second interview. Doctor and patient were discussing a recent quarrel between father and son; the son had come home late and the father could not settle down to sleep afterwards.

> I asked, 'Why couldn't he settle down?' She said, 'He is very strict, doesn't want anything to happen.' I said, 'Like what?' She said, 'You know what youngsters are these days, out late . . .' It came out that father's annoyance about his son being out with a girl might be more than just strictness. It was not difficult to link up that father could be very annoyed and frustrated by not having sex. She really reached these conclusions for me.

Three points emerge from this report. One is Mrs. P's need, and ability, to appear in a favourable light, to create the impression that she is sensible, co-operative, in fact, is doing her best. The other is Dr. O's emotional response; although he was trying very hard indeed to arrive at an objective professional assessment of his patient's problems, he could not help responding positively to her, that is, accepting her version as sincere.

This is a fairly common pattern of doctor-patient relationship, called in our seminars 'mutual seduction'. Mrs. P. felt that her doctor was most understanding, sympathetic, and helpful, while Dr. O. felt that his patient was appreciative, sincere, and most co-operative. This is a mutually satisfactory relationship, the only snag is that it is rather expensive to both partners. The positive feelings engendered in the doctor may prevent him from noticing any offending trait in his patient, while the patient is prevented from, or at any rate severely inhibited in, disclosing anything that might upset the benevolent and helpful doctor. A further serious consequence is that in this way patients become trained to expect this kind of treatment, and any future attempt by the same, or any other, doctor to confront them with some unattractive aspects of their character will meet with great difficulties or may even become impossible. A parallel inhibition is created in the doctor.

With this we have arrived at our third point, the influence of these interconnected emotions on the handling of the case. The first interview, fully reported above, was definitely unsatisfactory. We would be equally justified in blaming either the patient or her doctor. The patient, true to her compelling need, tried to be, and succeeded in being, cheerful and seductive in order to prove to her doctor that

73

she was a co-operative and grateful patient. The doctor, inhibited by his own emotions, could not see beyond this façade, although he was fully aware that something was not going the right way—for instance, that his patient and he colluded in the first interview to avoid discussing unpleasant matters. Instead of stopping here to examine his own emotions as possible symptoms of his patient's illness, he jumped to the conclusion that the unpleasant topic avoided by both of them must have been the patient's sexual life. We wish to add that nowadays, under the influence of psycho-analytic theories, this is often assumed as a matter of course, without any further examination.

Under the influence of this assumption Dr. O. tried valiantly to redress the situation in the subsequent interviews but, of course, in vain; the ultimate result was bound to be unsatisfactory. We have to admit that during the first and larger part of the discussion the whole seminar, including the leader, were still further off the mark than Dr. O. They too acted upon their emotions and saw in Mrs. P. only a seductive and insincere woman who tries very hard to mislead her doctor and prevent him from broaching any unpleasant subject. Except for one doctor—who protested against prescribing 'therapeutic copulation'—all of us felt sympathetic towards the husband and criticized Dr. O. for not being more firm with Mrs. P. Dr. O. on the other hand, under the influence of his positive feelings for his patient, could not help rising to her defence against the seminar's narrow-minded attack. In this way a rather heated but fruitless debate developed. It was only later in the discussion, after we had got rid of some heat, that we realized that all of us were sinning against our principles.

As a proper examination *by* the patient was not carried out at any time it is difficult to evaluate the case with any certainty. Probably in addition to her need to attract men by being really charming, Mrs. P. has an equally compelling need to frustrate them. As she is terrified that the disappointed man might leave her, she has developed an uncanny skill at involving two important men in a struggle in which both of them try hard to get her on their side. In this way she avoids the terrifying danger of being left alone, but only at the price of living constantly in a strained atmosphere. It is worth noting that it was only when we reached this formulation at our seminar that Dr. O. admitted that he had never been able to understand why Mrs. P's home had always been shabby and sluttish. If instead of colluding with his patient in creating the atmosphere of mutual seduction he had started by examining *with* his patient the meaning of her sluttishness, the whole therapeutic situation would have been different.

Our last case will show the same situation from yet another angle. In a recent seminar Dr. G. introduced his report as follows:

There is really nothing very much to this case except that some time ago you asked if we would try and make a note of any patients that we came across who we felt had been helped by reassurance. I think that this woman may have been helped but I do not want to make too big a claim, I only felt that the alternative to reassurance was beyond me; so I am afraid I did just give her reassurance once or twice and, well, she has certainly not been bothering me, as it were, or coming to the surgery.

CASE 10

The patient is Miss F., an unmarried woman of thirty-four, living with her mother in a nearby town where Dr. G. is trying to build up a branch practice; it was the mother who, on the recommendation of another patient, transferred six months ago to Dr. G. As the public transport between the doctor's headquarters and this particular district is very poor and the number of patients has not yet warranted the opening of a branch surgery, all the consultations must take place in the patients' houses.

While the doctor was attending to the mother's various psychosomatic complaints, she mentioned that she had been worried about her daughter who had pruritus vulvae, was always getting colds, was easily tired, and so on, and asked the doctor to take her on. Dr. G. learned also that the daughter was given cortisone by her previous doctor for the pruritus. They agreed that after the statutory fourteen days the daughter would be taken on the doctor's list.

When Miss F. was examined she told him that she got easily tired, perhaps because of her very long day. She was working in London about forty miles away, which meant getting up early, travelling morning and evening in crowded trains, etc. Dr. G. continued:

What struck me though really was the almost complete barrenness of her life: she seemed really to have nothing in life at all. It seemed to me—and this was reinforced by a talk with her mother later— that her main problem was that she was thirty-four and still single and she desperately wanted to get married. There didn't seem to be any men in the vicinity; true, she had met one or two—there was one man, a year ago, that she thought she was going to be engaged to, and she had suddenly discovered this man was married. This had been a great shock. . . .

I felt really this was terrible; here was a girl without hope. At week-ends she had a friend, a female friend of about the same age, and they used to go out and have a drink together, I think that they were just hoping to meet some man, which was fair enough . . . But there was nothing else in her life at all, and here she was, quite a presentable girl of thirty-four . . . I felt really I wanted to sort of say to her—well, look, there are lots of things in life, really you must not waste your life and let it go by, there are all sorts of wonderful things going on, why not get some pleasure and enjoyment from them; but I somehow couldn't do this because I didn't really feel I was in a position to.

So I had to go through the routine of taking her full history and I examined her and I couldn't find very much. I ought to add that her pruritus was better. And I just sort of told her and reassured her that there was nothing physically wrong and I thought perhaps that things were getting her down and I sympathized with her about this problem; we got this problem into perspective a bit more about her not meeting men and not having men friends and no immediate likelihood of her getting married and really I just adopted a reassuring attitude in that light, as reassuring as I could.

This is a very common situation indeed. The patient has various, fairly impressive complaints, no physical signs can be found to explain them, and the psychological situation is either much too complicated or much too hopeless. It is in this constellation that doctors resort to sedatives and 'reassurance'. In the previous chapter we tried to show the futility of this procedure and emphasized that every symptom—however complex or hopeless the situation may appear—must be properly examined together *with* the patient and, if possible, *by* the patient. This advice is easy to give but, because of their training, doctors find it very hard to follow. That is why time and again we asked the doctors taking part in the seminars to report any patient who apparently had benefited from 'reassurance'. It was to this request that Dr. G. alluded in his opening remarks.

His report clearly shows that he decided not to examine the origins of the complaints, instead he reassured the patient. This happened early in 1960 and when we discussed the case towards the end of June we had only the results of a four-month follow-up. During this time Miss F. only once consulted her doctor for a slight upper respiratory infection, otherwise she seemed to be all right. This impression was confirmed by her mother whom the doctor saw a few times during this period, so Dr. G's claim of having observed a case in which reassurance did work seems to be justified.

To get to a better understanding of the dynamic processes operating in this case, and in many similar cases, we propose to discuss four points. The first is the simplest. We have found time and again that when doctors report that they have reassured a patient they sincerely feel that they have done so; however, if they are asked to repeat as nearly as possible what they actually said, more often than not they do not remember the words used, and even if they can remember, the repeated words do not appear reassuring to themselves any more and certainly not to any third person who was not present when the 'reassurance' took place. Of course it is a still more complicated and ambiguous question what the intended 'reassurance' actually meant to the patient. We shall discuss this as our last point.

When we asked Dr. G. in the seminar to repeat the reassurance given to his patient he replied, 'Well, that she hadn't got any physical disease—that was what she was putting over to me, officially anyway —but underneath this of course was the problem that she hadn't been able to get married.' When pressed whether he told her that she still could get married Dr. G. answered, 'Oh no, I couldn't.' Then he went on telling us in great detail how he explained to Miss F. that travelling, especially in the winter, might be the cause of her tiredness and irritation but as she was happy at her present job perhaps it was worth while, and so on.

As we just said, this is the typical situation. The doctor cannot remember exactly what he said and what he can repeat does not really amount to reassurance.

The next point we wish to discuss is why the doctor decided to act in this way. His sincere report shows how strong his feelings were when he examined this patient; but instead of stopping and examining his feelings as possible symptoms of the patient's illness—as advocated by us—he acted upon them. When questioned by the members of the seminar he was able to express explicitly what he felt: 'She was not a terribly intelligent girl . . . but physically and materially she was well provided for, it was a comfortable home and all the rest of it . . . but the life she was living at the moment seemed too appalling for words . . . I was afraid rather of letting her know how I felt . . . and I was in a bit of a quandary what to do and I admit that the reassurance was partly because of that.'

During the discussion it was pointed out to him that apparently Miss F. is able to create a situation in which she must be rejected as a woman and some surprise was expressed that Dr. G., who was known to all of us as an interested, kind-hearted, and sensitive doctor, could not escape from it. Dr. G. replied: 'It certainly did create complete pessimism in me for days afterwards and in fact I found myself for several days asking myself isn't there any way out, as it were? It seemed to me that there wasn't, because I did think actually of taking it up and going into the problem with her, but I felt that somehow she wouldn't be able to accept anything that I could offer on those lines.'

We hope that these excerpts from a tape record enable the reader to form a clear picture of the dynamic situation. Dr. G. felt sincere sympathy with the unhappy and apparently hopeless situation around Miss F. He was convinced that he had found the connection between her presenting symptoms and her present way of life but he simply could not see any ray of hope for a change for the better. Although he had no doubt that physically Miss F. was quite a presentable woman he found her completely unattractive. The idea of any man being married to her appeared to him appalling and—remarkably—he accepted her lack of intelligence as a sufficient cause for it. In his embarrassing quandary the only thing he could do was to 'reassure' her.

As it was worked out—somewhat mercilessly—in the seminar, the reassurance was not a reassurance at all; it only side-stepped the crucial problem which, according to the doctor, was at the root of her trouble and tried to alleviate some anxieties about things that did not matter very much either for the doctor or for the patient. It is understandable now why the doctor could not remember the exact wording of his 'reassurance' and why what he did remember was so inadequate and weak. It is also understandable why for several days after this interview he had felt so depressed.

What else could have been done? May we repeat: if the doctor feels anything while examining a patient he ought to stop and examine his feelings as possible symptoms of the patient's illness. What were the doctor's feelings in this case? That no one could marry this girl, that she had an appalling life, that he could not say to her that she was a nice girl, with a nice home, having a friendly and happy relationship with her mother, and that she must be an attractive proposition for the right man. We must add that we learned from Dr. G. that, although he knew that Miss F. had been suffering from pruritus, he was satisfied when he was told by her that her itching was now better and did not examine her genitals. If one takes all this together the impression emerges that Miss F. must create around her an atmosphere in which she must be rejected as a woman. The doctor's emotions now appear as symptoms of this general condition. Her tiredness, her irritability, and perhaps also her pruritus may be considered as further symptoms of the same general condition.

As because of the doctor's emotions the investigation was not done properly and certainly not *by* the patient, we can have only guesses but no proof about the causes of her general condition. If a girl has to travel every day twice forty miles to get back to her mother for the night, then there must be some very strong bonds linking the two women together. During the discussion Dr. G. disclosed some further details which are in good agreement with this idea; it was the mother who persuaded Miss F. to change over to Dr. G.; the patient who originally recommended Dr. G. was a woman; mother was always present when the doctor wanted to talk to Miss F; the girl friend with whom she used to go out for a drink during the week-ends fits well into the picture; and lastly, there is one more important detail, while Miss F. was still in puberty father left the family without any warning and disappeared for good. Taking all this into account, Miss F. seems to live in an entirely female world which perhaps is intolerant of males. All her symptoms, viewed from this angle, serve the purpose of preserving this world by shying men away.

There is one more point to discuss and that is how it happened that the so-called 'reassurance' did have some effect, inasmuch as for about four months now Miss F. has not bothered her doctor. Unfortunately here too we have to resort to guesses. Her pruritus suggests that, for some reason or other, the pressure in her was possibly on the increase. If properly handled, under this pressure she might have been able to respond constructively to a new doctor who was apparently warmly recommended to her. When instead of helping her to open up Dr. G. 'reassured' her and did not even dare to examine what was wrong with her as a woman either psychologically or physically, she must have felt disappointed, hopeless, and rejected. Possibly she had enough energy left to let her shutters down and not to expect help from the doctor who apparently could not understand her and talked only about irrelevant matters. Perhaps the slight upper respiratory infection was a kind of last attempt, a hope against hope; when she received for it merely the routine treatment she was completely defeated and the only thing she could do was reinforce her repressions. How long she will succeed in it, no one can tell.

The four case histories discussed in this chapter are only illustrative samples of this most important general problem. It can be confidently stated that in any psychotherapy the doctor's emotions play a crucial part. If the doctor works on his own, without any opportunity to discuss his technical experiences and problems with an uninvolved colleague, much more often than not the influence of his emotions on his treatments remains largely unrecognized. As a rule he may not even become aware of the fact that emotions have been stirred up in him by his patients. This is especially so if the treatment—as it happened in our Case 8—takes a satisfactory course.

Another factor, active in this field, makes it still more difficult for the doctor to recognize the influence of his emotions. This is the self-selection of the patients according to their doctor's technique. In our research seminars we have been struck time and again by the immense difference between one doctor's practice and another's. Events which happened as a matter of course in one practice were absolutely unthinkable in another. Even the people who constitute the practice seemed to be characteristic of that particular doctor. This applies to every sort of practice but, of course, much more forcibly to a general practitioner's practice in which this selection process has sufficient time to show its might.

The dynamic cause of these differences is fairly obvious. If the doctor's individual technique prompted by his characteristic emotions suits the patients, they stay with him and benefit by his administrations; if not, they transfer to another doctor. Thus it happens that in his own practice, especially if it has been well established, the doctor has less and less cause for examining critically his habitual emotional responses. It is not at all impossible that something similar might happen even in the practices of psycho-analysts. In any case we have the impression that certain analysts habitually report about a certain class of patients and hardly at all about any other.

The standard remedy recommended against the undesirable effects of the doctor's uncontrolled or unconscious emotions is personal analysis. The impression just quoted and the co-existence of differing psycho-analytic schools suggest that this remedy may have its limitations. This does not mean that personal analysis should be discontinued as the most important part of psycho-analytic training, but it definitely means that its limitations ought to be recognized and discussed. What we said about psycho-analytic training applies much more forcibly to all other, less rigorous, training schemes for the many varieties of psychotherapy, all of which help the doctor or the therapist up to a point to become aware of, to recognize, and to control his emotions, instead of acting upon them. In our experience the limits of this kind of help are reached when the emotions engendered in the doctor belong to what is called sensible responses. By their appearance they avoid the normal watchful criticism and are accepted as part of the average professional psychotherapeutic attitude. The few cases reported here contain enough material to show how dangerous it is to rely on this belief.

We would repeat that we have not found the general remedy for this most important technical problem. We are fully aware that our advice: 'If the doctor feels anything while treating a patient, he must stop and examine his feelings as a possible symptom of the patient's illness but on no account act upon them', is simple and unobjectionable in theory, but it is very hard to follow it to its full extent in practice. The particular remedy that we found fairly satisfactory is the participation in an on-going case conference in which the uninvolved members of the conference may more easily recognize the doctor's emotions than the involved doctor himself.

In the previous chapter, when discussing the complex relationship between Dr. A. and Mrs. L. (Case 5), we reached the question whether our kind of approach amounts to a psychotherapy *of* the doctor and, if so, whether it is a fair and sensible procedure and what can be expected from it. We hope that the material presented in this chapter proves convincingly enough that every psychotherapist must be able to become aware of his emotional involvement in any one of his patients. Any psychotherapy, even the most superficial variety, demands a certain amount of self-awareness and self-control from the therapist. The deeper he intends to probe into his patient's problems, the higher will be this demand on him; therefore the acquisition of any psychotherapeutic skill is inseparable from an increased self-awareness and self-control, which is tantamount to a limited though considerable change of his personality. This is what might be called psychotherapy *of* the doctor and one of the most important aspects of this therapy is the examination of the doctor's emotional responses.

CHAPTER 7

The Present and the Absent Patient

Although the cases to be discussed here are only special examples of the complications caused by the doctor's emotions, and might thus have been dealt with in the previous chapter, none the less, because of their importance we decided to devote a separate chapter to them.

When consulting a doctor, patients often report about difficulties in their relationships with other people, in particular with their nearest relatives, and in many cases these difficulties seem to constitute a major part, if not the core, of the aetiology of their illnesses. The cases to be quoted in this chapter will amply illustrate this important point.

In every case in which there is a highly charged emotional relationship between two people and a third person is consulted about it, that person will find it difficult to remain objective and to avoid getting emotionally involved in the situation. Of course, his task in remaining objective will be incomparably more difficult if the problem causing the strain between the two people is similar to, or identical with, one with which he is himself struggling or for which he has been able to reach some kind of solution only with difficulty. There are two groups of problems for which very, very few of us are lucky enough to have found a satisfactory solution. These are the problems arising in the relationship between sexual partners and between parents and children. Unfortunately these two are exactly the problems for which doctors are consulted time and again.

There are several very common automatic reactions that must be watched most carefully in a psychotherapeutic practice. If the doctor has been lucky enough to solve the problem in question fairly satisfactorily for himself, he may honestly feel that his solution is unquestionably the best and will try to recommend it to, or even impose it on, everybody, even on those whose nature or character is incompatible with this particular solution. This is the simplest and most transparent case—at any rate, to an uninvolved third person, but many complicating factors may be present to obscure the issue.

One of them is the tendency to identify oneself with one of the two partners, seeing only his side of the problem to the extent of becoming almost blind to the other. Thus, in one of our seminars a particular doctor reported about a whole series of truly angelic women; they were affectionate and devoted to their children, looked after them impeccably, kept their homes in perfect order, although in more than one case they had to go out to work to supplement their family income, because their husbands were either severely disturbed people who could not work, or habitual drunkards, or gambled the money away, and so on, and so on. The reports were consistent and all the details fitted together excellently : these women were truly angelic. It was only after some considerable time that the seminar gradually discovered that these angelic women had some share, often a major share, in creating a relationship which eventually drove their husbands away from them.[1] It is noteworthy, however, that even after this discovery the doctor continued to report cases of angelic women and still needed considerable help from the group to see the not quite so angelic sides of their characters. Needless to say, the doctor was a woman.

Naturally this kind of idealization of a certain type is fairly general; the mechanism is always the same; it is only the type that changes. For one doctor, for instance, young, compliant, obedient women with little children were irresistible; they could do nothing wrong. Another doctor simply could not help rallying to the support of middle-aged, fairly cantankerous women, and did not mind even if they made his life rather unpleasant with their bitter and highly personal criticisms. A third doctor's type were upstanding, young, sportsmanlike men, who, because of some neurotic trouble, got into difficulties with their womenfolk, mothers, wives, or sweethearts. This enumeration could be continued endlessly.

There is, however, one type of emotional reaction which we must single out because of its technical importance. The usual pattern is as follows: a fairly neurotic man or woman comes to the doctor with various complaints, the origins of which, as a rule, can easily be traced back to a disturbed emotional relationship. Although it is clear that the patient present has his share of responsibility for the strained relationship, the partner's share seems to be so overwhelming that the doctor cannot help but sympathize with the present, and put the chief blame on the absent, partner.

The immediate results of this approach are usually, though not invariably, good. The doctor and the present patient then settle down

[1] In recent years several authors have studied the alcoholic's wife who apparently is not always an innocent victim of adverse circumstances.

together to try to do something about the absent patient who, if asked to come to see the doctor, sometimes refuses; if he or she does come, the resulting interview is more often than not unsatisfactory, thus reinforcing the doctor's opinion that the 'absent' partner is the really ill one. Of course, the present partner is very grateful, finds the doctor most sympathetic and understanding; at the same time the situation eases a little, but unfortunately the improvement is neither sufficient nor lasting; in due course, the present partner returns to the doctor with further complaints, now almost exclusively about the absent one. Thus, a vicious circle develops and the doctor and the present partner spend their energies in treating the one who really is never there. It is no wonder that in these circumstances the treatment is not very successful.

Our next case shows the first stages of this process. Although the doctor in charge of this case had had some considerable experience, because of his emotional identification with the present patient he was not able to see the full implications of his technique. A further factor which may have contributed to creating his emotional response was that his therapeutic attempts of the previous few years with the 'absent patient' had not been very successful.

CASE 11

John K. (*Asthma*) *Age fifteen.* In July 1960 the doctor reported that about six weeks earlier he had been called out at night to see this boy with a fairly bad attack of asthma. The family had been on his list for more than ten years and he had known the boy since the beginning of his asthma, but recently had seen him but seldom. The doctor felt a tense atmosphere between mother and son and soon learned that, against mother's wishes, John used to stay out late at the local billiard hall which was frequented also by teddy boys. Mother also complained bitterly that John's father was weak and it was left entirely to her to discipline John. On this occasion John was given an adrenalin injection and the attack soon cleared up.

Four weeks later the doctor was called out again in the evening because John had another attack. We quote now from the write-up of our discussion:

I sat down to discuss what might have brought the attack on. He is a nice boy, not unintelligent, but he does not show it, is very silent. When I asked him questions he would not answer, he nodded or closed his eyes; rather withdrawn at that visit. Mother was in

the room, and as I wanted to see the family together I did not ask
her to leave. I asked him what brought this attack on. On the previous visit mother had told me there had been a certain amount of
trouble at school; first, John had missed a lot of schooling through
his illness and, secondly, he had played truant for a day with
another boy. They had been found out and he had given up his
friendship with the other boy. John thought it might have been
something he had eaten that had brought the attack on. I didn't say
much but my face was dubious. Mother said, might it have been
the weather? I again looked dubious. Mother then started talking
about her attempts at disciplining the boy. She had treated him
leniently though she really did not like the teddy boys at the
billiard hall; John must be in at 10 o'clock, he must get sleep, his
health was not good.

John woke up a little and I said, 'What do you think?' He said
he wanted to go out, there was no harm done at the billiard hall.
I decided to side with the boy and I said, 'He is growing up, he is a
man now'. He brightened up a bit, started to talk, and the asthma
diminished. We were looking for causes for attacks in general and
for this attack in particular; mother and son thought that a row
he had had with his brother Peter, who is one year older, might be
behind it. Peter is very clever, goes to a grammar school, wants to
be a scientist, is very good at chemistry and mathematics, while
John is not brilliant, wants to be a market gardener. That struck me
as odd, being in the middle of a suburb, so I asked why. He has an
uncle (mother's brother) he likes very much who is a market
gardener and has chickens and pigs. Every week-end John goes
and looks after the chickens and pigs, and loves it. Mother said,
'Could that be the cause of asthma? He works hard there.' John
said no, he likes it and doesn't have to work hard. Uncle has
asthma too, the only other member of the family with it. John
wants to follow in his uncle's footsteps and become a market
gardener. I said, 'You want to follow in his footsteps and have
asthma too'. He laughed outright and brightened up and that was
the end of his attack.

Then father came in, a big aggressive-looking working man.
Though he looks like a boxer he is very meek and mild. We went
on talking about what could have upset John. Father joined in,
said he could think of nothing, everything worked perfectly, he
never told him off, though mother was sometimes a bit hard with
him because he goes out. Father did not mind, but the woman
runs the house, and there it is. Mrs. K. by that time had become a
bit anxious and she gave her point of view that children must not go

to bed late. John argued with her. The argument was now between mother and son, father and myself being onlookers. The attack had then finished. I gave John some tablets and said, 'Would you like to come to see me on your own? Perhaps we can discuss these problems.' He said he wouldn't mind but he has to go to school; perhaps during the holidays he might. He came on Tuesday for tablets. The asthma had been better and he had gone to school all the time. He said he might come during the holidays but the difficulty was he was going to uncle's to work in the market garden and he did not know what time he would come home, it depended on the amount of work that there was to be done. That completed the interviews.

I brought with me the cards of these people and I have not looked at them, I thought it would be better if I did it here. Mother has been a patient of mine since 1948. She had a thyroidectomy done and became myxoedematous. She was on thyroid medication for some considerable time, she developed some thyrotoxic symptoms until the dose was adjusted; during these years I saw her a good deal. In 1954 she came for an attack of depression. We discussed relations with her husband; it turned out she was frigid. She showed a lot of resentment against the children, the family did not understand her, she felt lonely and out of it. I saw her last in 1957 when she came with hot flushes. My partner saw her in 1958 and 1960. She had hydrocortisone ointment, I suppose she had dermatitis of sorts. She is obviously a very tensed-up woman; nice and pleasant but there is a lot underneath.

Husband is a bricklayer, a skilled profession, well paid too. Not a frequent visitor. Came last in 1958. Comes mainly for lumbago and sciatica.

John has had asthma since 1950. He went to an open air school and did not like it there.

Peter, the intelligent boy, is a very rare visitor to the surgery. I saw him once in 1958, he had a boil, and two colds. In 1959 he saw my partner, with a boil on his face, when I was on holiday.

Before discussing the many psychologically interesting implications of this report, we have to add a few more factual data which we learned from the doctor when we questioned him. John's asthma started about 1950 when two important events happened to him: he started going to school and his mother had her thyroidectomy. Now at ten years' distance it is difficult to say which of the two was more important. The fact is that neither son nor mother was offered psychotherapy at the time; on the other hand, all this happened in the doctor's pre-Tavistock period. Next we learnt that before 1954 the family consulted any member of the partnership who happened to be available, that from 1954 to 1957 Mrs. K. came regularly to our colleague, and a kind of close psychotherapeutic relationship developed between the two, but for some reason or other, since 1957 Mrs. K. had changed over to our doctor's partner.

The first technical problem that the doctor had to solve was how to conduct the interview. We heard (*a*) that John was rather a silent boy, not very forthcoming, and (*b*) that the doctor had tried with Mrs. K. but had not succeeded. In these circumstances it is understandable that the doctor decided to have a joint interview with mother and son. This meant that instead of tackling the resistances active in each of the two partners individually, the doctor decided to circumvent them. Whether this choosing the way of least resistance is or is not a good policy in the long run is difficult to say. In any case the joint interview was sufficiently productive but only at a price. As one of our members pointed out, all the attention was centred round Mrs. K. and 'the interview ended in a situation of three men (father, son, and the doctor) ganging up against the woman. As a family doctor this may cost you something.'

All of us agreed that in this case mother and son were tied up with each other but we could not decide whether it was a case of a domineering mother or of a dependent son who must have his mother's approval. We noted the fact that at his mother's request John gave up his friendship with the boy with whom he was truanting, but unfortunately this is compatible with either of our explanations. The same is true about his identification with his uncle who is mother's brother. Apparently the present material does not allow us to decide the issue.

The technical question is, has the doctor created by his approach a situation that will make the next therapeutic step easier or more difficult? His 'ganging up' with the boy against his mother is a typical case of treating the absent patient. This would be justified only in cases in which the present patient may be confidently diagnosed as the presenting symptom of the absent patient's illness. This, as our research has shown, is often the case when parents bring their children frequently with minor complaints to the doctor. Does John's asthma belong to this class, that is, is it the presenting symptom of his mother's illness? This is a difficult question to answer but on the whole one may say that, even though originally in the early 1950s the asthma might have been one symptom of the mother's illness, in 1960 it would be safer to accept it as an illness in its own right.

If this is so, then the doctor's technique in the joint interview must be criticized on two counts. One must ask how her recent experiences will influence Mrs. K's attitude to the doctor in the future. Unquestionably the answer is that as she must have felt criticized and let down in front of her son and husband, she will not find it easy to confide in the doctor. The other question is, how will John react? From what we said in the introduction to this chapter we would expect a temporary improvement in his state, a friendlier attitude towards the doctor, willingly agreeing with him that the chief blame has to be put on his mother, but also an increase of resistance which will block the way in any other direction.

When we asked the doctor whether John's attitude had been changed by the interview, he answered: 'John has always been a rather distant child, would not say much. He accepted injections and tablets but was very suspicious of me. The first time he talked was really when I took sides with him against his mother. The first time he came without his mother was the day before yesterday, when he was friendly and spoke quite freely. We have achieved a new relationship . . . he came as a mature person putting his case to the doctor, explaining why he could not come.'

This seems suspiciously near what we call mutual seduction. John behaves as the doctor would expect him to behave, the doctor is appreciative and likes the boy, and both of them accept that there are external difficulties, and tacitly agree not to examine the internal ones. This pattern was set when John and his doctor agreed that mother—the absent patient—was to be blamed. Among other things this enabled the doctor to feel that after all it was not entirely his fault that the therapeutic venture in 1954 to 1957 had proved a failure and in the same way enabled the boy to forget his inability to strike out independently to find a place for himself in life. At home he is tied up with his mother, in his leisure time with his teddy boys, and, at any rate for the present, in his choice of profession with his maternal uncle. Unless the doctor can extricate himself speedily from this mutual seduction, the prognosis for his therapeutic venture is not very good.

Next we quote another case in which the treatment of the absent partner had gone on for some years. A remarkable change took place when the doctor, under the influence of the seminar, altered his therapeutic approach.

CASE 12

Mrs. B. was in her early thirties when she first consulted the doctor eight years ago for feeling generally ill and tired. She was married for the second time; her first marriage had lasted barely a year when her husband was killed during the war. By her second husband she had one son who was four years old when she first consulted the doctor.

At the beginning of the treatment the patient spoke very little about herself though she frequently stated that her first marriage had been perfect in every respect and her second marriage could not be compared with the first. In fact, as gradually transpired, she had only lived with her first husband for brief periods during his leaves. The doctor commented that perhaps it was hard on the present husband to be compared so often with the first, but otherwise he accepted the patient's view that her present husband was indeed unsatisfactory.

Though Mrs. B. constantly complained of feeling ill and tired she was told by her husband and her mother-in-law to pull herself together. Eventually Mrs. B. was found to have pleurisy and T.B. and the doctor had to agree with his patient's criticisms of her husband and mother-in-law who had egged her on to an active life when she was really so ill.

She spent several months in a sanatorium; on returning home Mrs. B. found that her husband had been having an affair with a girl she knew. As she could not forgive him, she left him, taking her son with her. Her husband first asked her for a divorce but he soon changed his mind and wrote again saying that his affair had ended and he wanted his son back again. After about six months she returned to him and the couple tried to make a life together for the sake of the child.

We now quote verbatim from the doctor's report to one of our seminars:

The next thing was that the husband rang me up. He said 'I agree with you, I am a so-and-so. My wife came home and told me how appalling you thought I was.' I said I had not said that, though I might have accepted what she said. Subsequently I saw both of them together; she said she thought I had agreed with her, but I said I didn't say so.

I'm afraid I was misled into looking mostly at the husband until now. He was the illegitimate son of a well-known personality, who was married and extremely wealthy. This boy's mother was his mistress. He kept them in luxury and used to visit them. The boy felt ashamed of the luxury in comparison with his school friends and would beg the chauffeur not to meet him at school. When his wife died the father did not marry his mistress, but married a much younger woman. Up to the age of thirteen the boy

89

had not known he was illegitimate. His mother was romantic; regarded it as the love affair of her life. When the father died he left the boy very well off and he never had to work.

As a sixth-form prefect at 17 he ran away from school after a row with somebody. His housemaster thought he was very clever and got him into a College. He got very near his degree and then ran away again. He has never finished anything. According to his G.P. and psychiatrist, he would have been better with a little honest work. He took up a semi-artistic profession and became quite good at it, but couldn't earn much. He is a tall and diffident man, speaking slowly with almost a stammer.

It was at this interview that Mrs. B. started to talk about herself. She said she married her husband because he needed looking after. Her story is that when she and her sister were small, father left mother. She was brought up by grandparents in a small place abroad, where grandfather was highly thought of and practically ran the community. She has an enormous admiration for the grandparents—not for mother. Mother married again and she liked the stepfather. She said nothing about her own father at this stage.

The doctor then reported that after he had talked things over with his patient and given some help and encouragement, the couple got on rather better for two or three years and even decided to have another child, after which the doctor saw them only occasionally for contraceptive advice or when they had some troubles which were attributed to external circumstances, such as illness or domestic difficulties, etc. Then one night Mrs. B. rang up the doctor and reported another crisis precipitated by her husband's failure to want to keep any job. She asked him to come urgently. As during the next episode a dramatic change occurred we will quote verbatim from the doctor's report:

Then in September 1958 she rang up at about 10 p.m. and said, 'Please will you do something—we are at the end of our tether.' As she couldn't leave the children, the husband came to fetch me in his car. She was lying on a couch saying, 'I can't go on.' He sat in a corner: 'The only thing is to kill myself—there's nothing else to do!' I thought I had been looking at him all the time, and now I was going to look at her. I asked what was bothering her. She said she wasn't sure, but she thought her father was in jail. She poured out a lot of her home story. At the next interview she told me she had a letter from her stepmother to say her father had died of cancer, and what a brave, heroic man he had been. She had thought her father was utterly bad and that she was like him. Her mother hated him and used to say she was like father. She began to think perhaps father hadn't been in gaol at all; that it was a fantasy. Perhaps she too, like him, wasn't so bad.

Soon afterwards, so as to have something to do, the husband got a job in a small firm. Money was getting tight. Then she rang up again to say they had pulled themselves together. She came a few weeks later to see me and said she wanted to have a job, but couldn't because she was so preoccupied with the children. I asked why does she have to help her twelve-year-old boy to do his homework? Why does she protect her sons so much? She said she was afraid. I asked who was going to endanger them. Then she broke down and said she killed her first husband. He was away in the Forces for a year and wrote loving letters. Never let her quarrel with him at all—would always stop her if she was 'wicked'; managed her very well.

On the last occasion she had seen him on one of his leaves, they had had their first quarrel and she had written an angry letter to him. A few days later he was killed in a car accident; he was driving, and others had been killed too. Ever since she had been blaming herself that her letter had distressed him and made him careless. This is what was troubling her, and she had never dared to think of it until now. I asked if that was why she protects everybody, manages her husband, will not let him buy his own shirts, and must wear herself out decorating the house because she can't let him help.

After this interview she was very disturbed for several days, but when she came a week later she told me that an extraordinary change had occurred in her husband although she had told him nothing at all. He had got promotion in his job which he had threatened to throw over a few weeks before. He was taking much more interest in the home and children and, as she put it, 'He's quite different, seems to have wakened up to life'. He was taking initiative in the home, standing up to her and helping her and she said, 'He has changed—I don't know him.' I said perhaps she had changed. She said, 'I suppose I have—but he has gone and bought himself six shirts! I have stopped helping my son with his homework, for which he has thanked me. I don't know what has happened.'

Soon she was able to bring out more freely her resentment about his infidelity and relate it to her own attitude to him at the time it occurred. She disclosed that he had said, 'It would not have happened if I had not felt our marriage was already over. You made me feel you had no further use for me.'

I have seen her every week since. She says the home is so different —no outsize battles. Recently she told me that she could not bear to have intercourse because she was always thinking about the prostitutes her husband had admitted. This week she came and said they had intercourse several times in the last two weeks, and she has had an orgasm. I felt that this change happened because I started to look at the patient as well as her husband.

There is a whole host of absent patients in this case history whose treatment prevented the doctor for several years from seeing the real patient: Mrs. B. First, there is the seriously ill husband; it is hardly possible to find a better scapegoat. Then there is the 'wicked' father whom, because he was shrouded in his wickedness, neither the doctor nor the patient could see as a real person. There are the patient's mother and stepmother, and lastly, the patient's mother-in-law and, perhaps, her husband's natural father, now dead. All of them were made responsible for this and that, and at the end the patient emerged as a poor harassed woman who has been trying very hard to do her best. Only when the doctor became able to turn his attention away from the absent patients to the present one, did the situation change.

Correspondingly the case history is divided into two well-defined parts. The first part shows the characteristic atmosphere of mutual seduction. Doctor and patient agree that the real causes of all the troubles against which the patient seems to struggle so valiantly are external to her. The doctor is understanding and sympathetic, the patient co-operative and appreciative. This pleasant atmosphere, however, has to be paid for by an almost complete paralysis. The patient cannot do anything but suffer and struggle in vain while the doctor is unable to help and the only thing he can do is to give his patient sincere sympathy. It is only in the second part when the attention of both patient and doctor has been turned away from external causes towards the patient's internal world that the real examination starts. We wish to stress that it was a real examination, not only together *with* the patient but largely *by* the patient. In this respect this case could have been quoted as an illustration in Chapter 5.

It took several years before the doctor could see his way to a more effective approach. Admittedly the knot to be unravelled was most complicated in this case because both classes of the most commonly found problems were operating in it: those arising in a sexual partnership and those in a parent-child relationship. It would be an interesting task to follow up the interactions between these two classes of problems in this case, but it would lead us too far from our topic.

As this point—*if at all possible never treat the absent patient*—is of crucial importance for any psychotherapy, we wish to illustrate it with two more cases. The next case is fairly simple because the doctor, under the influence of our seminars, right from the outset took a straight line and never wavered from it. The general structure of the case is about the same as in the previous one, although in fairness it ought to be stated that the people in it were definitely less ill. On the other hand, here too we will find both classes of the most commonly met problems, those originating in the relationship to the sexual partner and those in the relationship between parents and children.

In August 1958 a doctor reported that he had recently seen Mrs. D., twenty-six years old. She came with her husband and for a few minutes the doctor saw them together. It was only the husband who spoke while the wife sat silent.

CASE 13

Mr. D. explained that he and his wife were unable to have normal sexual relations, though they had been married two years. They had attempted intercourse several times during the first six months with partial success, but I gathered they had made no attempts at all during the last eighteen months. The husband said there were faults on both sides. They start to make love quite normally, and then the wife literally forces herself away from him. At this point I decided to see the wife alone.

Her story is that she is one of three children—there is an older sister and a younger brother. She was proud of the fact that she and her brother had gone to grammar school, mentioning this several times during the interview. She was fairly happy at home, more fond of her father than of her mother, who was irritable and not very well, possibly owing to change of life. When Mrs. D. left school she took a job as a telephonist (in spite of the grammar school education). After six months she left home, by agreement with her parents, because of arguments, mostly with her mother, about coming home late from dances, and shared a flat with another girl. When the girl she lived with got T.B., Mrs. D. returned home and things settled down.

She met her husband's mother who was working at the same switchboard. Her future mother-in-law introduced her as a possible future wife to her son Bertie, who duly acquiesced and took her out! Mrs. D. does not like her mother-in-law, who is domineering. The mother-in-law's own husband left her when the boy was three, and she has had no one except her son to care about her; her own brothers and sisters threw her off because of her constant interference. She thinks of Bertie as her baby and wants him all to herself.

After they were introduced the couple went out together for four years. Mrs. D. had had previous boy friends, but they had not interested her sexually. She approved of Bertie because he did not go in for heavy petting and 'messing around'. There was a certain amount of kissing. He never suggested marriage, but she brought matters to a head by threatening to discontinue the friendship unless he agreed to an engagement followed by marriage. She was now twenty-three and all her friends were getting married. They were engaged for six months and then got married.

They had to live with mother-in-law for a few months and the two frequently quarrelled—faults on both sides. Now Bertie sides with his wife, although originally he sided with his mother. They bought their own home and settled down. About the same time she had some trouble with irregular menstruation, and that was the point at which they gave up trying intercourse. Her own parents emigrated and she missed them, particularly her mother.

There was quite a lot of difficulty in the sexual relationship. First Bertie failed to penetrate and the wife thought it was because she was too small. Mother-in-law gave her a book to read before marriage; this went into great detail, especially about initial pain at intercourse. They tried using a sheath for contraception, but this was very painful. Now she does not mind her husband starting to make love to her, but she becomes nauseated and has even vomited on several occasions. If he tries to go on she starts feeling pain as soon as he begins to penetrate. It is not really a pain; she cannot describe it—calls it a 'funny sensation'. Although she said she felt very guilty about her husband's frustration, she did not look particularly guilty. She apologizes to him afterwards because she thinks it is the right thing to do, as he is upset. Mother-in-law is anxious to have a grandchild and is urging them to have a baby, but Mrs. D. doesn't really want one. I offered to fit her with a cap but she refused. Yet she uses internal sanitary protection and has no difficulty in inserting it. She doesn't seem very disturbed about the whole affair. She hates her mother-in-law, and that is as far as we got.

The first question that we had to decide in the seminar was: who was the patient and who should be treated? In these complex cases we have two rules to help us; both are empirical rules only. The first is that, as a rule, the member of the group who comes first and asks for help is the least ill of the lot and therefore has a better prognosis than the rest. Our second empirical rule warns us that often one partner may be produced as the presenting symptom of the other partner's illness. If this is the case one should not waste much time and energy in treating the presenting symptom but, if possible, aim at a radical cure. As the policies advocated by the two rules are diametrically opposite, it is essential to reach a reliable diagnosis of the whole constellation right at the outset.

The diagnosis was not easy in this case. It was clear that both partners had failed in their sexual adjustment. The fact was that the husband came first but he presented his wife. Did it mean that he was the patient or that he was only the presenting symptom of his wife's illness?

Let us take the husband's case first. He is the only son of a domineering, interfering mother; his father left him when he was three, and since then he has been at the mercy of his mother who almost certainly turned all her pent-up libido on him, very likely in the form of aggressive, domineering affection; under these circumstances he could not develop into a mature and self-assertive male; we know that he obediently accepted the girl picked up for him by his mother and, in the same way, agreed to engagement and marriage when his future wife forced him into it; we know also that he was not very adventurous in his courtship, and his attitude towards his wife's sexual difficulties is definitely defeatist.

The wife's case is equally clear. She must be a fundamentally frightened and inhibited woman, which would explain her lack of ambition; after a grammar school education most people would aspire to become more than a switchboard telephonist. When we asked the doctor, we learned also that her dress and make-up were nondescript and unambitious; then there is her reticence against exposing herself to any sexual excitement, both before and after marriage; this general inhibition seems to extend to her physiological sexual development—as we have learned, she was suffering from dysmenorrhea and irregular menses. It is in good agreement with this idea that she chose as her partner a meek and considerate man, and not a forceful and sexually demanding husband. Then there are her slight hysterical symptoms, nausea and vomiting, when she is forced to endure sexual excitement, and lastly—a most characteristic symptom—her detached, smiling indifference. Mother-in-law, husband, everybody seems to be concerned about the situation and feels that something ought to be done, but she remains unconcerned.

After a long discussion we came to the conclusion that perhaps it was a better plan to treat the wife. We felt that her smiling indifference and slight hysterical symptoms were only a cover for a rather forceful personality. If the treatment could enable her to get in touch with her inhibited self-assertiveness and liberate it sufficiently, things would develop in the right direction.

A month later the doctor reported:

I have seen her twice since our discussion. The first time she was getting nowhere and still seemed unconcerned. As a child she knew nothing about menstruation and was frightened when it started suddenly while cycling. Her mother wouldn't explain it and sent her to an aunt. At the second interview she was much better, but now her husband was not 'obliging' and she felt depressed. She wants intercourse now but Bertie turns over and goes to sleep! She spoke to him and he told her to mind her own business. Now she begs me to see her husband. She may be making progress, but now we are meeting resistance from him.

This is a fairly frequent development and quite characteristic of this kind of case. What should the doctor do? Shall he accept the—apparently quite justified—description of the patient, stop her treatment, and turn his attention to the husband, or, also a frequently adopted measure, ask the husband now to come with his wife and have a joint interview with the couple? Both of these techniques are highly reasonable and it is easy to find arguments to justify them. The only trouble is that the price to be paid for them is rather expensive as they unavoidably mean that the main attention is shifted —partly or entirely—to the other partner, while at the same time the treatment of the first partner is slowed down or even made to fade out.

While we were discussing this case, this danger—diminishing the intensity of the present partner's treatment while turning our attention to the absent one—was constantly in our mind. Still there were many reasons why one could think Bertie ought to have some treatment. His potency was never particularly good, he started taking his girl out only at his mother's bidding, he was not very enterprising during the four years' courtship, his lack of interest in sexual intercourse as soon as his wife showed some keenness—the whole picture is rather impressive. For some time the discussion went to and fro, but at the end we all agreed with the doctor who proposed to concentrate his efforts on the wife and leave the husband alone, at least for the time being. One of the reasons that influenced our decision was that we learned from the doctor that in the last week Mrs. D. stood up against her mother-in-law and told her to mind her own business. This was definitely a promising sign suggesting that she was getting nearer to her self-assertiveness, so we agreed that her treatment should proceed, irrespective of the state of her husband.

As the course of the treatment is not important for our argument we shall quote only the doctor's final report which was given to the seminar five months after the initial interview:

> Mother-in-law was staying with them for several weeks, thoroughly upsetting the household; eventually she got a job in the country as a companion-help. Things settled down and Mrs. D. said she felt guilty coming to see me with nothing much to tell. I asked what she was keeping back—what did she want to tell me. She said she felt it was Bertie's fault, he was having premature ejaculation; and anyhow, he was too rough, wouldn't wait long enough for her to get interested. We left it at that but she went off and had a heart to heart talk with Bertie. I think we discussed in the seminar whether I should see Bertie; I decided against it, chiefly because I didn't feel strong enough. She went off and did it for me.
>
> Things improved after that. Mother-in-law came back but now Mrs. D. could cope with her. Another thing that may be significant is that her sister rushed off and married a black man, against everyone's advice. She, too, had been living with Mrs. D. for some time. The sister seemed happy and went back to Africa with her husband, though Mrs. D. thinks the marriage will break up before long. After her sister had gone, she suddenly got on much better with her husband and they have actually managed to have intercourse quite normally. She even reached orgasm once or twice. Bertie thinks it's because they have bought an electric blanket! The interesting thing is that everybody at work has commented on how she has improved. She has actually been upgraded in her job, and her husband also says she is more responsible in the house and is coping better. They want a baby and she is now discussing whether she is likely to produce one. They have never used contraceptives. Shall I go further or leave her alone?

We learned from the doctor that Mrs. D. was seen about once a fortnight during this time, that is, eight to ten times altogether, certainly a commendable result. Moreover—it was she herself who took matters in hand and was able during her 'heart to heart' talk to make her husband veer round; she must have gained considerably in confidence and also in her self-assertiveness. Undoubtedly all this would have been missed if the doctor had spoken to her husband or, still more, if the husband had been taken into treatment. Thus it was the doctor's choice of approach that created favourable con-

ditions for Mrs. D. But what about Bertie? Here we are not on the
same safe ground. We know he used to be an obedient son to his
mother and had some difficulty in transferring his allegiance from his
mother to his wife. Has the 'heart-to-heart' talk sealed his fate for
good, and will he now be for ever an obedient husband to his wife?
Would it have been better for him if, instead of his wife, an understanding and sympathetic male doctor had had a 'heart-to-heart'
talk with him? We must admit we do not know the answers, but we
must stress what we know, namely, that it was possible to carry out
Mrs. D's treatment to a fairly satisfactory conclusion by treating
only the present patient without any attempt at involving the absent
one.

In our last case it had to be accepted that the absent partner was
really ill; still it was most important that the present patient should
be properly examined, since failing in this would have meant missing
the opportunity to offer help to the present patient who, in fact, was
in very bad need of it.

CASE 14

Mrs. W. was referred to a psychiatrist by her general practitioner
with the following letter:

Thank you for seeing Mrs. W. I do not really know how best to
advise her.

She came to see me first a year ago saying that her husband was
exposing himself at the windows of their home and she feared that
the neighbours would complain. When the story came out it was,
of course, pretty grim, and I suggested that she should try to get
him to come and see me, but of course he would not do this. Mrs.
W. carried on for a year and then came again saying that really
she would like to leave her husband, but felt that if he were ill she
perhaps hadn't the right to desert him!

Mr. W. holds quite an important position and they have been
married about eighteen years. All through their marriage I should
say he has been impotent—she has never had any real happiness.
He takes every opportunity of insulting her in public, and frequently gives her a sly kick or pinches her.

She can, of course, tell her story much better than I can—
particularly as it is some weeks since I saw her.

Mrs. W. turned out to be a very well preserved woman of fifty-five,
looking more like forty-five, simply but attractively dressed, who start-

ed the interview admitting without any fuss that she was slightly deaf. She had a very good vocabulary and told her story confidently and convincingly. The picture of her husband which emerged from her description was coherent and without contradiction. In addition to the exhibitionism and impotence mentioned in the doctor's letter, her husband had a number of irritating infantile traits. He liked to go about the house, and in particular in the garden where other people could see him, literally in rags, deliberately tearing off the buttons of his shirt and trousers and tying his trousers round his waist with a piece of string, using a piece of string instead of his shoe-laces, and so on. According to Mrs. W. all this is done to call the neighbours' attention to his lowly status in comparison with his wife who is always properly dressed. On the other hand, whenever he can he uses his excellent brains to trip her up and humiliate her, especially when other people are present. This he does so skilfully that he can never be blamed for it directly.

More and more details of this kind emerged, which all fitted into the picture without any difficulty. Then she mentioned that she was her husband's second wife, he has a daughter by his first wife, but all of them live in great friendship. To the somewhat surprised question of the psychiatrist, she replied that the first wife had since married, yet the friendship still continued. In the last year, when things had begun to become worse, she had her first heart-to-heart talk with her predecessor and learned from her that Mr. W. was more or less impotent with his first wife too and simply could not tolerate that any consideration should be given to the young baby at his expense; for instance, he demanded that he and his wife should go out as before, leaving the baby alone at home. This she could not bear and after some months picked up her baby and walked out on him.

There can be no doubt whatsoever that Mr. W. is very ill indeed and badly needs help. It would have been quite easy to stop the examination at this point, reach the diagnosis of general immaturity, perverted sexuality, exhibitionism in an infantile personality, schizoid character, or something else of that kind—which, by the way, would all have been correct—to agree with Mrs. W. that her husband needed treatment, and then to send him an invitation, possibly through her, to come for an interview. Of course, this would again have been a case of diagnosing the absent patient. Instead of doing this the psychiatrist suspected a case of a pathological marriage in which one partner's patent illness is used as the presenting symptom to keep the other partner's illness in the dark. So when the interview reached this point—in about fifteen to twenty minutes—he asked the patient at what age she got married to this man, and why.

99

Several very garbled and muddled versions were presented and it cost quite considerable effort and attention to get the various dates clear. The end result was something like this. She is now fifty-five, the husband fifty-six. She got to know him when she was twenty-seven and got married to him at the beginning of the war, when she was about thirty-seven. She described herself as a normal young girl, popular both with boys and girls, rather sociable, who had quite a good job as staff officer in a big firm looking after all the women. Her wish was to get married to a congenial man, have children, and, as in fairy tales, live happily ever after. Several young men were interested in her but she could not herself decide. When her present husband turned up she did not take much notice of him, but he insisted and insisted until she realized that he really needed her and so she married him in the hope that he would be the right man. Here the psychiatrist pointed out to her that her wish to get married and have children could not have been very strong in view of the fact that she waited till she was almost forty to get married and to have her first inter-course and that she chose a man who turned out to be most inadequate. Mrs. W. who, until this point, was very composed, broke down and wept. The whole atmosphere changed from then on, her stiffness eased considerably, one might say that she accepted the psychiatrist as her ally.

In this relaxed or intimate atmosphere a number of characteristic details emerged. A most significant group consisted of her relation to sex. Although she was disappointed by her husband's impotence and indifference, she took them in her stride, perhaps because her own needs had not been very strong at any time. Then she returned to her husband's peculiar behaviour, and it transpired that he had to humiliate her mainly in front of women; similarly it was always women neighbours who made remarks about her husband's dishevelled way of dressing or said something which she interpreted as allusions to her husband's exhibitionism. The more her story unfolded the more women turned up in it, with conspicuous absence of any males.

Another topic that was interwoven with, and accompanied, the previous one was the couple's odd relationship to money matters. During their courtship and the first years of their marriage she earned well, almost as much as her husband, helped him to maintain his daughter, contributed her share to the household expenses, and helped also to pay for the purchase of a house. When this house was sold and another bought, her contribution was completely disregarded and the present new house is in her husband's name. At the husband's request she then stopped working and although she knows that her husband has quite a good salary she gets a minimal amount of housekeeping money and has no idea where the rest of the money goes. She realizes now that her husband is afraid of allowing her any freedom because he is afraid he might lose her, and so must keep her always under his thumb. Until now she has tolerated it, but now she thinks it would be a better idea if she went out and took a full-time job again which she thinks, with her excellent references, would be quite easy. She hopes that this would give her a better status and her husband would respect her and love her more.

In the last part of the interview she was able to talk warmly and simply about her sincere beliefs that this life of carnal pleasures is only a preparation for a broader and more important form of life and all the tribulations and problems such as she has to cope with in her marriage are only a kind of test for the future. Then she talked also about her psychic abilities; if she is in tune with people she just knows what they think and what they need.

Three characteristic and revealing episodes were mentioned by her in this part of the interview, the first of them as a response to the psychiatrist's question whether she had ever been in love in her life. Her whole face lit up when she told the story that at the time when they were negotiating the sale of their first house she got worried because her favourite cat, for which she cared almost as much as for a child, got ill as if he had broken one of his paws. She asked a veterinary surgeon to come and she knew that he was the right man for her. He did not need to ask any questions because she just gave the answers that he expected. The cat's illness turned out to be an abscess, which was easily dealt with. The house was sold and they moved into the country, but she knew that the man and she belonged together— perhaps not in this life, but it did not matter. He sent a nice Christmas card to the cat and she thinks that he might have written a letter to her too which almost certainly her husband intercepted. All this did not matter. She never thought for a moment of leaving her husband, because he needed her, needed her very badly, but from that moment on she has been quite certain that she and that man belonged together.

The other two episodes were reported spontaneously when, towards the end of the session, she returned to her main problem, what she should do with her husband. Should she try to stay with him or threaten him with separation? Her aim in reporting them was to give the psychiatrist concrete proof of the severity of her husband's illness. She repeated what she had already said at the beginning of the session, that her husband used to stand with wide open pyjamas at the bedroom window, although recently since she had it out with him he more or less pulls the curtains together. Still, one of her neighbours, a woman, said one day that they ought to have tall poplars in their garden. She had no doubt whatsoever that it was a clear allusion to her husband's misbehaviour. Then she added, recently one morning when she brought the coffee up to her husband in the bedroom, he came down the stairs to meet her with wide open pyjamas and an imploring look on his face. The psychiatrist asked whether the husband had an erection, to which she replied, 'Of course not, he was impotent', and the whole scene was meant to humiliate her. Then she mentioned the third incident. Her husband was working as usual in his tattered clothes in the garden and she called out to him that the afternoon coffee was ready. He immediately dropped everything, started to walk in a subdued way with head hanging towards the kitchen, and implored her with folded hands: 'Oh, may I have a break, oh, may I have a break'. To her this performance meant that he wanted to impress the neighbours what a cantankerous, bossy, woman she was, and what a poor hen-pecked husband he was.

As mentioned at the beginning, the aim of this interview was mainly diagnostic, to help the general practitioner to understand the situation better; moreover, the external situation was such that it appeared unlikely that Mrs. W. would be able or, in fact, would want to have psychiatric help. Thus the psychiatrist did not think it advisable to go further. In any case, this kind of highly organized defence, bordering almost on a paranoid system, usually does not respond well to a quick and penetrating therapeutic intervention. As a rule, these people need a long and well-tested contact before they can allow the therapist to take the liberty of seeing things in a different light from that in which they do. So the psychiatrist recorded his findings and reported them to the general practitioner in the hope that he would be able to use them in the future.

What then are the findings? In addition to the glaring picture of the husband's serious illness, he found a woman with a very meagre sexual life who waited to get married till she was almost forty and even then picked up a highly inadequate man; who fell in love for the first time in her life when she was almost fifty; the whole of this experience lasted only for a few minutes; it did not lead to any mutual, physical or emotional intimacies but remained an experience solely for herself. Then there is her life-long preoccupation with women, in her professional career, in her curious relationship with her predecessor, and recently with several women in her neighbourhood who seem to be all concerned with what might happen between herself and her husband. And lastly, we have these two episodes, which may be interpreted in her way but which may also admit exactly the opposite interpretation, namely, a desperate plea by her husband for mercy and understanding to her, a righteous and perhaps rigid and merciless woman. Almost certainly both interpretations will prove to be correct in the long run.

What about prognosis and therapy? Unfortunately both of them are rather uncertain in view of the severity of the illnesses of both partners. The husband is so frightened—and his fear will certainly not be eased by his wife's righteousness—that it is highly unlikely that he will come and ask for help. Until now the only thing that the wife was able to do was to consult doctors almost in the role of the prosecutor, of someone who has been wronged, who wants sympathy and help about how to bear all the wrongs done to her. As long as she remains in this mood, very little can be done for her, as is well instanced by her general practitioner's referring letter. The great question is whether the interview with the psychiatrist has helped her on the way to the realization that her role in her life has not merely been that of a passively suffering martyr but that of an actively contributing partner.

Although it is very far from certain whether she will be able to be helped along this road, we hope it will be clear that if the psychiatrist had accepted that only the absent partner was ill and had to be treated, she would not have had even this slight ray of hope.

CHAPTER 8

The Doctor's Responsibility

In this chapter we propose to examine yet another aspect of the therapeutic relationship between doctor and patient: what each of these two actors contributes to the developing drama and in what way its outcome is determined by these contributions.

A good starting point for our examination will be the customary names by which the two actors are addressed and described. Remarkably in all the civilized Western European languages the two actors are called by names borrowed from Latin which have already displaced, or are displacing, the native ones. One of the actors is called 'the patient' which literally means 'the sufferer'; moreover, 'passive', 'passion' and 'patience' are all derived from the same root. This is rather a curious mixture, but these four words taken together well characterize the contributions originating from one of the actors. The other actor of the drama is invariably addressed as 'Doctor' and the same word, though not invariably, is used for describing him or her. As we all know, its literal meaning is 'teacher'; moreover, the word 'doctrine' derives from the same root.

One can see the reason why one of the actors is described as 'patient' but why should the other be described as 'teacher'? Why did common usage reject words like 'healer' or 'comforter', 'wizard', 'witch' or 'sorcerer', or again 'caretaker', 'nurse' or 'nurser', and so on? The reason must be that somehow people felt that the functions described by the words just mentioned are not the most important attributes of the medical profession. According to the languages the most important function of our professional activity is that we teach. Here one may point out the curious inconsistency, at any rate, of the English language; though members of other academic professions may obtain a doctor's degree, it is unusual to address or to describe them as 'doctors'. By tradition, apart from the medical profession, only Doctors of Divinity are addressed as such; moreover, by the same tradition, all medical practitioners are called 'Doctors' although only very few of them have a University degree of Doctor of Medicine.

We, psycho-analysts, are reputed to make mountains of inferences out of little molehills of observations, so we propose, if we may, to remain true to the reputation of our speciality. Our thesis is that we doctors are called 'doctors' for good reason, which is that we do indeed teach something highly important to our patients while attending to them. During the course of teaching some patients may even be cured, but unfortunately this does not happen in every case. Not so seldom the patient has to learn how to be ill, how to live with his illness, how to adjust his life to it, and how to tolerate all the uneasiness, fear, and apprehension, discomfort, pain, and even disability, which may be the accompaniments or consequences of not a few pathological states.

This sort of teaching—how to live with an illness—amounts only to a short course of instruction if the illness is of the acute variety, but gains considerably in importance in chronic or recurrent conditions.

In this chapter we can only briefly mention one highly important aspect of this teaching, namely, that the patient has to learn how much and what sort of help he may and should expect from his doctor and, on the other hand, how much anxiety, discomfort, and suffering he has to bear unaided on his own; and further, when and under what conditions he has the right to ask for help or relief. This aspect of the doctor's professional work is but seldom stated explicitly, nevertheless, whenever a patient sees one of us—no matter whether in our consulting room or surgery, or at his own home—he invariably gets another lesson in this most important subject. We wish only to point out that the sum total of these lessons constitutes a highly important contribution to the developing doctor-patient relationship but, as just stated, this will not be discussed in detail.

The topic that we propose to discuss is that aspect of the doctor's teaching function which may be called the shaping of the patient's illness. This happens by an interaction that has been described elsewhere[1] as 'the patient's offers' of illnesses and 'the doctor's responses' to them. Using a simile from gardening, one could say that the patient grows an illness and it is the doctor who trains it by pruning some symptoms, allowing others to go on growing, while forcing yet others to take a direction that he prescribes to them. Of course, the doctor cannot do everything, his powers are as limited as the gardener's, but still, as our two cases will show, these powers are considerable.

We may use the simile of the gardener to highlight one more aspect of the doctor's function. Some parts of the garden are planned

[1] *The Doctor, His Patient and The Illness.* Chapter III.

for only a season or two, and in consequence the gardener is more concerned with the short-term effect of his methods. Other parts are meant to last, and there quite different methods are used, and the results are judged by long-term considerations. As we aim to study what sort of effects the doctor's teaching function may produce in a man's life we have to turn to patients who have been followed up for a very long time. In the two cases that we shall use to demonstrate our points the follow-up extended for more than ten years. This is the real domain of the family doctor. Follow-ups of this duration are such a rarity in specialist or hospital practice that their results are almost invariably publicized in articles about them in the literature.

The two cases to be quoted are of the common, every-day type, which may occur in every practice. The only difference in their treatment was the participation of the two doctors in our seminars which prompted them to take another look at the every-day events.

In the first case the doctor, though recognizing the problem in its real proportions, could not find a proper solution for it. It was only when we discussed his ways in the seminar that he realized that what he did was to teach his patients—it was a whole family—to accept the various chronic conditions and illnesses as part of their lives, and to live with them. In our second case, after some hesitation, the doctor decided on his own to use his excellent relationship with the patient and in fact succeeded in achieving quite commendable changes in the illness by teaching the patient to view it from a somewhat different angle. Again it was only our discussion that made him realize what in fact he taught to his patient.

CASE 15

As just mentioned, our first case will be a well-known story but we hope it will appear in a new light. We think it ought to be mentioned that it was reported to our seminars when we discussed parents who consult their doctors regularly about their children. The family— our Case 15—consisted of three people: Mr. F. who in 1958 at the time of the report was forty-six, his wife forty-one, and their only son aged thirteen. Mr. and Mrs. F. were working in their own small wholesale firm in the dress trade and consulted their doctor regularly every two or three months about their boy. Very rarely they asked him for a home visit when the boy had a cough or cold. They were described as grateful, appreciative people; true, time and again they consulted other doctors behind our colleague's back; this, however, did not cause any friction as our doctor did not mind it in the least.

As he said, it saved him trouble if someone else was made responsible.

Until this point this is a well-known story about over-anxious parents. Let us see now what is beneath the surface, that is, what the doctor himself contributed to its development or, in short, what he taught to his patients.

The doctor's connection with the family started almost immediately after their son's birth, that is, in 1946. It was then that Mr. F. came complaining about deficient erection and near-impotence. He was a very talkative man and told the doctor in great detail that this was his second marriage. He had no sexual difficulty with his first wife but she died of tuberculosis. He did not want any medical advice for his complaint because he knew that everything was physical and asked for drugs only. In order to escape his verbiage, the doctor agreed, and when the drugs did not help and Mr. F. asked for specialist examination he was referred to an endocrinologist. Prolonged and varied endocrine treatments did not change the situation; the doctor accepted this fiasco and, though he made it quite clear what his opinion was, did not press further; neither did the patient, who at that time was about thirty-three or thirty-four years old.

For some years there were no further complaints except what might be described as over-anxiousness about the boy. Quite often it was the father who brought him to the doctor which—as we found in our research—is always an ominous sign. In the last three years or so Mr. F. developed seborrhoeic dermatitis which was treated symptomatically without much result. Mr. F.—as is his custom—then consulted various hospitals and Harley Street specialists, some openly, some behind the doctor's back. No treatment had any lasting effect on him.

Of course we asked what the doctor knew about Mrs. F. Her story was that she had had no previous sexual experience when she got married at the age of twenty-seven or twenty-eight and had been frigid ever since. She had a typical background: the parents lived in an 'ideal marriage', she was brought up extremely strictly, was very fond of her father while mother was somewhat domineering and bossy, and sexual topics simply could not be mentioned. Like many of her type, she was terrified of pregnancy and childbirth and demanded that her husband practise withdrawal—rather a difficult task for a semi-impotent man. In spite of her precautions she became pregnant and it was in these circumstances that her son was born. Her experiences at confinement confirmed her fears and ever since she has mercilessly insisted on withdrawal. Our doctor suggested some more sensible contraceptive measures, whereupon Mrs. F. disappeared and this topic was never mentioned again by either of them. After some time

107

she appeared again consulting the doctor about her son's colds and coughs; we call this very frequent phenomenon 'the child as the presenting symptom of the mother's illness'.

In due course, after she had reassured herself that her doctor would not dare mention contraceptives again, she produced the usual array of minor psychosomatic disorders, such as severe indigestion, colics, various throat and nose troubles, occasional vaginal discharge, and on one occasion, a seborrhoeic skin rash. We wish to mention briefly an amusing episode. One day she came with a bad back. As our doctor is interested in orthopaedic manipulation, he asked her to undress and manipulated her back there and then. For her next appointment she arrived with Mr. F. who wanted to see—it is anybody's guess why—how the doctor manipulated his wife. Needless to say there was no further complaint about her back—an unquestionable success, unfortunately undecided whether due to proper orthopaedic treatment or to something else.

Remarkably the boy is quite a healthy youth, in spite of his many minor ailments, which do not amount to more than occasional colds and coughs. Recently he also developed seborrhoeic dermatitis, which greatly alarmed his parents, and the boy was taken to various Harley Street doctors. He likes the attention and the fuss about himself but does not seem worried at all otherwise.

Now what was the doctor's teaching in this case? He yielded, against his will, to the view presented to him, especially by Mr. F., that sexual problems are entirely physical, perhaps endocrinological, but certainly not to be talked about. By his yielding he taught, reluctantly though, that there was no overruling need to understand the underlying psychological problems; it was only the physical or chemical treatment that mattered. This teaching—or doctrine—was then further reinforced by his acquiescence; he did what Mr. and Mrs. F. demanded that he do, that is, he treated every 'little illness' phsysically to the extent of accepting and carrying out the specialists' recommendations.

What then were the results of this teaching? Perhaps most important from the doctor's point of view was the peaceful, friendly, and appreciative relationship between him and this couple. This, however, is coupled with an atmosphere in which nothing can be done. The doctor has been made as impotent in his profession as the husband in his sexual life. When he tried to be potent—about the contraceptives or when manipulating the backache in Mrs. F's case, or when pressing Mr. F. to accept that his sexual troubles were neurotic—either the symptom disappeared or the patients disappeared from his surgery and went to other doctors, saying almost in so many words the others were better. However, as the real problems could not be solved in this way a new symptom was produced, namely, the child.

In our discussion the doctor was severely taken to task about his teaching. It was pointed out to him among other things: that he had downgraded himself to the rank of a dispenser who merely carried out the treatment prescribed by the great specialists; that Mrs. F. succeeded in freezing out both her husband and her doctor, and this was not dealt with at all but tacitly accepted; that he avoided altogether coping with the real problem which was that of anxiety. At first the anxiety was about pregnancy in Mrs. F's case and about impotence in Mr. F's. This then changed to anxiety about their son and recently to that about their skin condition. True the doctor diagnosed the anxiety properly but never treated it seriously. In a way he recognized that the F's were troubled people, running from hospital to hospital, from doctor to doctor, but he could not do anything about it.

The doctor accepted all our strictures but said that, although he was aware of the problems, he could not make any fruitful contact with either Mr. or Mrs. F. He was quite sure that Mr. and Mrs. F. had known all the time that he was only yielding to their demands but that his opinion was other than theirs. Although Mrs. F. was willing to speak about her frigidity, during all these years the doctor could not see any possibility of making her recognize her frigidity as a pathological condition, she was completely identified with it. In the same way, although both of them knew that Mr. F's verbiage had been all the time a means of keeping the doctor at bay, the doctor could not see how to overcome this. These were the main reasons why he drifted against his will into the present situation.

Evidently we are faced here with a great and disturbing problem. Should a doctor insist against a patient's resistance and make him tackle a distasteful problem at all costs? The answer is anything but simple. Suppose he finds a positive Wassermann reaction, or tubercle bacilli in the sputum, there is no question whatsoever that he would, in fact he must, insist that the patient takes his findings seriously. In some ways the situation is similar in our case. The doctor could have said something like this: if you do not take seriously the woman's frigidity and the man's impotence, and do something about them, I can predict that you two will always be worried and you will probably have one illness after another, not only in both of you but also in your child. Can we state confidently whether the doctor should or should not say something like this? Of course, if he does, many complications will follow: both man and wife will have to face up to their own unhappiness and possibly will need treatment, there is even some risk that their marriage might break up, and so on.

But if we conclude that he should not say anything at all, then the result is the present situation.

Of course, he may shut his eyes and escape seeing all these implications; in this way he will not be put to the task of making a decision. Nevertheless a decision will be made and, unavoidably, by *him*, only he will make it blindfold. We hope that this case has shown sufficiently clearly that the decision is about what to teach the patient, or patients, as in this case. It is a painful responsibility to realize that *teach we must—our only choice is what to teach.*

Our next case is about the same problem, only it will show it from a somewhat different angle. It is also a long history, that is, a true general practitioner's case. There will, however, be a difference from the previous case, namely that here the doctor decided what to teach.

CASE 16

The patient, Mr. K., is a man of thirty-four, married, with no children. He has been on the doctor's list for thirteen years, that is, since his marriage. Still, he is a comparative newcomer, as his wife's family was already in the practice when the doctor took it over from his predecessor. Thus he has known Mrs. K. since she was a little girl. Mr. K. is a well dressed, sportsmanlike, pleasant, and very considerate man, and the doctor-patient relationship has been excellent all the time.

He has been complaining of dyspepsia for many years now. Although the doctor diagnosed it as 'functional', he first tried antacids which seemed to help; in consequence during all these years the patient has come to collect them regularly every two or three weeks. Being a keen footballer he has turned up occasionally with minor injuries, when he has asked—quite justifiably—for a couple of days off work.

In November 1957 quite unexpectedly Mr. K. turned up in a bad state, depressed, shaky, and very tense. The doctor happened to be very busy at that time—as most general practitioners are in November —so he noted on his card 'proper interview next time' and for the time being gave him some amytal. Next week as the doctor was still very busy and the patient reported to be 'better', things were left at that.

In March 1958 Mr. K. was again depressed, but this time the doctor—like most general practitioners—was not so busy so he offered him a 'long interview', which means usually an hour, by appointment. He learned from Mr. K. that his depressions started about three years ago when his father died. Father was an ex-boxer but suffered severe injuries in the 1914-18 War and became in consequence deaf and crippled; he could not work and lived on his Army pension. Mother and the rest of the family nagged at him and treated him very badly so Mr. K. was glad when mother and the other children were evacuated during the 1939-45 War and left him in London with his father. When mother returned Mr. K. joined the Navy, got to know his wife while on leave, and married her soon afterwards.

Three years ago he was asked to be best man at his brother's wedding which—being a shy man—was a very great strain on him. Thus it happened that he did not take much notice of father's repeated complaints. A few days after the wedding father collapsed in the street, was taken to hospital and died a few weeks later. Mr. K. still reproaches himself for not noticing the seriousness of his father's condition. At home father's name is never mentioned; in spite of this Mr. K. visits his mother regularly but, remarkably, cannot go to see his father's grave.

Then Mr. K. spoke of his marriage. He is very fond of his wife, they are very happy indeed. They have no children by choice because they are afraid the child might come between them and so they practise withdrawal. Recently—a very rare event indeed—they had a row. He felt his wife provoked him like mother used to provoke father. He was badly wrought up and was afraid that he might become violent.

Then he spoke about his fondness for football. He is very keen indeed; whenever he can, he goes to the nearby marshes and kicks the ball on his own 'to get it out of his system'.

As the doctor was well acquainted with the family he knew that Mr. K's father used to be a good boxer and Mr. K. himself was of great promise but he gave it up eventually because he felt he could not come up to what was expected from him. Using this the doctor interpreted to Mr. K. that apparently he must cope with more anger than he is really capable of and added that perhaps this was an additional reason why he had to give up such an openly fighting and manly sport as boxing. This seemed to make sense to Mr. K. who mentioned in response to the interpretation that he was a keen follower of his Club, usually got very excited and could not refrain from using abusive language against the referee or the opponents if things did not go right for his Club. Though afterwards he was terribly ashamed, he simply could not help it.

The doctor then pointed out that giving up boxing, kicking the ball on his own, his abusive language at the matches, all showed that there was plenty of anger in him and that he found it rather difficult

111

to cope with it. The recent event of welling up of violent temper against his wife created a very dangerous situation indeed; he must have felt that if he lost his temper, it might destroy his peace and happiness, which meant so much to him.

The doctor then concluded that apparently Mr. K. could not accept his intense anger, nor could he find an acceptable outlet for it, so the only possibility open for him was to turn it against himself and become depressed.

When questioned by the seminar, the doctor said that he was fully aware at what point he stopped in his investigations and treatment. He did not draw a parallel between Mr. K's anger at his wife and at his mother, though this was clear enough, nor did he try to show him that he had chosen his sweet wife because she was the exact opposite of his fierce mother. Secondly, though Mr. K's extreme loyalty to his father was properly discussed, no attempt was made to examine Mr. K's critical attitude towards his father, which could easily have been done, using his shouting at the referee, an obvious father figure, as an entry. Thirdly, the doctor did not try to get at the roots of Mr. K's loyalty to his father and to his wife, although here too there were plenty of clues, such as his ready submissiveness, his lack of drive, giving up boxing, accepting withdrawal as a contraceptive measure, fear of a child as a potential rival, and so on.

Now the follow-up. Next week we heard that Mr. K. reported, 'Much better. I know now I have got it inside me so I must get it out of my system.' The doctor agreed and recommended for that purpose football matches and kicking the ball on his own. The next week Mr. K. reported completely well.

In mid-April 1958, that is, six weeks after the first interview, Mr. K. relapsed and was depressed again. He told the doctor that during his Easter holiday he visited his mother and this stirred up everything in him. This did not seem to be a sufficient explanation to the doctor who, of course, knew that Mr. K. visited his mother regularly, and so he asked for more information. After overcoming some resistance, Mr. K. told him that the previous Easter he drove past the cemetery where his father was buried but he could not make himself visit the grave. Doctor and patient then went over the same ground again, tying up some loose ends; in particular the interpretation about controlling his anger was repeated. Mr. K. felt better immediately and next week reported all right.

In November 1958 he came with an abscess on his elbow and in December with a typical follicular tonsillitis; each time they had another short interview and Mr. K. has been all right ever since. The doctor sees him only in the street when they wave to each other.

We wish to point out a remarkable side-effect. The indigestion and dyspepsia for which he came for several years regularly have completely disappeared. Tablets are not mentioned any more.

Now let us survey here too what this doctor's teaching was. First that emotions may cause trouble; it is especially so with anger, it must be got out of the system. In addition the doctor taught two methods for dealing with emotions and in particular with anger: one is self-control and the other sublimation in a socially acceptable form such as kicking a ball or shouting at football matches. The results of this teaching so far have not been too bad. Indigestion and dyspepsia have gone, depression probably has gone also. But there are also negative sides of the doctor's teaching. These are somewhat more difficult to put into words as they have not been properly mentioned during the treatment, that is, instead of the patient's words here we have to use our own formulations. First, a kind of axiom, which says that you must not hate or be angry with people that you love, such as your wife or your father, because this might be dangerous to your happiness. Second, it is unnecessary, perhaps even undesirable, to be an aggressive, self-assertive man, like a boxer, or one who would not spare his mother from justified criticisms. Another aspect of the same teaching is that it is acceptable to be somewhat anxious and to go on using withdrawal as a proper contraceptive measure. And lastly, that it is not so important to have children.

Although we know quite a lot about Mr. and Mrs. K. it is not so easy to predict what will happen with them. One thing, however, is certain, and that is that the contact between Mr. K. and his doctor is now so good that, whatever may happen in the future, the contact will prove a valuable and most useful asset. Thus the prognosis for the near future is fairly good; should any trouble occur Mr. K. certainly will be able to get help from his doctor. The question is whether this harmonious but somewhat precariously balanced situation will be able to stand up to the strains of time. Will Mr. K. be able to find sufficient outlet for his angry emotions, especially if they increase, and can Mrs. K. remain for good the sweet, not nagging, wife that her husband so badly needs, or will she turn into a hard and resentful woman as so many childless women do? Should this happen, will they turn against their highly-valued doctor and reproach him that he missed several opportunities to warn them while there was still time that they ought to use some more sensible method of contraception than withdrawal and that they ought to re-examine their apprehensive attitude about having a child? Evidently we shall need about another ten years to find out what the real value of the doctor's teaching has been.

We hope that these two cases prove our point, namely, that whatever treatment or diet the doctor prescribes, willy-nilly he teaches his patients what their illnesses mean and how they should live with them, or without them, as the case may be. Thus he really deserves the form of address given to him all over our Western world. Everyone talking to him calls him 'Doctor', that is 'Teacher'.

We wish to stress again that *it does not matter whatsoever whether the doctor shuts his eyes and refuses to see what he is doing or accepts his role and chooses consciously what he teaches—teach he must*; but we have not yet discussed what determines what he will teach to his patients. As it happens, the two doctors just reported apparently agreed on one point, namely, that a proper, free, and satisfactory sexual régime is not all-important; other things are more important. We hasten to add that there are plenty of doctors who will teach exactly the opposite, namely, that every human being has an absolute right to have a satisfactory sexual life and all sorts of other considerations must take second place to it. Sexual satisfaction is only one of the innumerable aspects of human life with regard to which such diametrically opposite teachings exist; some of the others are self-assertiveness, altruism, sense of duty, honesty, sacrifice, love, hate, and so on and so on. It is rather alarming to realize that these diametrically opposite teachings exist in practically every instance of what are generally called the highest human values. It will be only a meagre consolation to the doctor if he is told that this constitutes just one more instance of the general ambivalence which pervades human life. This knowledge may increase his understanding but will not lighten the burden of his responsibility.

We have to accept the fact that the world, including theology, philosophy, ethics, and science, does not offer the doctor unequivocal advice about the crucial decision of what to teach. On the other hand —as we have tried to prove in this chapter—he must teach, the only thing he can do is to choose what to teach. What then decides his choice? One of us (M.B.) described in his book, *The Doctor, His Patient and The Illness*, that every doctor seems to have a vague but almost unshakably firm idea of how a patient ought to behave when ill. Although this idea is anything but explicit or concrete, it is immensely powerful and influences practically every detail of the doctor's work with his patient and, in particular, that aspect which we call teaching. It is almost as if every doctor had revealed knowledge of what it is either right or wrong for patients to expect and to endure and, further, as if he had a sacred duty to convert to his own faith all the ignorant and the unbelievers among his patients. This was called 'the apostolic function' and, although we got more and more impressed by its importance as our research work progressed, its real significance dawned upon us only when we started to study the development of patients followed up at least as long as the cases reported in this chapter.

This, however, ought to have been expected. If a gardener consistently prunes a tree in the same way, the effect of his conscientious work will show up more and more impressively as the years pass by. The same is true about the doctor's teaching. A short and dramatic contact may have a fundamental influence on a patient's illness and life but the causal connection between the doctor's teaching and the patient's mode of life is difficult to prove. With a long-term follow-up, these connections emerge clearly, provided one is willing to see them. If doctors wish to learn more about how to use better and more efficiently the immense powers of their teaching function, the most profitable way open to them is to study their patients in some such way as is described here.

CHAPTER 9

The Place of Psychotherapy in Medicine

The fact that a chapter had to be devoted to this topic shows that the place of psychotherapy is an unsettled and controversial problem. So let us start with that part of the field about which there is general agreement.

Unquestionably any therapy must be rational and as far as possible capable of validation. Our first question is what do we mean by rational therapy? Rational therapy—as taught nowadays at the teaching hospitals—means a technique that will try to approximate at least one of the following three aims:

(a) The elimination of the cause that is thought to be responsible for the pathological condition, in the hope that the restitutive powers of the organism will be strong enough to restore things to normal. Examples are: stopping the further growth of, or even killing off, the invading micro-organisms in an infection by the administration of antibiotics; fixing the pieces of a broken bone in a correct position, and so on. All these methods are intended to create a favourable condition for the restitutive powers of the organism to do their job.

(b) The therapy may consist of removing the diseased organ altogether, in the hope that the rest of the organism, though now mutilated, will be able to survive the mutilation and return to health after filling the gap by scar tissue. Most surgical operations belong to this category, such as appendicectomy, partial gastrectomy, radical mastectomy, and so on.

(c) The therapy will have the aim of helping the organism to cope better with the pathogenic noxa. Most medical treatments belong to this class. Examples are: digitalis medication in heart failure; morphia in myocardial infarction; insulin in diabetes; barbiturates in epilepsy; various diets in obesity or anorexia; diet and some drugs in peptic ulcers or constipation. In some diseases all that we can do is to help the organism to cope better with one

116

or the other symptom of the illness, for instance, when we prescribe, say, 'Dramamine' for nausea or vomiting due to any cause.

In most of these cases there is no inherent, self-evident connection between the patient's complaints and the rational therapy. This connection, which is the rationale of the therapy, must be supplied by the doctor. For instance, there is no inherent sense why a patient who is prone to attacks of unconsciousness should take a sedative. This sense is supplied by the doctor who knows that certain attacks of unconsciousness are due to a disturbed rhythm of the brain and that these abnormal rhythms, if they are due to epilepsy, can be controlled by barbiturates. This example is the model of all rational therapy, the basis of which is always *a theory about the causation of the illness and the control of this presumed cause*. Unfortunately, as the history of medicine shows, theories are anything but permanent and when they change all therapy based upon them must change with them.

A very impressive example of this change is the pre- and post-operative treatment of a patient undergoing a major surgical intervention. One of us (M.B.) remembers that when he was a student the accepted pre-operative treatment was that the patient had a very light meal plus a fairly large dose of castor-oil on the previous night and practically nothing from then on until after the operation, certainly no fluids; on the contrary, early in the morning he was given an enema. After the operation he was nursed flat on his back, the permission to use even a very small pillow was given with great misgivings and only to very exceptional or very awkward patients. The patient was not allowed to move or raise his head and in order to immobilize him fairly heavy sandbags were put at his side and across his abdomen. Today every item of this régime would be considered as a major mistake. Patients are encouraged to take fluid and glucose or other carbohydrates before the operation, castor-oil and enemas are practically unheard of, and, in particular after abdominal operations, the patient is nursed in a semi-recumbent position and is often encouraged to get up and walk about a few days after the intervention. The reasons for this fundamental change are the changes that have taken place in our theories about what matters in or after an operation.

It is understandable, therefore, that doctors have become rather uneasy about therapeutic techniques based solely on pathological theories. They have had far too many unsettling experiences with techniques which seemed beyond every doubt firmly established and validated one day, and disappeared into the limbo a few years later.

117

To reassure themselves they had to look round for a safer foundation.

It soon became clear that clinical experiences with therapeutic techniques were not quite reliable in themselves. Time and again a second experimenter was able to demonstrate that not only had the factor which the first experimenter thought to be solely responsible to be considered, but that there were other factors active which had an equally important, if not more important, part in the favourable results.

In order to create reliable conditions, and in particular to free the judgement of results from any subjective bias in the observer, in this century a new method of validation has come into fashion: the *double-blind experiment*. In this, two groups of patients are selected who are matched for sex, age, and social status, all suffering from the same illness; both groups are treated by pills which look the same, taste the same, and so on, but one class of them contains no therapeutic agent, the other does. The experiment is arranged so that neither the patients who take the pills nor the doctors who give them and observe the results, have any knowledge whether the pills are real or fake. This is known only to a third person who remains completely uninvolved, who, if possible, does not even see either the patients or the doctors in charge of the treatment, and to whom the observed results are then submitted for final judgement. It is hoped that in this way any proposed therapy can be judged impartially and objectively.

Undoubtedly this method—the double-blind experiment—is highly scientific, objective, and reliable in its results. Furthermore, *its results are independent of any theory, and thus remain unchanged however fundamentally our views about the causation of a disease may change*. The only trouble with this experiment is that its application is painfully limited. This very serious drawback is usually forgotten or not mentioned and any therapy which cannot be tested by this method, or one of its less stringent modifications, is liable to be considered as not beyond suspicion. Is this judgement justified?

As just stated, the double-blind experiment can be applied only in a very limited field. Let us survey now some of the factors that cause this limitation. The first factor is that, in order to be safely controlled, the patient's participation in the experiment must be kept minimal. It is definitely not necessary for him to know what the diagnosis of his illness is, why this kind of therapy has been prescribed, and how it is supposed to work. In particular his insight into the interaction of the various pathological and therapeutic factors is entirely immaterial and irrelevant. Nor is it necessary that his complaints and the therapy prescribed should together make sense for him, since *in principle the double-blind experiment can be carried out by coupling any kind of therapy with any kind of illness or complaint.* With some exaggeration one may say that giving no explanation whatsoever to the patient makes the experiment still more scientific and objective. The only thing the patient is called upon to do is to swallow reliably the pills prescribed and to report any sensation and especially any change of sensation to his doctor. Even the doctor who treats the patient may be limited in his participation. True, he must be a reliable diagnostician, must be able to match patients according to sex, age, and social status, and lastly, must be a reliable observer; but he need not even know what sort of drug is under trial. The only one for whom the whole set-up must make sense is the master-mind, the third, uninvolved doctor. It is only for him that the theory of pathogenesis and the theory of pharmacodynamics must make sense together.

The reason why this double-blind experiment is so limited in its application is that it presupposes an entirely objective situation in which any doctor may treat any patient with any illness with any sort of therapeutic agent provided their emotional involvement in each other and in the therapy can be kept minimal. True, in certain double-blind experiments the patients were given a full explanation of what was expected from them, since it was found that their co-operation became safer in this way. This, however, diminishes somewhat the scientific value of the experiment since the patients were given some suggestion of therapy, though admittedly not very much.

In all cases in which the condition of emotional detachment cannot be fulfilled, in which the therapy is based essentially on an emotional understanding of the pathogenic processes by the patient, as it is in most psychotherapies, any idea of a double-blind experiment is out of the question. The reasons are many. First, it is evident that to match patients according to age, sex, and social status is sadly insufficient, in view of the many further determining factors that crucially influence the issue. To mention a few of them: the occurrence of deprivations in early childhood and their exact chronological spacing; the patient's attitude to authority, such as his doctor inevitably represents; the degree of sexual maturity of the individual patient and his ability to obtain regular sexual satisfaction; and last, but not least, there is the immense, mostly uncharted, land of characterology. Whatever the illness in question may be, an obsessionally reliable man will give utterly different results in any psychotherapy from an over-excitable, highly-strung man, and so on.

A further difficulty which makes a valid matching of patients in this field well-nigh impossible is that our knowledge of certain illnesses is not yet reliable. It must be borne in mind that diagnoses containing the adjectives 'functional', 'emotional' or 'psycho-neurotic' are about as precise as when we label an illness as Bright's disease or angina pectoris. Any matching based solely on diagnoses of this kind must inevitably defeat its purpose since there is no guarantee whether patients described by the same diagnostic label will have many or very few common features in their pathology.

All this, however, is only a minor difficulty compared with the impossibility of giving placebos in psychotherapy. Psychotherapy is either a proper and honest attempt, and is recognized as such by both patient and doctor, or is nonsensical, when again both of them must be aware of this fact. Equally it is utterly impossible to offer the patient at a given moment, according to a time-table, pre-arranged interpretations of a certain kind of sympathetic understanding, as prescribed by a third uninvolved doctor. Any such procedure would be meaningless. Even if it were prescribed by a real master-mind, no colleague of his would be able to follow exactly his instructions, however correct and profound they might be. And lastly, whereas it is easy to persuade a patient to 'swallow' a pill, whatever its contents, it is impossible to make him 'swallow' a piece of understanding or an interpretation that does not make sense to him at that moment.

Evidently we have to do with two different classes of therapy: one which can be carried out without much co-operation from the patient, he need not even understand it or accept its implications; and another which can be effective only if the patient's individual history, his character, his present complaints, and his whole illness on the one hand, and the therapy offered to him by his doctor on the other hand, can make sense together. Roughly the same holds true for the doctor. During the therapeutic work belonging to the first class, he may remain detached or distant, there is no need for him to identify himself with his patient; but if he undertakes therapeutic work belonging to the other class, he cannot avoid becoming involved in the therapeutic relationship; true he must—as was shown in Chapter 6—be able to control his involvement, but—as described in Chapters 10 and 11—it is only on that basis that he will 'understand' the illness and be able to offer meaningful help to his patient. Although this classification sounds very sensible and even pedestrian, in fact it is a revolutionary principle, as will become clear if we examine some of its repercussions.

Any one of the case histories reported in this book can be used to demonstrate this difference, but in order to simplify matters we shall use only the three cases from Chapter 5. Our chief reason for choosing those three is that examination *by* the patient is the necessary precondition for any therapy of the second class, that is, one which makes sense to both the doctor and the patient.

The simplest to discuss is Case 5, Mrs. L., because in her case the doctor was not able to induce her to take part in the examination. In consequence, her whole treatment was carried out according to our first class, with the result that all her 'minor illnesses' were efficiently dealt with in their turn, but her general condition remained unchanged.

In the other two cases the doctors were able to induce their patients to take part in the examination, and in fact in Case 7 most of it was carried out *by* the patient. As both doctors recorded when and how this change occurred, the difference between the two kinds of therapy can easily be demonstrated.

May we recall that when Mrs. X., Case 6, presented her clicking rib as her third illness in eighteen months, her doctor was not satisfied by merely examining her physically but tried to induce her to help him in examining her whole life situation. There can be no doubt that a number of doctors would have accepted it as proper treatment if, after ascertaining that there were no major pathological changes in the lungs and bronchi, the doctor had treated the patient's complaints by restricting her smoking and prescribing something for the bronchial irritation. Moreover, this kind of treatment—exactly in the same way as the treatment a year ago—could have been examined by a double-blind experiment; after establishing the fact that the patient was suffering from a condition that we agreed to study—a somewhat uncertain duodenal ulcer, or spastic colon, or a bronchial irritation, functional in origin—and after matching her properly with a similar case, she could have been treated as prescribed by a third, uninvolved doctor, using any sort of diet and drug. The results of this kind of approach would have taught us a good deal of what we shall call hospital or scientific medicine.

Our registrar, however, went further than this towards what might be called *a diagnosis in depth*. He established the fact that Mrs. X. had refused sexual intercourse for at least two years and possibly had had a very unsatisfactory régime for much longer. It was during this time of abstinence that she developed three diseases which were apparently independent of one another and which were diagnosed as follows: probable peptic ulcer, spastic colon, and the clicking rib syndrome. Looking at them from this new angle we cannot exclude the suspicion that they might be secondary consequences only of an underlying general condition. Moreover, the husband's periodic drunkenness might be considered as a fourth syndrome or illness stemming from the same general cause; probably he too was forced to find some vicarious outlet for his pent-up tension. As already mentioned, we call this last phenomenon 'one partner as the presenting symptom of the other's illness'. Taking now the husband's drinking together with the three so-called illnesses presented by the wife, we find here another instance in which a patient who has been labouring with an insoluble problem comes to his doctor with various 'offers' to which it is the doctor's task to respond with a proper diagnosis. As discussed in the previous chapter, not only the future development of the illness 'offered' but also the patient's whole future life may depend to a great extent on the interplay between the doctor's responses and his patient's offers.

The situation is more difficult and perhaps less exact if—like our registrar—they decide to go 'deeper'. Whereas any properly trained doctor who is familiar with the present state of medical knowledge can prescribe the right sort of treatment for an uncertain peptic ulcer, a spastic colon, perhaps even for a clicking rib, and certainly can be instructed by a third especially well-trained doctor as to what to prescribe for any of these conditions, the situation is utterly different for the kind of treatment that we think is advisable in a number of cases. This treatment, a kind of psychotherapy, cannot be prescribed by any third doctor because the only way to make it efficient is to discover it by the one patient and the one doctor in a joint effort. In other words, for this therapy to be efficient it is unconditionally required that it should make sense to the patient and to the doctor at the same time.

To distinguish between these two kinds of approach let us call the one advocated here 'diagnosis in depth' and contrast it with 'diagnosis in rigorousness or precision' which is largely taught and practised by specialists in hospitals.[1] Undeniably, diagnosis in depth, and with it therapy in depth, that is, psychotherapy, because of their multi-dimensional nature, are of necessity always somewhat imprecise as compared with standard hospital diagnosis or treatment. That this lack of precision is not tantamount to a lack of effectiveness is clearly shown by Mr. G's history, Case 7.

[1] While 'diagnosis in precision' is a fairly adequate term we are not so happy about our second term, 'diagnosis in depth'. Our analyst colleagues will feel, rightly, that the various 'diagnoses in depth' reported in this book are rather superficial, especially when compared with what analysts would accept as 'deep'. We considered calling it 'diagnosis in breadth' or 'encompassing diagnosis' but could not decide on either of them. Each describes correctly one aspect of what we have in mind: that in this kind of thinking the whole personality and life situation of the patient must be examined, but each leaves out the other—in our view more important—aspect that the examination must be oriented so that it should proceed from the patient's 'offers' towards what lies beneath them. 'Depth' thus ought to be taken as denoting the direction, and not necessarily the level reached.

At the end of the interview in November 1958, after examining the many past illnesses presented by Mr. G. to the medical profession, doctor and patient reached together the conclusion that in future they could relate Mr. G's ill-health to his feelings about his present work and the world around him. We would stress here that neither doctor nor patient felt it necessary to distinguish carefully between so-called organic and functional illnesses, they talked merely of ill-health; many people will feel this an unforgivable generalization, perhaps even a retrograde step, unworthy of a scientifically trained doctor. Still, this highly imprecise formulation—we would like to, but dare not, call it diagnosis—and the treatment that it represented worked better than all the rigorous and precise diagnostic formulations and the treatments based upon them, contained in the thirty-four letters written by specialists and preserved in Mr. G's file. Further, when in February 1960 Mr. G. complained of an exacerbation of his stomach pains, the doctor did not send him for gastroscopy or barium meal, which would be unavoidable steps towards a proper diagnosis in rigorousness and precision, but asked him whether he had experienced any new difficulties in his life. This enabled Mr. G. to realize—one step ahead of his doctor—that he felt threatened that even the little personal relationship that remained to him would be taken away by the automation; again, rather a tentative and not at all precise formulation.

This kind of diagnosis, and of course the treatment based on it, is very far from being precise or rigorous. It certainly cannot compare in this respect with any of the findings of the many specialists who treated Mr. G., for instance, the orthopaedic surgeon who found his crushed vertebra, or the gastroenterologist who saw the small ulcer on gastroscopy.

Then there is another important point, and that is that although we prescribed a proper psychological examination for a complicated case, we had no idea that the examination would turn out to be also therapeutically effective. But even if we had decided in advance that Mr. G. should be selected for, and be given, psychotherapy, neither we nor anyone else could have prescribed what sort of therapeutic understanding, in what dose, and in what sequence, should be given.

One body of medical opinion, and it ought to be stated that most academic teachers belong to this, maintains that any progress in medicine must be towards more rigorous and more precise diagnosis and towards a rational therapy based on this. They can marshal very powerful arguments for their claim; almost all of the magnificent achievements in medical science during the last hundred years or so have been achieved in the way they advocate.

No one wants, or, for that matter, is able, even to challenge their argument. Medicine has indeed developed magnificently under the influence of this scientific spirit, but perhaps we are allowed to ask what has been the price that all of us, doctors and patients alike, have had to pay for it. One of the answers has been often given: the price has been the parcelling out of medicine, and with it the patient, among the ever-increasing number of specialists. Admittedly each of them does his own job very well indeed; the trouble is that all of them tend to close their files as soon as the patient or his illness has moved over to another specialist field. Mr. G., Case 7, had collected thirty-four reports of specialists and was still ill, although it is beyond any doubt that, for instance, the surgeon who operated on his anal fissure, the orthopaedist in charge of his crushed vertebra, or the neurologist diagnosing his jerks, had closed his case as finally dealt with, possibly even as successfully treated.

On a minor scale, something similar was about to happen with Mrs. X., Case 6, and it was just by chance that this outcome was prevented. If the patient's doctor had been more meticulous he could have referred her first to a gastroenterological department where both her doubtful ulcer and spastic colon would have been treated successfully and her case closed. Next year she could have been referred to a lung specialist, who would have treated her cough and clicking rib also successfully. True, in her second case history, under previous illnesses, her successfully treated duodenal ulcer and spastic colon would have been mentioned, but would an average chest physician have realized, or even cared to realize, that her past and present illnesses were probably due to the same cause?

Apart from parcelling out the patients and their illnesses, the other great shortcoming of standard hospital practice is the restricted nature of any follow-up. One aspect of the restriction is the comparatively short duration of the contact between hospital and patient, the usual length of which is from a few weeks to a few months. True, in some cases the contact extends to several years, but this is not the general rule. The other, still more important, aspect of the restriction is the field in which the specialist is interested. Let us suppose that Mrs. X., our Case 6, had been followed up either by a gastroenterologist or a lung specialist, it is hardly thinkable that either of them would have enquired whether or not her husband was an occasional drinker or whether the couple had a proper sexual régime. The demand for precision and rigorousness apparently involves a restriction of the field under observation.

The whole world is different for a general practitioner, at any rate as we know him in England. His relationship with the whole family is lasting, quite frequently not only over years but over generations, and so his follow-up is automatic. He need not write letters and implore his patients to come for a check-up because he sees them anyhow. Moreover, he simply cannot restrict his field of observation as the specialists do. He has to look after the family whatever their need or complaints may be, or, to quote extremes, from antenatal examination till the death certificate. Of course his routine does not allow him to be as precise and rigorous as are the hospital specialists, and as he was taught to be. In the present medical atmosphere this painful fact is rubbed into him time and again and in consequence he truly feels himself inferior to his colleagues in the hospitals. This prevents him from realizing that his practice is a real goldmine from which, with some honest effort, he can extract scientific observations as valuable as any found in the hospitals. Thus it appears that the second price to be paid for the great achievements of precise, scientific medicine is the acceptance that general practice is a second-rate kind of medicine compared with the 'proper' variety practised in hospitals.

This, however, is not all. There is a third, a very high price, to be paid as well, and that is the abandonment of the idea of the illness as a meaningful stage in the development of the individual, and the degrading of any form of psychotherapy to a not quite 'proper' status. We mentioned at the beginning of this chapter the three possible functions of a rational therapy, as taught today, (1) to eliminate the pathogenic cause and to create favourable conditions for the restitutive powers of the organism, (2) to remove the diseased organ and so help the organism to close the wound by growth of scar tissue, and (3) to help the organism to cope better with the pathological condition.

Psychotherapy does not fit into any of these three categories. The main reason for this is, perhaps, that these three categories of therapy are based on a conception of the illness as a kind of accident befalling a human being, an accident with which he had no previous connection. Of course, it will immediately be argued against us that everyone knows that there are congenital states, such as Friedreich's ataxia or polycystic kidneys, and so on, and that in many illnesses the importance of the pre-morbid personality is fully recognized. We readily admit that there are many transitional states that make a clear distinction most difficult. Still, one may contrast the idea of an illness as an accident with another idea according to which illness is due to a lack of integration brought about by some disturbance in the relationship between the individual and his environment. This would mean that illness or 'ill-health' must be considered as a meaningful phase in a person's life-history. If this idea is acceptable, and the cases quoted in this book certainly fit in well with it, then we come to *a fourth category of rational therapy* the task of which is *to help the patient to achieve this integration which he was not able to do on his own.* This of course can be done only if the meaning of the illness, the lack of integration, is understood.

The more an illness resembles an accident, the better are the results of hospital medicine, and it is here in this field that the proper application and value of the double-blind experiment lie. On the other hand, the more an illness is due to a lack of integration the less effective will be the so-called scientific treatments and the less applicable will be the double-blind experiment.

Of course, as just mentioned, a number of illnesses represent transitions between these two extremes, thus they constitute a borderland with inexact boundaries and unsettled proprietary rights—a most important field, that is, for research. Fervent lip-service is paid to the urgency of this research, foremost in the United States, under the slogan of *comprehensive medicine.* Unfortunately in most hospitals this means merely the enlisting of the services of a few more specialists, among them psychologists, sociologists, social workers, nurses, health visitors, and so on. True, at any rate in theory, all the various specialists concerned with one family congregate together and discuss in a joint consultation the whole field of problems. In reality, however, some of the specialists—and this is more true for the medical than the non-medical ones—are represented in these joint conferences mainly by paper reports. A further puzzling fact is that although the investigation and diagnosis are carried out under this comprehensive banner, the treatment is not. This is delegated, as is customary in every teaching hospital, either to the most junior member of the staff or to a student, and since students and junior members change rapidly, when the patient or another member of his family turns up a few months later for a second piece of advice or a follow-up, he will meet probably the same social worker or the same nurse, will certainly have the same file, but hardly ever the same doctor who treated him on the previous occasion.

This apparently means that scientific or hospital medicine tacitly maintains that it is not necessary that the same patient should be treated by the same doctor; it works on the principle that any doctor with the same training and experience can treat the same patient equally well, and therefore doctors can be changed without any detriment to the patient. Stating this in these blunt terms might provoke some resistance. Hospital specialists will argue that the Head of the service and possibly his first Assistant remain the same and they will see to it that their junior staff will do their job properly and sympathetically. For the sake of argument, let us agree that they succeed in achieving this; still there cannot be any doubt that the quality of the junior staff varies somewhat from one person to another, maybe even greatly, and that their personality and character are certainly never the same as those of their predecessors. However hard the senior staff try to maintain a uniform service, this service can never be uniform, except if it is so standardized that it becomes inhuman.

This is a very difficult problem indeed. To change it, the whole structure of the teaching hospital, the real home of scientific medicine, ought to be changed, which it is unrealistic to ask. What then is the solution? Are we really to recognize the existence of these two kinds of medicine, (1) the scientific or hospital medicine as it is taught and practised in pure form at the teaching hospitals, and in a more or less impure form in other hospitals with lesser resources, and (2) the other kind of medicine which might be called medical practice? The aim of scientific medicine should remain, as it is now, a diagnosis in rigorousness and precision, a therapy based on this sort of diagnosis and validated under as strict conditions as possible on the model of the double-blind experiment. For quite a time to come this medicine will be the science of specialists who possibly will have only a limited contact with their patients and, most important, will be able to observe only a limited field, that is, their speciality.

The other medicine, called here medical practice, for quite some time will have to forgo the ambition to become as exact as its sister branch. The ambition here will be less diagnosis in precision than diagnosis in depth and it will take much work and many years, possibly generations, before doctors will be able to refine their findings, and their language for describing them, in such a way as to match the achievement of scientific medicine. As their long-term contact with their patient compels them—at any rate those of them who are not completely under the influence of hospital medicine—to look more at the man than at his 'illnesses', the techniques they must use will always have a strong psychotherapeutic element, and will not lend themselves to a validation according to the model of the double-blind experiment. They will have to develop new criteria, a different kind of scientific objectivity which may be called *whole-person pathology or whole-person medicine*, in which the principal task will be to understand the meaning for the person of the complaints and illnesses that he offers to his doctor. The aim of therapy will then be *to enable the patient to understand himself*, find a better solution for the problem facing him, and thus achieve the integration

127

which has not yet developed, or has broken down because of a disturbed relationship between him and his environment. This is the place of psychotherapy in medicine.

If the existence of these two kinds of medicine is to be recognized, what can we expect from the future? A number of doctors will feel that there is no need for controversy or competition, or for subordinating one medicine to the other. Each of the two medicines could, and should, work side by side for the greater benefit of the ailing population. What must be done, however, and must be done from both sides, is to find out in an honest research what sort of conditions can be treated best by what kind of methods. It is here that great difficulties have to be expected. For many hundreds of years the teachers of medicine were general practitioners. It is only since the era of scientific medicine that the teaching role has been taken over by the specialists, or hospital scientists, with the result that their methods are now considered by tacit agreement to be far superior to anything else. There are increasing signs that this system will have to be revised. It is true, and we readily admit it, that in many conditions the specialists' methods are indeed superior. On the whole we would characterize such conditions as being ephemeral, but highly dramatic or critical, and often involving danger to life; yet having said this, may we claim for general practice and for proper psychotherapy, the other field which covers everyday life—the many little or greater irritations of human existence, involving not so much life or death but, what are perhaps equally important, contentment and human happiness? Maybe these are too exaggerated ambitions, so may we express the same idea in more modest terms: the aim of general practice and psychotherapy is to free people as far as possible from the unnecessary miseries of human life.

Acquiescing in the separate existence of these two kinds of medicine is one possibility. Is there any other? Are there any ways that would make a re-integration of medicine possible? There are some unmistakable signs that many doctors feel that this would be highly desirable. We have just mentioned the idea of 'comprehensive medicine' to which may be added the principle, heard more and more often in recent years, of 'one patient, one doctor'; the oft-quoted axiom that not the illnesses but the patient should be treated; the establishment of general practice units at more and more teaching hospitals; the increasing interest in psychotherapy among general practitioners, among non-psychiatric specialists, and—a highly important sign— among medical students. Thus it is quite possible that a number of people will feel that we have dwelt too much on diagnosing a condition from which medicine has suffered for some time but from which

128

she is rapidly recovering. Our answer is that this is a somewhat optimistic view.

In our opinion only symptomatic or palliative treatment has so far been offered for an insufficiently clearly diagnosed condition. Radical treatment would mean accepting very different points of view, as perhaps will have by now become clear to readers of this book. The points of view and ways of thinking we are advocating cut across existing ideologies and convictions firmly held, but nothing milder or less drastic will serve to re-integrate medicine, and in the long run ideas such as ours will have to be introduced into the teaching hospitals. This means more than merely allocating a few weeks of the students' already overcrowded time-table to a psycho-therapeutic outpatients' department. Three weeks or, for that matter, three months, are insufficient to obtain a training in psychotherapy. If the teaching hospitals should decide to offer proper training in psychotherapy to their students, then the whole structure of teaching would have to be modified so that each student would be able to remain in contact with his patients, when needed, for years. We know that a number of specialists feel strongly the need for some such arrangement.

Thus it seems that for some time to come the present split in medicine will remain as the official policy which, however, will have to defend itself against an increasing demand for reform. It is certain that the demand will stem from both camps, that is, from specialists as well as from general practitioners. The great difference is that the official policy has the power and its supporters are well organized, whereas the supporters of reform consist merely of individuals. True, their pressure has been strong enough to induce the official policy at least to adopt palliative measures. These, however, in the same way as in any type of therapy, can only mask, and never cure, the underlying condition.

PART III

THEORETICAL CONSIDERATIONS

CHAPTER 10

Understanding People Professionally

As a first approach to our problem it could be said that there are two kinds of understanding. One might be called intellectual and the other emotional. It is easy to quote situations that demand an intellectual understanding. This is the case with a mathematical or an engineering problem, in fact, with the whole field of exact and applied sciences. In this kind of understanding emotions play no part, or at most have a minor role. When trying to understand a problem intellectually, more often than not emotions are felt to be a nuisance or even a serious disturbance. Intellectual understanding is more easily achieved and is felt to be the more reliable if emotions can be kept at so low a level that their effect on the problem may be disregarded. Intellectual work should be performed in an 'unemotional' or 'objective' atmosphere.

The further away the problem lies from the field of the exact sciences, that is, the more the influence of the human element makes itself felt in it, the less reliable will become the results of a purely intellectual understanding of the situation and the more we shall need to understand the various emotional factors contained in it. This emotional understanding, as we will call it, is in many ways more complicated than a purely intellectual understanding. The first difference may be characterized as mutuality. To solve a mathematical, engineering, or scientific problem, it is as a rule sufficient to understand the external problem; there is hardly ever any need to understand ourselves as well. In contrast, any emotional understanding presupposes a fairly keen appreciation of what the emotions under observation mean to the observed and to the observer. A further difficulty is caused, as pointed out on several occasions, by the nature of our language. We have developed fairly precise and unequivocal means for the description of objective facts and unemotional events but it is hardly possible to give an exact description of what an observed person feels and what the meaning of this feeling is for ourselves, the observers.

133

This difference between intellectual and emotional understanding is largely responsible for the different approach to a patient's complaints in organic medicine on the one hand, and in psychological medicine on the other. In the first approximation, physical medicine treats the patient's complaints as a physiological, that is an intellectual, problem which has to be solved by the physician-observer objectively and unemotionally if possible. This is certainly true of diagnosis, but also, though to a lesser extent, of therapy. In a somewhat exaggerated way, it might be said that the patient is considered to be a very complicated piece of physico-chemical machinery; his complaints to be signs of trouble in the works; diagnosis has the task of discovering which parts of the machinery do not work properly, and the therapy must then endeavour to restore these parts to normal working order. During this intellectual undertaking the patient's feelings and emotions, though observed, count much less than the physical signs. In consequence, the doctor's first concern is to understand intellectually the physical signs, and by comparison he bothers much less about understanding his patient emotionally.

In contrast, all psychotherapies are based on understanding a fellow human being not only intellectually but above all emotionally. This is true no matter whether the therapist is a general practitioner, a social worker, or a non-psychiatric specialist. All of them have the task of understanding their patients in a professional capacity. Presently we shall return to discuss in detail what this difference between private and professional understanding means.

What we are going to contribute to the study of 'professional' understanding will apply in many fields—anywhere in fact where some understanding of human relationships is desirable if things are to go smoothly between two or more people. In the medical field, at one end of the scale we find full-scale psychotherapy; at the other end the understanding that can be given during an ordinary visit at the surgery or at home. Perhaps the best way to demonstrate in what way we intend to use the term 'emotional understanding' is by comparing and contrasting two fairly common but quite dissimilar experiences.

We may start with the experiences of a family at the arrival of their first baby. This should be a simple and happy occasion but often enough it is complicated and confusing to the parents, who then ask their doctors for advice or turn to books to help them to understand their child. Moreover, it happens frequently that the parents find both the doctors and the books unhelpful, and instead of being reassured they become annoyed and even more confused. Although they are convinced that there must be straightforward answers to their puzzling problems, and usually have no doubt that the doctors and the books have these answers, they cannot get at them, and so they conclude that their trouble must be due to their own short-comings; for instance, they may feel that somehow they were not successful in asking the right questions. Gradually they discover that what they have to do is to get to know their baby better by watching and noticing him more. It is only reluctantly that they can accept that there are no simple questions or answers to their problem, which is really one of human relationships.

We come upon a rather similar experience when we try to under-stand an unfamiliar piece of music or poetry, or a picture which at first may appear particularly meaningless or insolubly puzzling to us. In this instance too we may try to get some help towards understanding the music, the poetry, or the picture by talking to other people who know more about these things or by reading books, but we only really gain in understanding when we learn to look or to listen in a different way.

The most important aspect of this difference is *identification*, which is the basis of all emotional understanding. Though identification requires a certain amount of conscious effort by the observer, it depends much more on a willingness, and indeed a desire, to under-stand, and on an ability to sympathize with the person under ob-servation. To identify, the observer must be in tune to such an extent that for a brief time, perhaps only for a few moments, he may feel as if he were himself the person observed or the creator of the object under observation. The observer must be free, and secure enough, to part with his awareness of himself and of his role, his likes, dislikes, and individual idiosyncrasies, so that for the moments during which he identifies, he may feel what it is like to be the other person or the creator of the object.

Thus if the identification succeeds, observer and observed have a mutual experience. Conversely, no identification is possible unless the observer is prepared to have new experiences and wishes, or even expects to learn something that may be alien and even alarming to him. On the other hand, once an observer has identified himself with someone or something, he will find it difficult to feel objectively about that person or thing again. Every form of psychotherapy requires this biphasic effort. The psychotherapist must first identify, and then withdraw from the identification and become an objective professional again. In addition he must be able to respond constructively without too much delay.

When the observer is a mother and the person concerned her own child, the withdrawal from the identification need not be, and in fact

135

never is, complete; mothers are not meant to become objective about their children. It is only in professional relationships that this biphasic process becomes signally important. One could even say that understanding by a professional person occupies a borderline position between intellectual and emotional understanding.

This biphasic task—sympathetic identification followed by withdrawal into objectivity—is one of the characteristics differentiating a private from a professional relationship; or to restate this in a way that fits the scope of our book—differentiating a doctor's personal relationships from those he has while giving medical treatment to his patients in an expert capacity.

There are of course many other differences. The first is connected with the kind of setting in which the relationship is to take place. In a private relationship the setting can vary to any extent. It can take place anywhere and it can develop whether the two people concerned are alone or in a crowd; whether they meet regularly or irregularly; or whether there is a plan or structure in their relationship or not. In a professional relationship things are stricter. Here the relationship depends on a limited involvement between the doctor and the patient, and a stable setting in which, as a rule, only the two people concerned are present and which dedicates itself, so to speak, to the professional relationship for limited uninterrupted periods.

Very often the professional relationship exists only in this setting and stops abruptly when the two people concerned leave it. In fact, in many cases when they meet outside the setting, an ordinary private relationship replaces the professional one. Of course, there are exceptions to this rule; for instance, a general practitioner when meeting a patient in the street may decide in some circumstances to continue his professional relationship. It must be added here that geographically the setting need not be, but usually is, the doctor's consulting room, but it can be the patient's bedroom, the hospital ward, and so on. Whatever the actual setting may be, it has for the time being to take on the characteristics of a consulting room, that is, it must appear to be private and dedicated to the relationship, at any rate for a limited period.

Secondly, the forms of communication in a professional, as distinct from a private, relationship must be limited. Understanding is conveyed largely by words, seldom by action. The doctor hardly ever encourages his patient to have contacts with him outside the limited setting and tries to avoid becoming a permanent part of the patient's life. This means that the patient has to rely on his private relationships for all instinctual gratifications other than those that can be conveyed by words in the professional setting. Thus, the professional relationship is in many respects basically frustrating, and any attempt to avoid or mitigate this tends to dilute it and merge it into a private relationship, with the consequent advantages and disadvantages, assets and liabilities, characteristic of these kinds of relationship.

Thirdly, all parties in a private relationship inevitably develop emotional ties with one another which are lasting and, as a rule, *mutual:* the mother *and* the baby; the husband *and* the wife. But in all cases its intensity is limited more by what the partner can enjoy and tolerate, and less by what the individual wants and needs. In a professional relationship the doctor's emotional involvement must remain far less intense than the patient's. The interactions that take place between them, and in fact their whole relationship are centred one-sidedly on the patient, and the doctor's interests, emotions, ideas, and problems should be ignored as far as possible. Thus the intensity of the interaction is determined more by the patient's wants and needs, and the doctor must be prepared to endure the impact of emotions of very high intensity, which may even tax his resources. Of course, in this respect individual doctors will vary a great deal. The doctor is able to accept all the strains caused thereby because it is for a limited period only and because his own private relationships are not—or at any rate should not be—too much interfered with by his professional life. The patient, when starting a professional relationship, must accept these hard and seemingly rigid limitations; true, they help to protect the doctor from too intense a strain, but it is these limitations that provide the basis for the development of a professional relationship, which is the precondition for all forms of psychotherapy.

A further difference between professional and non-professional understanding is that the doctor starts the relationship without previous emotional involvement. He wants to do a limited task and then to fade out of the patient's life. True, he gets paid for it and would probably like in addition to have some gratitude and appreciation, but he is in no need of any lasting emotional ties with the patient. The fact that he is paid for his work means that he gets a reward for the relationship, which in this way may be kept more easily unemotional.

Lastly, the most important external criterion for differentiating private from professional relationships is the existence of a special and relevant kind of knowledge and skill in one of the two persons. In addition to having the ability to identify in the right setting while having only a limited involvement with his patient, the doctor must also possess some expert knowledge and have this knowledge at his fingertips apart from, and before, the actual relationship with his patients. In Chapter 12 we shall attempt to show how every psychotherapist is affected by his training; but here it is enough to say that there is an obvious connection between knowing things and events, having prior information about them, and being familiar with certain kinds of situations caused by them, and being able to observe them correctly. In this book we lay more emphasis on that part of psychotherapy which may be characterized as observation, attention, and experiencing, than on that part which may be called learning and knowing. This, however, must not be taken as if we wished to minimize the importance of the latter part; on the contrary, we are fully aware that observing and experiencing are closely linked with knowing in advance what to observe.[1]

In fact the *sine qua non* for all that we have been describing as professional understanding is the professional's knowledge and skill, which is the outcome of what he knows and what he has learnt to do irrespective of the patient that he is with. There are great dangers, however, in the use of theoretical, that is to say, general knowledge applied without discrimination and without proper skill. The professional must be able to use not only his general knowledge, but also his actual observations. For instance, there is a danger that the observer might see some conflict or anxiety in a patient during an interview and try to explain it to him entirely from his understanding gained from another patient, or from books, and ignore or fail to perceive because of his 'book' knowledge what the patient is showing him at the moment. To give an extreme and perhaps ridiculous example, he might say that the patient is suffering from an oedipus complex, or that he is frightened that he wants to kill his father, because he shows anxiety about his father's health. Although it is necessary to know about the existence, and the working, of the oedipus complex and of the unconscious, this knowledge in unskilled hands can merely enhance a rigid way of thinking about, or handling, the patient's problems.

The doctor's first task as a professional is, then, to listen to and observe what is there in the present and to understand it. As we have said, the basis of this professional understanding is identification and knowledge. This listening and observing, however, is not a wholly passive affair; it is an alert and participating listening, but—as a rule—no other activity is needed. Most people when in the position of interviewer, or when responsible in any way for other people, feel an urge to offer, or even to give, something, or to be active in some

[1] In the Introduction we have already discussed the limitations of textbook knowledge.

tangible way. At a party, drinks are often handed round to begin with, or food is offered; this makes both the guests and the host and hostess feel better, and so indirectly helps the party to start well. Drinks are not usually offered by doctors, cigarettes sometimes are—and may help, particularly the giver. In place of these symbolic gifts, doctors are apt to give interpretations or explanations as something 'good', to prove—at any rate to themselves—that they are worth visiting and it is not a waste of time talking to them.

In the effort to help the patient to overcome his initial difficulties, and to give proof of being worth while, some doctors think that they have to adopt some special attitude towards him. Some of them try to appear as a kind of permissive maternal figure, others as a strong, dependable, trustworthy father. We shall discuss the problem of these, almost standardized, attitudes in Chapter 12.

Furthermore, we have found that nearly all the doctors in our groups, when starting to try to understand their patients' emotions, are afraid that they will not be able to do so in the first interview or, if they do, that they will soon get lost and will not be able to follow the next move. On the other hand, if they take a reliable and exhaustive medical history they feel safe because they are using something sanctioned by accepted authority as 'good'. When going deeper into the events, it is almost invariably discovered that the patients themselves are not so bothered—they do not expect to be understood in the first interview or to be followed closely all the time. Thus the doctor's compulsion to 'give' must be watched, as it should be determined by the patient's needs, not by his own. In other words, the doctor must be able to feel acceptable and secure enough not actively to *need* to give anything 'good' except himself, that is, his room, his limited but reliable time, his full attention, and his professional skill during that period.

The doctor, then, has to provide this kind of setting and to be able to observe freely, not to behave automatically; convey the observations dynamically, not turn his back on unpleasant facts or confessions; and refrain from giving when it is not called for, so that the interview with him will be determined by the patient's problems and difficulties and thus become for the patient a vital experience. It would make things far easier and certainly much more reassuring, particularly for beginners, if a kind of Baedeker for psychotherapists could be devised, giving them some general advice on how to plan the journey and pointing out by one, two, and three stars, objects of particular interest worth visiting. Admittedly something of this kind was attempted in Part II of our book, but we are fully aware that its value is very limited indeed. It would, of course, be easier too if the would-be professional could have his teacher with him while he is with his patient, but this too is usually impossible and he has to manage on his own without props or guides or rules of the road.

But his difficulties do not end here. If anyone who is not a psychiatrist, whatever his training or background, attempts to do work that can be labelled psychotherapy, he will at once come under fire from many quarters.

For instance, it is sometimes thought by people who have some acquaintance with psycho-analysis that in any psychotherapy it is essential for the therapist to obtain information about and to understand the patient's emotional development. It is felt that it is only if psychotherapists can understand why a person behaves in the way he does in terms of his emotional or libidinal development, that they may be able to help him to change. Or other people would say that any understanding, however exhaustive, except when revealed in the course of proper psycho-analytic treatment, is of very little use since it is too rough and ready, too undynamic, and inadequate to deal with the deep unconscious conflicts that must be uncovered, understood, and resolved, if any change is to take place in the patient's illness. These people would say that psychotherapy has no justification except as a sympathetic supportive treatment and that anybody who attempts any more than that runs the risk of doing merely unprofessional amateurish work.

True, it may be agreed that a doctor may be able to understand some of the factors, conscious or unconscious, that led to a patient's illness or relationship difficulties, but it is questionable whether this 'understanding' will be therapeutically effective in itself. To illustrate this point, we quote the case of a woman in her mid-twenties who came to her doctor complaining that her husband wanted to help her to look after her baby, and this she simply could not tolerate. It soon became clear, when she began to talk to her doctor, that she felt very inadequate as a mother and was jealous of her husband's role as a man. It also transpired that, as a child of five, she had been very jealous when a brother had been born; this event apparently had some connection with her inability to share her feminine role with her husband. This interpretation was made but did not help her to get on better terms with her husband, though it probably allayed the intensity of her feeling and slightly eased the strain. In other cases it may even happen that by this sort of intervention some extra strain will be imposed on the patient; the interpretation may make more difficult the use of some of his customary defence mechanisms without enabling him to use himself better and more freely.

A corollary of this problem is whether psychotherapy can be of any real value unless the patient's fantasies and dreams can be understood, or unless his inner world can be revealed and properly understood in the treatment. It could be said that the source of all neuroses and character disturbances lies in these areas of the mind and there can be no value in superimposing changes when the structure underneath remains unchanged, so that the identical struggles will continue without abatement, perhaps even with increased force. Does it follow that in such cases nothing can be done apart from a proper psycho-analysis, except perhaps the sympathetic supportive treatment, mentioned above, that may relieve some conscious guilt feelings and offer some reassurance? If no analysis can be provided, is this all that should be attempted?

It does seem, however, that quite ill people may change for the better, and there is also such a thing as a spontaneous recovery and adjustment. Can these changes be understood in any way and, if so, can the understanding of the underlying processes be used by psychotherapists who for some reason or other cannot undertake analysis in a particular case? Will our use of the terms emotional and professional understanding help us here? It is well known that sometimes when reading a book or looking at a picture something may click and make sense to us that has never made sense before; as the saying goes: 'the penny dropped', and we are clearly aware of some shift of tension in us. For instance, such an experience may mean that we have learnt that some problem of ours, which we have never been able to formulate and which may be incapable of verbal formulation, is shared by a poet or a painter, and that his solution is not unlike one that we ourselves have been trying to reach; or that we can be moved or made to feel alive by someone else's communicated experience.

This kind of experience cannot be planned; it seems to depend on chance and coincidence, although one might guess that it can only occur when one is on the look-out for, and in need of, such an experience. Successes in psychotherapy show, however, that it is possible to provide a patient with an experience of this kind in a planned way. In certain cases, in fact, psychotherapists are able to understand enough of a patient's illness and, furthermore, to give him a creative experience that enables him to find a satisfactory solution to a problem and to discard an unsatisfactory one. In other words, psychotherapists may be able to provide vital dynamic experiences for their patients in a professional setting. We intend to examine this more fully in the next chapter and then to go on in the last chapter of this part to discuss the various techniques used by psychotherapists in this field.

CHAPTER 11

Enabling People to Understand Themselves

As we have already said, the doctor, while using his familiarity with other patients and his knowledge gained from books, must be aware that his patient is unique, and each interview, each anxiety, each complaint, different from any other. The patient will not be able to make use of generalities learned from books, but needs to be understood in a professional setting at a time when he is conscious of the need for help, and therefore prepared for change.

Before going further, we must discuss why and how the gaining of new understanding may have a therapeutic effect on the patient. As we have said, the doctor, by giving enough attention and by bringing experience and knowledge to clarify what he says, can help the patient to see new things about himself and the world he lives in. The patient can then, on the basis of his new understanding of himself, make a conscious effort to correct some of his automatic ways of behaving and thinking. Though what he finds out about himself may contain some unpleasant elements, none the less highly acceptable new ideas and feelings may emerge in due course. For instance, it may be very unpleasant for him to discover that the reason he is so intolerant of a colleague at work is that this colleague so much resembles certain aspects of himself; but later he may become more tolerant when he finds that the hateful part of himself that he has hitherto only recognized in other people hides a fear that he is not lovable and will never be accepted by others. We must emphasize here that this kind of understanding is not necessarily therapeutic, but that it can be so in favourable circumstances.

For instance, a woman consulted a doctor and told a story about her married life and her childhood in which there were conspicuously no complaints at all. She had a good husband, very nice children, plenty of money; she had received a good education and her mother was a good and kind mother. Her only complaint was her own irritability. She clearly felt guilty about asking for help, and at

142

the end of the first interview the doctor was able to point out to her (and by this time she was very near to tears) that perhaps her life was full of things that had not been wept over or complained about up to now; everything had been so good that she had felt there really was nothing that she could legitimately weep about. This interpretation had an instantaneous effect on her and enabled her to discover how much she hated her good mother who had kept her away from her father, and how much she had loved her father who had hardly existed for her before this interview, and how unhappy she was at times with her husband because she treated him in the same way as she treated her mother, as she felt it was her duty to be happy and cheerful with him all the time. By means of the interpretation she was given permission, so to speak, to be unhappy about what seemed to her trivial, unreal, unimportant, intangible events and feelings. In fact the help she was given was largely due to the acceptance by her doctor that the illogical and stifling events of that part of the world until now felt by her to be unreal, were as important and as dynamic a force in her life as those which she felt real and logical happenings.

Secondly, when a patient is given a new understanding of himself it may help him to feel less alone; thenceforth he may feel more a part of, and more related to, other people. It seems that it is one of the eternal aims of mankind to regain in adult life the lost feeling of merging into the universe, of being at one with the world and not separate from it, which has been valued so much since infancy. When a patient recognizes something new in himself and finds that this something is understood, and therefore shared, by another, his world may at that moment be enlarged. New parts of the external world, perhaps of someone else, are felt to correspond to parts of him, and he is to that extent enriched and changed. Ideas and emotions that he has suppressed, or repressed, either because he felt shame or guilt about them or because he felt they were queer, unrealistic, or even mad, can be acknowledged, and he can therefore use more of himself and experience or feel more in his relationships with other people.

It would seem that the internal changes we are just discussing are somewhat difficult to achieve, no matter how much people may wish for them, and it follows that, in order to enable people to achieve such changes, something unique and really worth while has to be offered to them. We shall leave on one side why it is so difficult for people to change, because this would lead us into a most difficult problem of psychotherapy, namely, why people feel so intensely threatened if they are expected to give up a part of themselves, however useless this part may be. Unfortunately, much too little is as yet known about these processes.

Returning to our main train of thought, it is well known that, on the whole, it is much easier to help those people who spontaneously come asking for therapy than those who come unwillingly, under pressure. This everyday clinical experience demonstrates convincingly that understanding alone, which may be given with both classes of patients, is in itself not necessarily therapeutic; something else is needed over and above mere understanding by a professional person. One of the aims of this book is to examine the various opportunities available to the therapist in his own setting for providing his patients with this something else.

To illustrate the great variability of this 'something', let us recapitulate very briefly what we said about the professional's setting in Part I. For instance, as we have shown in some detail in Chapter 2, the on-going professional contact that a general practitioner has with a whole family for a very long period gives him unique opportunities for intervening during any important moment in his patient's life. The general practitioner's setting admits more flexibility than that of any of his professional colleagues; the patient can either be given a great deal of 'attention' at one moment when he really needs it, or he can obtain small doses of it over a longish period if this is the form in which he can make good use of it. Thus the patient may rest confident that his doctor is always there for him and that he need feel isolated only if, and in so far as, he wants to. It is important to bear in mind that at certain periods a patient may *want* to feel isolated or, in other words, private, and it may even be so during most of his life; nothing is worse for such a patient than to have a doctor who is always ready to give some 'understanding' whether he is asked for it or not—let us say, each time the patient has a cold or 'flu—just because such an 'understanding' was asked for, and was most welcome, on a previous occasion.

Neither the on-going contact, nor the danger of unwarranted trespass into a patient's privacy exists for other psychotherapists. In Chapter 3 we discussed another setting, that of the specialists. While the general practitioner's psychotherapeutic setting is characterized by its great flexibility and its continuing contact with the patient, the specialist's setting is essentially ephemeral but spectacular. We can only repeat here that the specialist normally has only one chance—at most a very few; his time spent with the patient is much shorter and his contact thus more concentrated and intense than the family doctor's. On the other hand, this means also that the patient need not live with him and this allows him to see and even to discuss things that a patient would not like his family doctor to know. For further details we must refer to Chapters 2, 3, and 4.

Of the many possible settings of social case-workers, we are most familiar with the type in which help in marriage difficulties is offered; we would quote it briefly as a contrast since here a different kind of opportunity may be studied. When complaining about marital problems, the patient will show the case-worker many important aspects of his usual way of relating to people, as the marriage difficulty often is a more or less representative sample of the most important conflicts in the patient's life. It is therefore relatively easy for the case-worker to gain an entrance to the crucial areas in the patient's conflicts and to deal with them only so far as they relate to the marriage and without the need to delve more deeply into the whole of the patient's life. Moreover, the insight in this kind of work is not gained by one person alone, but by the couple—husband and wife; in this way the emotional upheavals can be expressed not only in the treatment but in the marital relationship. Consequently the change becomes more easily bearable because both partners are involved in it.

After this short recapitulation, let us return to our main topic and ask why is it that something happening in a therapeutic situation —a professional setting—may act therapeutically, whereas if the identical event took place in a non-professional setting it might have no dynamic effect at all? We would suggest that the first reason for this is that, in a therapeutic situation, what happens occurs at the moment when it is needed; secondly, because the doctor provides a setting for the work to be done, and for the event to happen, and this setting thus acts like a boundary or a frame separating the whole occurrence from the rest of the world. What happens within the framework of treatment sometimes has a dream-like quality; the patient may not feel he has had a real experience at all and he may even totally forget what happened in the treatment. If asked what happened, he may say 'nothing' while realizing that in fact he had an intense experience but that there are no words to describe it. Sometimes even the changes brought about by the treatment, which are obvious to him and his friends, are attributed to some other happening outside the treatment, and the treatment itself is then discounted. We saw an example of this in Chapter 7, Case 13, when the improvement in the sexual relationship between Mr. and Mrs. D. was thought by Mr. D. to be due to their purchase of an electric blanket.

Each interview with the doctor—as well as the whole treatment— has a beginning and an end. Even if the patient comes to see his doctor the next day or the following week for some other—or even the same—complaint, a psychotherapeutic interview is a limited experience. Though, in the setting, the patient may reveal a good deal about himself, and his relation to his doctor may temporarily assume dependent, infantile qualities, all this happens within a frame that helps him to preserve his independence, and instead of further regression and dependence he may even grow up and mature while working with a mature person. We shall have to return to this important point in the next chapter.

When a patient consults a doctor about an emotional difficulty, he brings with him inevitably a whole segment of his life, in particular that in which he finds himself now and in which his difficulty lies. This segment may start from the time when he made up his mind to seek help, or from some earlier time when his illness began, or when he suddenly realized that everything was not going well with him. Included in the segment and forming a very important part of it, is the patient's relation to all the intimate people in his personal world. The doctor's task is to see, as it were, the whole picture, and to help the patient to see it in a new light, so that it may make sense to him. The doctor's role in the psychotherapeutic setting, though important, differs considerably from the analyst's; true, both of them will sooner or later replace or represent important people in the patient's present or past, but the doctor can adopt the role of a kind of additional or subsidiary ego whose chief function is to watch and to understand the empty patches, the stumbling blocks and blind spots both in the patient's personality and in his life-history, without much emotional involvement. He must accept the *whole* of the muddle presented by the patient—the story, the confusion, the unrealistic or contradictory feelings—and must not push unpleasant or illogical bits out of sight. If this can be achieved, the present and the past will no longer be separated, they will be talked about in turn, one leading to the other. The patient will illustrate what he is saying about the present by a memory of the past, and vice versa. Thus, a kind of matching process will develop in the interview situation between patient and doctor, as well as in the patient's mind.

We have described in the previous chapter the kind of setting that the professional person creates for his patients and in what ways it is different from the setting in which ordinary, non-professional conversations take place. This has led to the other aspect of professional work, under what conditions understanding by a professional may be therapeutic. We called this aspect enabling people to understand themselves, which is tantamount to psychotherapeutic technique. These two aspects of our subject, creating a setting and helping people to understand themselves so that they may change, are so interwoven that the task of disentangling them has caused considerable difficulties. We shall now, in the next chapter, concentrate more on the problem of technique or variants of psychotherapies—when the aim is to help people to understand themselves so that they may achieve change.

CHAPTER 12

Variants of Psychotherapy

We have already seen in Part I how techniques vary according to the setting in which they are used. In this chapter we shall discuss how they vary, on the one hand according to the therapist's training and, on the other, according to the therapeutic goal. We shall leave on one side the psycho-analytic technique, which is beyond the scope of this book, and will concentrate on psychotherapeutic techniques with more limited aims.

The techniques we use in our therapeutic work will depend to some extent upon how much skill we have acquired in our training—no matter whether it was systematic or empirical, under supervision or autodidactic; it is our skill that determines the limits of our understanding and the kind of interventions that we think we can make and that we expect to be useful. Apart from this, our training will influence us in another way as well. What we have in mind here is not so much the obvious consequences of having been taught, or having picked up, a technique—which may be a rigid copy, or may serve as a basic pattern to be adapted freely to suit the individual doctor or patient—but rather the unavoidable results of having been trained in any form of psychotherapy. This aspect has less to do with the therapeutic method itself than with our ways of thinking and the observations on which the treatment is based. Although we shall not describe the psycho-analytic technique itself, for the sake of simplicity we shall illustrate this point by a discussion of the influence of training on psycho-analysts and on therapists trained by psycho-analysts.

It is well known that psycho-analytic techniques vary greatly; these variations have been amply described and discussed in the literature; in spite of this fact the techniques used by various psycho-analysts have many more similarities than differences. Roughly the same will hold true if they apply psycho-analysis to another field, e.g. to psychotherapy or psychiatric diagnosis. The reason for this is that no one, not even a well-trained analyst, can fundamentally change his way of observing, of thinking, and of fantasying, all of which

148

are largely determined by his training. For instance, analysts have learned to recognize transference phenomena and, no matter whether they interpret them to the patient or not, they cannot avoid their professional handling of the whole therapeutic situation being influenced by their knowledge; moreover they understand the patient's behaviour and verbal communications in a certain way which is bound to lead the emerging material in certain directions. True, no two analysts will lead the material in exactly the same direction, but the general trend will invariably be towards uncovering defence mechanisms and unconscious ideas in the patient's inner world. Some analysts, when undertaking psychotherapy, will make a particular effort to avoid the development of anything similar to an analytic situation and will refrain from using any interventions which seem dangerously near to analytic interpretations, but they cannot fail to understand the material broadly in the same way as they do when they are analysing, and their total knowledge, experience, and fantasy world will be mobilized by the patient whether they mean to use them openly or not. Thus the patient will get from an analyst something different from what he would from someone with no analytic training and experience.

Similarly, psychotherapists who have been trained by psycho-analysts, or have developed under a strong psycho-analytic influence, will have more in common with one another than with psychotherapists who are totally uninfluenced by psycho-analytic ideas. In their case too, familiarity with their own unconscious experience and fantasy will be reflected in their work, and the amount of awareness that they have of the patient's dynamic unconscious, and of their own, will be used whether they are aware of it or not.

Generalizing, this means that psychotherapies may be classified also according to the training of the therapist and, conversely, one can know something about the technique used if one knows something about the psychotherapist's training. This applies of course to the authors of this book, both of whom are psycho-analysts, and the discussion about technique which follows must be read with this in mind.

It is more difficult to show how techniques vary according to therapeutic goals. To begin with, goals are seldom clear-cut and precise and still less frequently stated explicitly; that is why it is far from easy to isolate them. Moreover, when it comes to describing or isolating techniques relating to specific therapeutic goals, any attempt to do so briefly will inevitably turn complex and fluctuating processes into orderly and over-simplified abstractions. In spite of all these difficulties, as a first approach we have isolated two main therapeutic goals and will describe some techniques causally related to them.

Before doing so, however, we would point out that the problem of therapeutic goals is, in fact, closely linked with that of diagnosis, whenever a patient first consults us, our chief task is to make a diagnosis and, on the basis of that, to decide on a goal. The subject of diagnosis will be discussed more fully in Part IV; here it will suffice to mention the well-known fact that whenever a doctor listens to a patient's story in a professional setting and with some therapeutic skill, therapy will start even if it is his intention only to make a diagnosis. Nevertheless, a proper diagnosis must be made, particularly when the aim of therapy has to be limited, because accepting a limited aim is tantamount to deciding how deep an understanding a given patient will need.

Mere listening to the patient's story will seldom provide a sufficiently firm basis; we have in addition to do something with the story in order to arrive at a safe diagnosis. Here is a good illustration: a patient came complaining about headaches, and during the course of his story told the doctor rather bitterly about his nagging and unbearable wife. The doctor wondered why the patient married such a woman and made an attempt to find out what had brought these two people together. The patient then added that his wife lived in the same village as he did when they were young, and he came across her accidentally later at a time when he was lonely and had no friends, and they had then quickly drifted into marriage. She had always liked him but he had known her very little when they were young. This story, if properly understood, could tell the therapist a great deal, and as a next step he could try to discover whether this kind of drifting behaviour followed by resentment was something that had happened before in the patient's life and also why it was that he was lonely, and so on. In other words, the doctor could put out feelers, the responses to which might in the end help him to arrive at a diagnosis. We may conclude that unless the therapist is capable of noticing that there is more behind some of the patient's remarks than meets the eye, and of discovering by his feelers what it might be, he could not get to know about the depth of the patient's illness. In order to put out the right feelers, the therapist has to be able to identify with the patient in the way we described in Chapter 10.

Another patient, while complaining of depression and confusion, told a story in which she reported that she had been quite happy as a child although she had had no brothers and sisters; her father died when she was young, and her mother was an alcoholic. Since she had grown up, she had had many love affairs and a successful business career. For some time the doctor listened to her story in which more and more details were given, including real childhood memories. The doctor then felt quite at a loss as to what to do because, although he apparently knew everything about his patient, he understood nothing about the cause of her illness. He therefore made a fresh start and tried to find out what it was that he had not been told in the story; why, for instance, the patient had never enjoyed any of her love affairs and whether he was right in suspecting that the patient's mother was still the most important person to her. This enquiry led to floods of tears and a confession that the patient had never got over not being with her mother, who had died two years before, and that what she had most desired was to spend her life looking after her mother.

Though in this kind of way it is possible for a doctor to learn a great deal about his patient in a few interviews and to build up a picture about the nature of the patient's most pressing problems and usual object relationships, he might quite easily be mistaken about the nature of the illness. In other words, he might make a partly correct but partly wrong diagnosis. In spite of this it is bound to be on the basis of such findings that it will be decided whether or not the patient should be treated at all and, if so, in what way, by whom, and with what treatment goal in view.

As mentioned, we have isolated two principal classes of psychotherapeutic goal. In the first class, the therapist's chief attention is upon readjusting the patient's *external behaviour* with important people in his environment; the focus of the work is on what the patient does and why he does it and the aim is to help him to behave differently. In the second class, the therapeutic aim is to help the patient readjust some of his *internal problems*; the therapist concentrates the work on the patient's intrapsychic problems and pays less attention to how these internal problems affect the patient's external behaviour. The external relationships of patients treated in this way might be as bad as those in the first group, but the internal strains appear to be so pressing that the therapist comes to the conclusion that they cannot be altered merely by behavioural or external changes.

We would stress that it is not the symptomatology that decides the therapeutic goal. A patient might present a symptom of insomnia, some phobia, or headaches, or might merely complain that he is always worrying about something or that he can never stop working; he may even say that what is wrong with him is caused by someone in his environment, a husband, a wife, a parent, or a child, and may ask the doctor to do something about one or the other of these people. No matter what sort of symptoms or complaints the patient offers to his doctor, it is the doctor who has to decide whether this particular patient can be helped by readjusting his external behaviour or his internal problems.

Let us suppose that the doctor decides that the patient's difficulties can be best helped if he is enabled to understand something about how his behaviour restricts and hinders him in his relationships with other people, and how his own behaviour influences other people's attitudes towards him. For instance, a woman came to her doctor complaining about her husband's indifference and lack of love for her, and was helped by the doctor to see how in fact she was rejecting all her husband's approaches and so preventing him from feeling capable of satisfying her in any way.

Here the technique was focused on helping the woman to see what she was doing with her husband. This turned out in fact to be the reverse of what she thought she was doing when she came for treatment. This, however, was not too painful for her and it was not necessary to show her, except in a very superficial way, why she had felt rejected by her husband. The therapist hoped in this case that this one piece of fresh understanding of herself would pave the way for others which were likely to follow in due course.

It is easy to assess the results of this technique, which may be called readjusting external behaviour; after treatment, either the patient can function better in his environment and make better relationships, without increased tension or the development of new symptoms and complaints, in which case the treatment might be thought of as a success; or his relationships remain as bad as they were when he sought treatment, when it is regarded as a failure. However, this behavioural goal can seldom be kept completely pure, and it usually includes our second goal, which is to help the patient towards a better internal adjustment; for instance, in the case just quoted the therapist might have tried to show the woman her ambivalence to her husband which made her reject him, and also perhaps her fear of hurting him or being hurt by him.

The principal aim set by the therapist, however, has an important influence on the technique, and consequently on the results that emerge. For instance, if the aim set by the therapist is to help the patient in his external relationships, the therapeutic work will inevitably be directed also towards helping the patient to overcome some dependent and childish wishes and attitudes, and any marked improvement in his symptoms or in his behaviour may lead to the termination of the treatment. If, however, the aim is more in terms of adjusting intrapsychic problems, a symptomatic improvement might encourage therapist and patient to continue as it would indicate a favourable prognosis for further work; the patient, too, would willingly forgo some immediate independence if he could feel he might be helped to reach the inner disturbance which was a burden to him, and do something about it.

Whatever the goal, many psychotherapists start treatment by encouraging their patient to talk freely about whatever seems to be relevant at the time of the interview. On the whole, under the influence of psycho-analytical thinking, they try to *understand the present genetically in terms of the past*, that is, to make the patient aware of how his difficulties are connected with what happened to him when he was a child. We have discussed some implications of this technique in Chapter 10 and found that it is questionable whether this kind of understanding will be therapeutically effective in itself. This technique may be applicable when the aim of the therapy is to help the patient to see and comprehend important aspects of his present behaviour of which he has been unaware, namely, when the therapist has our first goal principally in mind. The patient may then come to see in the light of his past why he behaves in the way he does and why his expectations about other people's behaviour towards him are of the particular kind they are. Arising out of this, he can be shown how his expectations cause him to like or dislike certain people and how this behaviour causes people to like or dislike him and to expect him to behave in the way he does.

The remembered past, in fact, in this kind of work is brought in to explain and illustrate the present. The patient is given a fresh picture of himself in his environment and can reassess some of his habitual ways of thinking, feeling, and behaving. The therapist, when using this technique, is not so much concerned with understanding the patient's unconscious fantasies which lie behind his overt patterns of behaviour, but concentrates on what is actually happening in an overt way in the present. He may have to interpret some fear or anxiety to loosen some defences before the patient will start work at all, but once confidence and a minimum of insight have been gained, work can often proceed fairly easily.

A good example of this kind of approach is the treatment of Mrs. S., a woman of thirty, who had been married for thirteen years and had a son of eleven—she was referred for help because she and her husband had had no sexual relations for three and a half years. She had consulted her general practitioner three years before because she felt that the problem was all hers and was due to the fact that her own parents had been on such bad terms; but after discussing the matter with her doctor she had emerged with the conviction that she was perfectly normal, and that the fault was all with her husband, who refused intercourse. This conviction was brought to the first interview with the psychotherapist along with a good deal of hostility and hopelessness and an absolute refusal to accept that she had any share in the present impasse; however she was able to admit that she found intercourse disappointing and that she was terrified of having another child. She asked for help and advice but did not allow the therapist to make any real contact with her.

She agreed to come for a second interview in a week's time but she saw to it that there was a fortnight's interval before the second interview by coming on the wrong day. In the meantime she had provoked a quarrel with her husband which had led to a temporary separation. The husband came in to see the boy every day, but was not living at home at the time of the second interview. Mrs. S. was even more hostile and forbidding at the beginning of the interview, but she looked so hopeless and despairing that the therapist commented on this fact and remarked that anybody would understand how awful she felt. This led to a dramatic change, the patient broke down, started to cry, and dropped her rejecting and forbidding behaviour. In the same interview she could accept an interpretation to the effect that she had to get her husband out of sight so that she should not see the awful effects of her treatment of him, and soon after she was able to realize that it was her own resentment and guilt towards her husband that made it well-nigh impossible for him to make love to her.

By the fourth interview the husband had come home and asked for treatment for himself. The work with Mrs. S. then centred on her obvious preference for her son, and the boy's knowledge of this. She was then able to discuss her attempts at controlling the relationship between her husband and her son and to see its connections with her own oedipal problems.

One important, but usually unrecognized, side-effect of a technique which includes understanding the present in terms of the past, is that the patient gets reassurance from the therapist even if no actual reassuring remarks are used. This is so because this kind of therapy may imply that whatever the patient does is not really the patient's fault, but that he behaves in the way he does because of his early relationships, over which he had no control but which were bound to influence him. We are not suggesting that whenever a psychotherapist interprets the present in terms of the past he does so in order, so to speak, to sugar the pill and to make the patient's present inadequate behaviour tolerable. This, however, is an important aspect of work of this kind which, if not watched carefully, can be abused. To take an extreme case, it is possible for a patient to be encouraged to feel during therapy of this kind that he has only loving feelings and that his 'bad' behaviour is not his fault, does not even originate with him.

The therapist is well advised to bear in mind at all times when using this technique of understanding the present in terms of the past, the dangers of ignoring the patient's unconscious feelings of resentment and guilt which may otherwise have to find outlets outside the treatment. To give an example: a man of thirty was enabled during treatment, probably for the first time in his life, to feel and to express feelings of a loving kind and to experience the therapist as a kind parent substitute. The results seemed excellent until, some months after the end of treatment when a follow-up was done, it was discovered that during the treatment the patient had had severe gastric troubles which he had not reported to his therapist and which had led eventually to a gastrectomy. During treatment he had preferred to keep painful topics away from his therapist as if they did not belong to him. The patient had then sought out and joined a religious group, and this seemed to him a satisfactory outcome of his treatment. However, just before the follow-up he had a severe accident at work. Here in both the present and the past the patient's resentment and guilt had been ignored, although they were dynamic and in need of interpretation. His loving feelings and his painfully destructive ones were kept at a distance from one another.

As an alternative, the therapist may try to avoid using the past events in his patient's life to 'excuse' or 'explain' the present, but in this case he will leave the patient to bear without implicit reassurance all the resentment, shame, and guilt that emerges during treatment. If this is too painful, patients often introduce the past in their search for explanation and reassurance. The therapist may remain more or less aloof and, though listening with interest and attention, refrain from making 'reassuring' and 'explanatory' comments, especially when he thinks that it will be more therapeutic if the patient is allowed to take full responsibility for what he sees is happening in the shelter of the psychotherapeutic setting. In any case he can hardly ever be absolutely sure that any particular childhood experience has 'caused' or may 'explain' the present trouble. The therapist, by showing freedom from anxiety about the patient's resentment, shame, and guilt, provides an opportunity for him to become more mature and independent.

We now come to our second goal; here the emphasis is on helping the patient to overcome or solve some *intrapsychic and unconscious conflict* without offering him a full-scale analysis; in all these cases, of course, the chief attention is focused on some unconscious conflict rather than on the result of the conflict, the patient's behavioural patterns. Here are some examples in which this kind of work was thought to be needed and was successfully used: a young girl experiencing difficulties in growing up because of unconscious fears of her mother's jealousy, and a young man who could not progress in his business career because of an unconscious fear of his homosexual wishes. The young footballer described in Chapter 8 is another case of this kind of technique.

At the beginning of treatment the technique is similar to that in our previous group. The psychotherapist listens in the same way to the patient's history as it unfolds itself, intent on discovering anything in it which might throw light on the symptom or conflict about which the patient has sought help; but here the therapist must listen to the material in a different way. He will not try to show the patient how he behaves, or why he behaves in the way he does, or the effect that his behaviour has on the people in his environment. Instead the therapist will concern himself chiefly with what might seem to the uninitiated observer to be unimportant details in the history, with casual references, omissions, under- and over-statements, and in particular with any unexpected display or lack of display of emotion. In this type of therapy, pauses will be as important as the narrative itself and will have to be understood in their context. The therapist must also follow the associations of one idea or topic with another, that is, he must observe carefully what follows what in the flow of talk in order to discover if this throws any light on the area of difficulty which he has been asked, or has set out, to treat.

In other words, repressed half-conscious or unconscious ideas, which need not necessarily be understood in psychotherapies which are chiefly concerned with behaviour problems, must be understood here. The attention is focused, not on hitherto unrecognized ways of behaviour but on recognizing irrational ideas, anxieties, and fears, daydreams and nightmares, in order to give the patient insight into some area of his inner world. The therapist, in fact, has to try to understand, and to make sense of, what he hears and sees, not excluding the 'drama' which is taking place in his room during the interview. But the sense he has to make of it is not the rational or logical kind of sense we are used to, but a special kind which belongs to this particular patient alone. It is more like a code which must be deciphered, but which is the patient's way of thinking and experiencing in the illness or conflict area of his mind. The patient himself is, as a rule, unaware of this code and so the therapist has first to decipher and then to explain it to the patient.

To take a simple example: an intelligent girl came to her doctor asking for sleeping tablets. She said she was quite well but she had been taking some examinations lately and was unable to sleep and felt rather exhausted. The doctor thought this was very reasonable and gave her the pills. Later, however, it emerged that the girl had not consulted her doctor or asked for the pills until after she had learnt that she had passed the examinations. 'Logically' she should have needed them earlier, but it was success that brought her sleeplessness.

Before her doctor could help her, however, he had to listen to her story with his ear attuned to this kind of 'sense'. Once the therapist starts to listen for this kind of logic, he will expect to hear different sequences and different causal connections. He will, in fact, have a new kind of expectation about what goes with what. If, however, during the ensuing discussions his expectations are shown to be wrong (i.e. if he learns that the girl patient can enjoy some successes), he has to re-examine his assessment and to ask himself whether he was wrong before, i.e. whether he made a wrong kind of sense out of the patient's previous communication; perhaps the patient has now changed, or perhaps the new piece of information can really add something to the incomplete understanding achieved by him before. For instance, in our example, the girl who was anxious when she passed examinations was anxious only when competing with men, not with women, and then probably only with particular kinds of men. The therapist must never try to force his 'theories' into the patient's story and may have to bear *not* being able to make sense of what is indeed a real confusion. In this latter case his job then is merely to note the confusion and not to try to clear it up at all costs, for some time at least.

In some treatments, what the therapist has to do is to accept the illogical, irrational parts of his patients, take them seriously and, even though they are only fairy-tale-like wishes or fears, not deny their importance and power. It is no good asking patients to test and to make do with reality unless the therapist himself can accept his patients' fantasies. It is no good asking them to accept the fact that they are lucky—or unlucky—before he knows what their inner world is like and what the contrast is between their internal fantasy world and their real external world. One example of this kind of treatment was given in Chapter 11, where the married woman with no complaint except her own irritability was enabled to weep about seemingly unimportant, irrational facets of her life.

As we said before, none of these variants are mutually exclusive. They are all probably used to some extent in every treatment; the therapist will always have some hunches about why the patient behaves in the way he does in the present in the light of what he hears about his early family life; and on the other hand irrational fantasy material is hardly ever totally disregarded, but is taken into account to some extent in all forms of psychotherapy. Equally it is rare for psychotherapists to ignore a patient's fear and anxiety which manifest themselves at the opening stages of treatment and to deal only with past events and symptoms.

All techniques have their advantages and also their dangers. A fairly general danger is that, although the patient appears to be much improved on the surface, his anxieties may be even greater than before treatment and they may force him to some other forms of neurotic behaviour or even to a physical illness. Another danger is the development of a dependent relationship with the therapist. If the therapist's chief concern has been to get hold of and to interpret unconscious fantasies and dreams, all of which may be done with but little co-operation from the patient's conscious ego, the patient may become so involved in this fascinating experience that his only wish will be to continue to understand his dreams and fantasies and he will have little extra ego strength and interest to enable him to use his new insight in everyday life. In consequence, the patient may be willing to continue with his treatment, though it has done him little good, provided he can do so on his terms, i.e. without really changing or getting deeper in a meaningful way into his area of conflict.

We must return here to the point we raised briefly in the previous chapter, namely, how the therapist's attitude affects his work. We feel that whatever technique the therapist adopts, his attitude to the patient will be as important as any verbal communications that take place between them.

In our view, the therapist must always have the courage to be himself and be willing to accept as much of his own peculiarities, weaknesses, and strengths, skills or limitations, as he is able. He must not try to 'put on an act' for his patient. This does not mean that he must always be the same with every patient, any more than that he is rigidly the same with the people that he meets in his own environment; but he must try not to adopt a set role whether it be as an ideal therapist who knows everything or, on the contrary, as a poor doctor who has very little insight and should be careful of what he does. It may be only too easy for him to present himself as a strong, dependable father figure who has some magical insight and inexhaustible patience, or as a stern figure who will stand no nonsense, or as a permissive, good, lovable mother, and so on. It is often, if not always, very difficult *not* to give some false impression of this kind as very often the therapist does in fact feel that he could be more dependable or more loving than the patient's real mother and father.

If possible, then, the therapist should be relaxed and quiet and at ease with his patients, particularly so in difficult cases if he feels that only a miracle can help and the patient really needs more money or love or different housing or an entirely different past history if he is to be helped at all. In these situations more than any other a quiet, attentive, alert and even curious attitude is called for if the therapist wishes to be of any help. He must never forget that he is a professional and that his task is not to love or to be strict or to make good the deprivations in the patient's past or present, but to listen attentively to what is said and to understand it in a professional capacity, as we described it in Chapter 10, and, in particular, never to forget that there is always something new to understand. What he must be on the look-out for are not faults in the patient's environment or history, but misunderstandings, exaggerations, painful contradictions, and omissions, which characterize and colour the patient's present wishes, hopes, and vision. He must always know that there is more to understand than appears at first glance and his only hope of understanding is to wait and to listen. If he feels in a hurry to understand, his attitude may be over-confident and omnipotent, and this more than anything else will prevent a useful relationship growing up between him and his patient.

We have to conclude this chapter on rather a gloomy note. We have many times said that psychotherapy is a skill and that it cannot be learned by attending lectures or reading books, but that those who wish to practise it have to be trained to do so. The reason for this will now perhaps have become clearer. There are so many 'instructions' in this chapter which can only be followed if one already knows how to use the skill. We hope, however, that we have conveyed to our readers a rough outline of our ways of thinking about technical problems in psychotherapy.

PART IV

THE PSYCHIATRIC INTERVIEW

CHAPTER 13

Comparison with Medical Examination and Psychological Testing

1

The diagnostic interview is the pivot of every form of psycho-therapy. All of us—general practitioners as well as psychiatric and non-psychiatric specialists—are equally interested in it since every therapy inevitably starts with an initial diagnostic interview; and so all of us have some experience in it. Surprisingly, the techniques of interviewing have received much less attention both in psycho-analysis and in psychiatry than those of therapy. There is even a story about Freud who, when asked what he did with people who came to consult him, answered that his main function was to impose a fine on them for disturbing his peace.

This relative neglect is rather odd in view of the fact that a good interview technique is the crux of psychological diagnosis; with some exaggeration one may even add that the whole of psychotherapy happens within the framework of the psychiatric interview which is, therefore, the indispensable vehicle for diagnosis as well as for therapy. All doctors interested in psychological medicine—except perhaps the general body of psychiatrists and psycho-analysts—are keenly aware of this fact; moreover they seem to feel that we psychiatrists have a kind of esoteric knowledge of the right technique which is jealously guarded as a secret of our trade. Time and again we were surprised when one group of doctors after another almost implored us to reveal to them some components of this secret.

We have, thus, a twofold task before us in this part. We want to show our non-psychiatrist colleagues the many problems that await solution in this field so that we may reckon with their continued interest; we also want to stimulate our psycho-analyst colleagues by demonstrating how important these problems are, not only for a reliable diagnostic technique, but also for psycho-analysis in the strictest sense. As will be seen from the following pages, it is our opinion that a close collaboration between these two groups offers the best prospects for solving these thorny problems. The first condition for a fruitful collaboration is a good acquaintance with each other's problems, which is why we have assigned one whole part of our book to this topic. In addition we hope it will prove to our non-psychiatric colleagues that we have not many trade secrets.

As we have mentioned, it was only with reluctance that they accepted the fact that for many psychiatrists there was not much of a problem here. For the latter a psychiatric interview is merely a special form of the medical interview, with a patient suffering, or suspected to be suffering, from a so-called functional or psychiatric condition. The aim of a medical examination or interview is to enable the doctor to understand the patient's complaints, symptoms, and physical signs, and to integrate them into a cohesive picture; in other words, the doctor's task is to discover the true nature of the disease, assess its severity, and find out whether it is stationary, progressive, or improving. A further aim is to enable him to prescribe adequate treatment. Ideally the treatment should reverse the pathological processes and restore health or, at least, should arrest the pathological process and enable the patient to adapt himself, without undue suffering, to his present illness.

We must repeat here what was said in Part III, namely, that a basic assumption of this way of thinking is that the doctor can examine the patient almost as an engineer would examine a machine. This ideal is realized to a very large extent in certain types of examination, such as x-ray of a fractured bone, or listening to the heart sounds, and still more so in the pathological laboratories where there is no need even for the patient to be present; all that is required is a specimen of his sputum, urine, etc.

Although the situation is more complex in the so-called 'clinical examination' it approximates to this ideal fairly closely. Since our whole training as doctors is based on the 'clinical examination', our attitude when meeting a patient for the first time is strongly influenced by it. This is understandable, because what is called 'proper clinical examination' is the result of several centuries of hard thinking, searching criticism, and sound clinical observation, shaped into a smooth procedure by the pressing demands of efficiency. In fact, a proper clinical examination can be performed in ten to fifteen minutes, without much embarrassment or suffering for the patient, and yet it enables the doctor to form a reliable picture of his patient's overall condition. Moreover, if the classical routine is conscientiously adhered to, the doctor can be confident that it is highly unlikely that he has missed anything important. And last, but not least, the clinical examination can be repeated as many times as necessary either by the first examiner or—theoretically—by any number of his colleagues, thus offering the safety of verification should any problem or doubt arise.

The situation is utterly different in a psychiatric interview. First, there is no approved and settled routine; second, however objectively the doctor tries to behave, he must, willy-nilly, enter into a personal relationship with his patient, and the result of his examination will depend, to a very high degree, on his subjective experiences and attitudes in this relationship. Consequently a repetition of the examination may not yield exactly the same results, and we must look further and use more complex methods if we need a verification for the findings of a previous examination. This point will be further discussed in the next chapters.

Let us now survey the first two points in further detail. It is true that several attempts have been made to devise a routine for the psychiatric interview. We all know of the many so-called 'case sheets' or 'record forms' available for this purpose, and a number of us psychiatrists have tried our mettle at devising new ones. Although admittedly these routine case sheets, designed on the pattern of those used in the medical wards, are helpful by reminding the doctor not to overlook certain aspects of the case, their usefulness does not go much beyond this. It is a common experience that—unlike a medical record—a psychiatric case sheet completed by one examiner is of but little use to another. One reason for this is that, although it contains a number of useful and important pointers, somehow the picture of the whole patient and his present state does not emerge clearly from it. One way to deal with this difficulty is to leave the 'case sheet' or 'record form' almost bare, enabling the examiner to record his findings in an unobstructed way. As often as not the result is a long and meandering description, often verbose and boring, or even unpalatable, for any third party. Obviously there is still a great need to devise, for psychiatric cases, something akin to the efficient routine clinical examination and the equally efficient way of recording the findings made during it.

The other difficulty mentioned is the absolute necessity in a psychiatric interview of establishing a personal relationship between doctor and patient. To show the difference in this respect between a medical and a psychiatric interview, let us imagine a passively unco-operative and monosyllabic patient. Although the medical examiner may have some difficulty, he can proceed without much hindrance to examine the patient's reflexes, breathing, heart sounds, and so on. Quite possibly he will have some difficulty in palpating the patient's abdomen, but not too much, and almost certainly he will be able to overcome it. All the time his patient might remain indifferent and monosyllabic. The situation is utterly different in a psychiatric interview. If the doctor is not able to make a good enough rapport with his patient, the result of his examination will be unsatisfactory, patchy, or even misleading. All this is well known, but the implications of this state of affairs have perhaps not been pointed out sufficiently. With a psychiatric examination it is almost as if while determining the level of blood sugar the doctor were to feed his patients with sweets. Obviously the values for the blood sugar will then depend not only on the patient's 'internal milieu', but also, and to a very high degree, on the amount, form and nature of the sweets offered by the doctor and on the willingness or reluctance of the patient to accept them.

The fundamental difference between medical and psychiatric examination can now perhaps be stated more clearly. The classical medical examination is almost entirely a physiological and anatomical examination which belongs, to use an important concept stated by John Rickman,[1] to one-person biology or psychology. A psychiatric examination is simply unthinkable if restricted to this field, as it is essentially the examination of a human relationship; thus it belongs to the field of two-person biology or psychology. This is the reason why all attempts at developing a routine, based exclusively on the pattern of the classical medical examination, must prove, and indeed have proved, futile.

Having established the fact that the psychiatric interview is essentially a phenomenon belonging to the field of two-person biology or psychology, it follows that its course will depend on the contributions of both participants. Nevertheless, the aim of the interview is to assess the mental state of only one participant, the patient, by studying his contributions to the relationship. A whole host of difficult theoretical problems emerge here, which we cannot propose to solve. Our aim is to point out their importance and discuss the influence of only a few of them.

Although to some extent the 'routine medical examination' is also a two-person relationship, its results are interpreted and recorded entirely in terms of one-person biology. Let us take a well-known and often quoted example, that of blood pressure. If a patient is anxious or tense, his blood pressure will rise, but this raised value is usually not recorded at all. Textbooks and the everyday clinical

[1] 'Number and the Human Sciences', reprinted in his *Selected Contributions to Psycho-analysis*. London: Hogarth Press, 1957.

teaching recommend all sorts of techniques for easing the patient's tension before observing and recording what is called the real value of the pressure. The real value, in this sense, means the level of the blood pressure when the patient is, as far as possible, protected from the impact of the two-person relationship. Similar routines are adopted when counting the pulse, when examining certain reflexes, determining the B.M.R., etc. etc. The basic assumption in all these cases is that the influence of the examiner, or the fact of being examined, is a disturbing factor, the effects of which must be eliminated as completely as is compatible with the investigation.

This, obviously, cannot be done in a psychiatric interview. Everything that happens there represents an interaction between two persons, each responding to the other's needs and demands in his own individual way. Or, in other words, the psychiatric interview is the sum total of the patient's reactions to a particular doctor, at a particular moment, in a particular setting; and as nothing of this can be left out from the interview, what in fact is examined is exactly this interaction. Therefore, what can be a disturbing element in a routine medical examination becomes the essence of the psychiatric interview.

The third problem, still more difficult than the two previous ones, is our way of recording the findings. Practically all our psychiatric terms describing neurotic or psychotic illnesses or mental states have been either borrowed from, or coined on the pattern of, the one-person biology, i.e. anatomy and physiology; to quote a few: hysteria, neurasthenia, schizophrenia, drug addiction, epilepsy, general paralysis of the insane, senile dementia, anxiety state, melancholia, nervous instability, and so on. They are intended to describe anatomical or physiological states and only secondarily human relationships. This means that, although everything that we observe in a psychiatric interview is essentially a phenomenon of a two-person relationship, we must describe it in terms belonging to one-person biology. As one of us (M.B.) pointed out elsewhere,[1] this is reminiscent of the procedures in projective geometry, where the task is to represent an $n + 1$ dimensional body in n dimensions, the best studied example being the representation in a plane of shapes and movements in space. Although representation is possible, it is always poorer than the original and, as projective geometry teaches us, there are many tricky situations which may fool anyone but a highly cautious expert, and sometimes even him also.

[1] M. Balint (1952). *Primary Love*. London: Hogarth Press. Pp. 234–5.

2

Returning to our main theme, we have seen that the psychiatric interview is essentially a two-person relationship built up from the contributions of both participants. The aim of the interview, however, is to study only the patient's contributions, in order to arrive at an assessment of his present mental state, and then to describe it in traditional language, which is unfortunately rather inadequate for this purpose.

In order to study the patient's contributions to this two-person relationship, one might think it essential that the doctor's contributions should be more or less rigorously standardized. Obviously, if we subject every patient to the impact of the same treatment, then the observed differences in reactions may be considered as an acceptable scientific basis for our conclusions. Something similar is aimed at, and allegedly even happens, in psychological testing. Each test, whether its aim is to measure the intelligence, assess the personality by various projective techniques, or even to ask only for some perfectly innocent information by the use of a questionnaire, prescribes a rather rigid technique of administration without which, as all the authors agree, the results might not be valid. However, if we survey the situation more closely, we discover that the psychologist's approach to the test situation is rather similar to the doctor's when taking his patient's blood pressure. There is, in fact, a strictly prescribed routine for taking the blood pressure, but before it can be started the patient must be put at ease, that is to say, his fears, tenseness, etc., must be dealt with. Exactly the same is true for all psychological tests. The administration of the test itself is a fairly rigid procedure, which, however, is preceded in almost every case by a period of 'putting the patient at his ease'.

This 'putting the patient at his ease' is supposed to be achieved by what may be called the *standard blurb*.[1] This is supposed to deal with the standard (common, most frequent) apprehensions, hostile attitudes, fears, etc., of the patient. In most cases it proves quite useful but, when it succeeds, the psychologist does not stop to enquire what he actually did; that is to say, what his own contribution was. Only when the 'standard blurb' fails to achieve the intended result and the psychologist has to do something else in addition, does he realize how important his contribution is. To

[1] A good descriptive term used in a discussion by Mr. G. Hutton, to whom we are grateful for the suggestion.

168

illustrate what we mean, we would like to include a report on the administration of a T.A.T.[1] to an unco-operative patient. She was a woman suffering from ulcerative colitis and undergoing group therapy at a psychiatric outpatient clinic.

Although she came by ambulance, the patient was about half an hour late in arriving, and when asked to come upstairs said she wasn't ready yet and went off to the lavatory. She was a plainly dressed, squarely built woman, with tight lips and narrowed eyes; the total effect being rather unpleasant.

She was rather ill at ease at the beginning of the interview, and fiddled vigorously with her wedding and engagement rings. She spoke with a good deal of grimacing and to the accompaniment of frequent forced laughter.

When asked how she was, her first complaint was that she was constantly snapping at people and she added, laughing, that they snapped back.

When the purpose of the test was explained to her she laughed and announced she was no good at that sort of thing. She was told that all that was required of her was that she try as best she could, and the test proceeded.

Her immediate response to the first card was, 'Doesn't convey a thing—looks like somebody in a fog'. After four minutes' silence, during which she held the card so that it screened her face, she added, 'It doesn't convey a thing to me'.

This pattern was repeated for the next two cards. With these, as with all subsequent ones, she used the card as a screen behind which she industriously sucked her thumb. When she had finished with the third she was asked what the difficulty was. She forced a loud laugh and said, 'Don't ask me, maybe I'm dumb', the latter statement being produced with a defiant and challenging air. She made no reply to the suggestion that she was not as dumb as all that, and continued to suck her thumb.

After the next card she was asked if perhaps something in her feelings about the whole situation made things difficult. She looked rather scornful at this and said, 'It doesn't worry me',

---

[1] T.A.T. means Thematic Apperception Test. The test material consists of a set of cards depicting simple scenes, involving one, two, or three people, or groups. The patient is asked to make up stories to the cards about how the situation has come about, what it means to the people involved, and how it ends. It is assumed that the pictures act as stimuli, eliciting responses from the various parts of the patient's internal world which the patient then 'projects' onto the cards. It is on the basis of this assumption that the stories produced are interpreted. The various 'projective' tests have the same structure in principle; the chief difference is in the stimuli that are used, that is, the cards that are presented.

adding in a playfully threatening tone, 'Only if you don't get to the bottom of this, I'm going to be very disappointed'.

Her manner changed slightly after this in that she dealt quickly and briefly with each card and showed some overt hostility in her glances.

It was suggested later that perhaps she felt somewhat resentful at being asked to do the test and at having to come here at all. She said, in a surprised tone, 'Oh no, it doesn't worry me—makes no difference to me'.

When the blank card was introduced and she was asked to imagine for herself a picture on it she laughed and almost shouted, 'Oh no. No, you'll never get anything out of me.' She added that she had done something silly in coming without her glasses. She described the card—'It's just a blank piece of cardboard—rather grubby', and fell silent, staring out of the window. Asked if she felt she could try, she replied that she was no good at imagining things, and went on to tell how at school she had been told she hadn't any brains.

The interview was ended here, and as she was leaving she said, 'Doctor wants a report from you, but it won't be ready, will it? Not much good going, is it? It messed things up when you had to cancel the last appointment' (referring to a previous appointment she had cancelled on a plea of sickness). She walked off without saying goodbye.[1]

Though the observations made and recorded by the psychologist are highly significant and may form the basis for various inferences about the patient's character and illness, the interview must be called unsatisfactory, as it failed to reach its aim, viz. to elicit responses from the patient to the test cards. In this sense the psychological test situation is a more suitable subject for study than the psychiatric interview, because its aims are fairly well defined: if patient and tester fail to accomplish them, there can be no doubt that something has gone awry. In the psychiatric interview, the aims are only vaguely apprehended; one may even say that everything can be considered as grist to the mill, and therefore it is much more difficult to decide whether the interview was successful, and if so, how far. In Chapter 15 we shall try to define some criteria on the basis of which this decision may be approximated, but before doing so we propose to continue our discussion of the simpler situation of the psychological test.

In the case just mentioned it is almost certain that the patient's

[1] We are indebted to Mr. A. Pollock for permission to use this report.

hostile attitude was caused, at any rate partly, by insufficient preparation by the doctor who sent her. That means that her unco-operative attitude was also due to a transference from her doctor to the tester. This, however, is only of secondary importance for our discussion. The report conclusively proves that there are two phases in every test procedure. The first is the preparation of the patient, which may be done either outside the test situation, that is, by the referring doctor, or inside the test situation by the tester himself. The aim of this first phase is to create an atmosphere in which the patient will fit into the role he is required to adopt. This preliminary procedure is usually treated as a necessary but not very important incident. Its techniques, that is, the tester's contributions, are hardly ever recorded, although the bare fact that the tester had little—or great—difficulty in winning the patient's collaboration is usually mentioned in the report. After this preliminary phase there follows the second, the test proper, in which the tester's contributions are strictly standardized. This phase is recorded in detail so far as the parts contributed by the patient are concerned. The tester's contributions, being standardized, are taken for granted; as they are practically identical in all cases they need not be recorded.

It is instructive to follow in our unusually candid report the psychologist's emotional contributions, how the whole situation developed between the two partners by each of them reacting in turn to the stimulus presented by the other. This interaction resulted here in a vicious circle, ending in an unsatisfactory result. In our case the starting mechanism was fairly clearly stated by the patient in the beginning of the interview when she said that she was 'constantly snapping at people' and added, laughing, that 'they snapped back'. That is exactly what happened in this interview: she snapped at the tester and made him cross, and then the tester, though all the time at pains to control his irritation, had no alternative but to snap back, though admittedly in a mild way.

What else can be done in a situation of this kind? In the seminar in which this case was discussed, two methods were suggested. One was to remain calm and give the patient a sensible explanation about the aims of the test and the collaboration needed from him, the advantages he may expect from the test, and the reasons why he should co-operate. This method could be described as *the appeal to reality*.

Another method suggested could be called *structuring*. This would mean pointing out in more detail to the patient what material is presented to him on the cards and leading him patiently but firmly to see what sort of response is expected from him. In other words, the tester's attitude in adopting this procedure could approximately be described as one of 'I know what is best for you; come along with me, there is no need for you to be frightened, angry, awkward, or hostile'. We may call this adopting the role of a kind, understanding, but firm and unshakable adult towards a child.

It was soon recognized by the seminar that both these methods are present in a rudimentary form in the 'standard blurb' and are only, so to speak, its extensions. Looking at the standard blurb and its extensions in this way, they may be considered as ready-made clothes, cut for standard figures; although in a number of cases they fit tolerably well, they hardly ever fit perfectly and are useless for irregular figures.

Yet another method of dealing with this situation would be for the tester to allow feelings and emotions to develop in him and then to admit to the patient that this had happened. We described similar situations in Chapter 6, and wish to recall Case 8, when the doctor became angry with his patient partly on account of the patient's irritating behaviour, but partly because of irritating events in his own life which happened prior to his contact with the patient. In that case the doctor made use of his anger and showed it in a deliberate way. In our case the tester might have said to his patient, 'You seem to have succeeded in making me annoyed and I know you expect me to snap back at you. But let's get down to work.' Or he could have shown by the expression on his face or the tone of his voice that he was annoyed, while admitting that nothing could be done if the patient was determined that he should 'never get anything out of her'.

The rationale for this kind of procedure is to allow the patient to see that he is in the presence of a fellow human being who has feelings not too unlike his own, and to allow him to have some triumph without raising in him too intense feelings of guilt, contrition, or fear; hoping that, after having made a relationship with the tester of a real but unproductive kind, he might be able to relate to him in a more useful way, i.e. to collaborate in completing the test. The great problem with this and similar procedures is that they are rather shots in the dark. We do not know, we only guess, how the patient will react, and so must hope for the best.

The same uncertainty adheres to yet another way of dealing with this situation: by remaining tolerant and unperturbed, by *really* not becoming angry, i.e. *not reacting* at all to the patient's provocation. This is another shot in the dark, since the result may be as bad as after snapping back; we all know that, for instance, children can turn frantic or become uncontrollable, 'mad', if their aggressive, hostile, and destructive impulses are not checked in time. The same might be true of a patient who is allowed to frustrate the interviewer. Similar criticism must be levelled against still another kind of preparation, which would openly admit failure to the patient and ask him to come for a second interview, in the hope that collaboration would then be possible. Clearly this is yet another sensible shot in the dark.

If we disregard the rare possibility that the patient has a compulsory biphasic pattern—after having satisfied his hostility in the first place, he will be able to co-operate in the second—then the aim of any 'preparation' is to change the patient's pattern from unco-operative (in this case snappy) to co-operative.

3

To repeat, we have seen that the patient comes to the interview with a ready-made pattern and it is the interviewer's task to manage the situation in such a way that it develops into a co-operative relationship. It is important to bear in mind that the test situation (and still more the psychiatric interview) is essentially a two-person relationship and any development in it depends on the contributions of both partners. We have recognized the 'standard blurb' and its extensions as a good enough, ready-made contribution by the tester. If his standard devices prove unsatisfactory, he may try a few 'sensible' shots in the dark—some of which were discussed in the previous section—which may perhaps create the desired atmosphere. It would, of course, be preferable if, instead of shooting in the dark, proper aim could be taken.

The first condition for aiming is an understanding of what has happened up to now and what is going on at present; for only if we understand the developing two-person relationship will it be possible to choose our contributions purposefully. Here a highly important problem arises, just as important for the psychological test situation as for the psychiatric interview, although in the latter its importance is usually neglected or even glossed over. The problem is whether it is advisable, or even permissible, for the tester to change the patient significantly by the test, in other words, whether the patient has not the absolute right to leave the test situation in the same state in which he arrived. This is another important difference between medical and psychiatric examinations; it is extremely rare that a medical examination raises this problem, while a psychiatric interview almost regularly does. It will readily be admitted that to stir up the patient unnecessarily, to arouse in him inordinate fear or anxiety, is inadmissible, and that every precaution should be taken to prevent such an occurrence. Some test manuals even contain brief instructions on how to reassure or calm down the patient in the case of such an untoward event. There are, however, a number of other by-products which are not even discussed, such as the advisability of allowing expectations to develop in the patient, especially if it is not possible to follow up the test or the interview with proper therapy.

A similar problem faces us, perhaps still more pressingly, in cases in which some interpretations are considered to be necessary in order to secure the patient's co-operation; a further complication is that thereby a kind of therapeutic process might be started which has to be broken off at the end of the interview. An easy solution, at any rate as far as the psychological test situation is concerned, is to advise the tester not to try very hard. In cases where the standard blurb and its extensions prove of no avail it may be better—in order to prevent the tester from becoming too much involved in the struggle with the patient—to abandon the test altogether. More likely than not, with these patients the result of the test will anyhow be unreliable and, in addition, the observation of the patient during the attempt at preparation may be more important for a psychiatric diagnosis than a test which has been forced upon him.

But what is true of a psychological test is not true of a psychiatric interview. The psychiatric interview allows much greater latitude because its methods and procedures are essentially flexible and, above all, it has no rigidly defined aim towards which it must work. This, however, is a mixed blessing, since this greater freedom makes it much more difficult to decide whether the interview has achieved its aim or not. After all, whatever the patient says and does can be interpreted in psychiatric terms and can be integrated into a psychiatric diagnosis which will be correct as far as it goes. But what criteria are to be used to judge whether all, or at any rate most of, the *relevant* facts necessary for a proper assessment of the case have been obtained? Or to what extent the phenomena observed during the interview were characteristic of the patient's condition and to what extent of the doctor's interview technique?

The psychologist administering a projective test is not bothered by this problem, as it has been settled by his colleague who devised the particular test. It is well known that every test has its limitations, and psychologists all over the world are busy devising new tests and new methods to extend the present boundaries or to cover new areas. It is the inventor's—and the validator's—task to delimit the

174

area covered by the test and to see to it that the standard method of administration should be capable of collecting all relevant facts belonging to this area. Although it is not always stated explicitly, every test implies the acceptance of, and acquiescence in, these limitations. The psychiatric interview, as a matter of principle, must reject any such acquiescence.

To describe the same difference in another way: during a projective test the psychologist offers to the patient his cards as the chief stimuli. True, the tester and the whole situation act also as stimuli and thus cannot be completely disregarded, but it is fair to say that the patient's attention is consistently directed to the cards within the whole situation. We have discussed the function of the 'standard blurb' and its extensions and found that they are meant to structure the whole situation so that the patient's responses should be stimulated as far as possible by the cards.

After this follows the second phase in which the psychologist offers standardized stimuli and records the responses. In a third phase then, detached from the emotional impact of his contact with the patient, the psychologist evaluates the responses on the basis of his experience and knowledge.

In the psychiatric interview all these various phases and roles are intermixed. The psychiatrist represents the cards, that is, he has to act as a stimulus, records the responses, and, while still under the emotional impact of his encounter with the patient, has to evaluate them; moreover at every step he has to decide—on the basis of what he has been able to observe in the interview up to this point and what he has deduced or inferred from his observations—what the next stimulus presented to the patient should be. Furthermore, the psychiatrist has—in contrast to the few cards of the test—an enormous range of stimuli to choose from; his choice, of course, will be prompted partly by his conscious, and partly by his unconscious intentions. The range begins with friendly or frosty silence, and progresses through the simple encouraging 'hm', challenging, disapproving 'hm', bored 'hm', questions about objective facts (which may be more or less emotionally charged for the patient, e.g. how many brothers and sisters he has, what he earns, whether he is satisfied in his marriage, etc.) or about subjective involvements, leading questions, confronting the patient with his contradictory statements, pointing out topics deliberately avoided or dropped, to fully fledged interpretations.

Moreover, though the psychiatrist may intend his silence or his questions to be friendly or encouraging, his unconscious, not quite controlled, emotional involvement may turn them into something

175

utterly different, or the patient may feel them as utterly different from what they were intended to be. But whatever the interviewer does, or refrains from doing, he will inevitably stimulate his patient in some way; an attempt at avoiding any emotional interactions—if it succeeds at all—will result in an interview which can only be understood in terms of a patient's responses to an interviewer who tries not to exist while conducting the interview.

From all this it may be seen that the psychiatrist's is a much more complicated task, and no wonder that it is far less well standardized than the various roles of the psychologist. One aim here was to stress this difference with its many and varied consequences. Since we cannot see a solution to this problem from this direction, we propose to approach it from another.

CHAPTER 14

Psychiatrists and Psycho-analysts as Interviewers

1

The comparison of the dynamics of psychological testing and of the psychiatric interview revealed fundamental differences. Summing up these differences, we may say that the various roles in which the psychologist functions during a test are not only fairly well standardized but also isolated from one another, both in time and in space. In contrast, the psychiatrist must function simultaneously in many roles that are far from being standardized; on the contrary, they are only vaguely apprehended. We have found in our survey that the psychiatrist—in addition to putting his patient at ease, establishing a good rapport, or creating a suitable 'atmosphere'—has to *act as a set of stimuli*, that is, like the cards of the projective tests, has to *record* the patient's responses to the stimuli offered, and to *evaluate* them on the spur of the moment. All these four roles are intermixed, whereas for the psychologist they are cleanly separated in time as well as in space. The situation, however, is still more complicated for the psychiatrist because he must function also as the designer of the test since he has to *devise his stimuli and the methods of administering them to the individual patient* as the interview proceeds. True, all of us have developed a more or less routine form of interviewing for our own use, but these forms are, so to speak, secrets of the trade; they have never been adequately described and, of course, still less examined or validated.

In striking contrast to this state of affairs the psychologist's responsibility is limited. Nearly always he functions as an assistant, whereas the psychiatrist's responsibility is as absolute as any physician's or surgeon's. It is he who—on the basis of his findings, aided perhaps by the psychologist's report—has to decide what should happen to the patient and then take full responsibility for his decision. How difficult this task is and what sort of pitfalls the psychiatric profession constantly encounters are well illustrated by the many unfortunate controversies between psychiatric witnesses in criminal cases or in those concerning certification.

Thus it is no wonder that in order to cope with this uneasy and unpleasant situation, psychiatry mobilized the two defensive mechanisms most commonly used in such circumstances: denial and idealization. On the one hand, psychiatrists behave as if there were no problems at all—denial; and, on the other hand, pretend that they have reliable methods for coping with them—idealization. Remarkably, this is one of the rare fields in which academic psychiatry and psycho-analysis are in complete harmony. With very few exceptions, workers belonging to both camps imply by their behaviour that a psychiatric interview presents no exceptional problems and they know how to conduct it. It is only in the last twenty to thirty years that research workers from both fields have become increasingly interested in the study of what happens during psychiatric interviews and are now trying to devise standardized techniques and methods for validating them. As often happens in science, the pendulum seems now to be swinging in the opposite direction, and in recent years a number of thick volumes have appeared dealing with the psychiatric interview on the basis of verbatim records. Some of them go so far as to accompany the printed transcript with tape or gramophone records. One project that we know of has gone still further and analyses phonetically every phrase used either by the doctor or by the patient.

These, however, are exceptions, or maybe they are harbingers. The main body, both of psychiatrists and psycho-analysts, is still using denial and idealization. To take the psychiatrists first, their advocated method is to be comprehensive. This means collecting every available fact from all the fields that may have any bearing on the patient: his heredity, his constitution, his personality, and his possible psychiatric condition. Since psychiatry has as yet no criteria to decide which facts are relevant and which not, the working principle— almost as in an anxiety state—is 'the more, the better, and the safer'. Apart from causing the doctor an enormous amount of work, the result is a vast array of facts, as a rule disjointed, a very large part of them irrelevant for the diagnosis, the whole leading to an atomistic collection which is then arranged under extrinsic headings that have hardly anything to do with the individual patient and so, more likely than not, obstruct the emergence of a picture of the patient as a whole person.

The psycho-analysts' idealization is based partly on Freud's technical advice that the analyst should behave like a well-polished mirror, reflecting back to the patient an undistorted picture of his illness and character, and partly, as we discussed in Chapter 12, on his knowledge of and familiarity with the workings of the unconscious. Although nowadays it is generally admitted in analytic practice that the ideal of the well-polished mirror can seldom be achieved and that everything that happens in an analytic treatment has to be understood also in terms of the relationship between the doctor and patient, this finding has not yet much influenced the attitude towards the diagnostic interview, except in the broadest and crudest sense. For instance, a patient's anxiety or manic behaviour in the interview will be understood chiefly as symptoms of his psychopathology, but hardly as responses to the stimuli provided by the doctor's behaviour and verbal communications, and any criticism will centre rather on whether or not he was able to reflect an undistorted picture of the patient's illness and personality, than on an examination of the interaction between his interview technique and the patient's responses elicited by it.

The usefulness of understanding the unconscious areas of the mind for diagnostic purposes can also be over-estimated. True, the analyst will notice and understand a great deal that a non-analytically trained doctor may not even see, but the use of this understanding for diagnosis has been insufficiently explored. In addition it would appear that the opinions we form about our patients in a diagnostic interview are not as reliable as we would wish. Though it may be true that in a diagnostic interview we analysts elicit in a deeper and truer sense more information about the patient than do other doctors, our inferences from this information appear not to be much more reliable than those of other interviewers.

To prove this we may mention a well-established clinical fact, about which innumerable jokes circulate in the oral tradition. This is the high failure rate occurring when a patient who consulted a senior analyst is referred for treatment to one of his, as a rule junior, colleagues. As these events happen in private practice, no official figures are available and, to our knowledge, no one has taken the trouble to investigate this field, but according to hearsay information a conservative estimate would put the failure rate at one in four to one in three.

Turning now to non-analytic practice, what happens when a patient is interviewed by a non-psychiatrist—or even by a psychiatrist, always assuming that he is not under surveillance by a strict hospital routine? The method commonly used is a rough and ready mixture, consisting partly of a shortened version of an academic collecting of disjointed facts and partly of watered-down psycho-analysis. In our view there is not much possibility that anything useful will emerge in the foreseeable future either from the academic approach or from the humdrum of everyday practice, so our discussion will centre chiefly on the psycho-analytic approach to interview technique, the more so since—both of us being psycho-analysts—this is the field in which we are interested and have gained our experience. Our aim is to examine the obstacles and resistances which, to our mind, have hindered psycho-analysts from turning their attention to this interesting and rewarding field.

The reasons why 'pure' psycho-analysts are, on the whole, not so interested in a critical study of their interview techniques are mainly historical. The patients that a student treats under supervision are, as a rule, selected by his Institute or his supervising analyst. When he starts his private practice, his first patients are, more often than not, referred to him for analysis by his senior colleagues, and the only problem that faces him in the first interview is how to start treatment. It is only after some years that gradually his own independent practice develops. By that time he has discovered that clinical diagnosis is more or less irrelevant for his own practice; the chief question that has to be solved by his diagnostic interviews is whether the patient is analysable or not; if not, there his responsibility ends. It is only when his practice has developed still further and he has a full load of patients most of the time that further questions will have to be decided by his interview techniques. They are roughly as follows: Is it advisable or necessary to start treatment immediately or can the patient wait for the next vacancy? Should the patient be referred to some other analyst, in which case should he be given one name only or several names? Thus, for many years the only two questions that a 'pure' analyst has to decide are: is the patient analysable or not; is the patient referrable or not?

A further reason why psycho-analysts are, as a rule, not so interested in their interview technique stems also from this historical development. A psycho-analyst whose professional development happened according to the pattern just sketched is first and foremost a therapist; during practically the whole of his working days he sees patients for therapy only. Especially in his formative years, it is only a sporadic event that someone consults him for diagnostic purposes, and even in his later years his consulting practice amounts only to a fraction of the whole. Thus his main concern is to refine his therapeutic technique, which depends on the psycho-analytic situation, and is so devised that it should preserve and maintain this situation. It is not surprising then that the constant preoccupation with therapeutic considerations and the relatively small importance of consulting practice lead to an over-valuation of therapeutic techniques and to a comparative neglect of diagnostic methods.

It is possible that things may change in the future. More and more analysts are engaged, during their training and in their first years of independent practice, as assistants—registrars or senior hospital medical officers in Great Britain, residents or junior professors in the United States—to a psychiatric department. During these years they have to interview patients regularly but, as far as we can see, for most of them this is not a welcome opportunity, merely an acceptable but not very interesting way of eking out a number of lean years. In consequence they consider the refinement of their psycho-analytic technique to be their first concern and little, if any, of their libido is left over for the problems of interviewing. Signs are, however, increasing—at any rate in some of our younger colleagues—that under the impact of these experiences a new interest is gradually awakening. This slowly progressing change has not yet much influenced the prevailing psycho-analytic climate, which still considers the diagnostic interview techniques as of not much importance, not really worthy of a psycho-analyst's attention.

Thus it happens that when seeing patients for consultation, the psycho-analyst is tempted either to use his therapeutic technique, admittedly in a somewhat limited or watered-down version, or to revert to the collection of disjointed facts as taught by academic psychiatry. The psychiatric interview is, however, essentially an ephemeral relationship which in many respects differs fundamentally from a true psycho-analytic situation. Thus the well-proven therapeutic techniques of psycho-analysis have only a limited usefulness in the consultative interview. A move that would mean an important progress in psycho-analytic treatment, as it establishes a reliable and lasting relationship between therapist and patient, is not necessarily a gain in a psychiatric interview. On the other hand, a mere collection of facts is an unsuitable basis for assessing the patient's personality, and thus insufficient for a proper psychological diagnosis.

The more extended an analyst's practice becomes, the more varied the patient material he has to look after, and the greater will be the impact of extra-analytical experiences on him. On the other hand, the more strictly analytical his practice, the more he will be under the sole influence of his analytical experiences and, in parallel, the less he will feel any need for a critical examination of his interview technique. He will be satisfied if he can select from among the people who consult him those who either are suitable for analysis by himself or are referrable to one of his colleagues, surrendering the care of all other patients to the medical profession in general. In many respects this policy is sensible and realistic; moreover, superficially it conforms with the medical tradition: if a specialist finds that a patient is not

181

likely to benefit by his specialized methods, the patient should be referred back to his doctor. The only fallacy in this policy is that other doctors, as a rule, are still less capable of assessing the psychotherapeutic chances of the particular condition and so, in fact, the patient is not helped, nor has the doctor who referred him learnt anything from the consultation.

We have discussed in Chapter 4 some of the facts that ought also to be taken into account when deciding on treatment and might considerably modify the procedures just quoted. In any case, various forms of psychotherapy have firmly established themselves, and pressure of external circumstances might compel even the purest psycho-analyst to consider whether to advise analysis or one of the alternative methods of psychotherapy. These other methods include Child Guidance treatment, group therapy, the various forms of short-term therapy or therapy with limited aims, to which we would like to add, on the basis of our experience of many years, general practitioner psychotherapy and consultant psychotherapy, as described in Part I of our book.

Of course the decision whether to advise psychotherapy and, if so, which form, faces the non-analyst practitioner or consultant still more urgently. Apart from some haphazard empiricism and some preconceived ideas, the criteria which in most cases decide the issue are financial considerations and the availability of time, both of them compelling, but neither of them very sound or inherently connected with the patient's illness or personality. What are badly needed are some criteria in the patient's illness and personality which would enable the doctor to decide which of the various forms of psychotherapy would offer the best prospects in any particular case.

However, it will not be easy to discover, to define, and then to validate these criteria as the resistance is very great on all sides. Academic psychiatrists admit only grudgingly the value of psycho-analysis or psychotherapy, whereas psycho-analysts, as already pointed out, consider analysis incomparably superior to anything else. What we urge is a more objective, more realistic attitude all round, accepting that other methods may yield therapeutic successes, studying which method has the best successes under what conditions, and then working out diagnostic interview techniques directed so that they should inform the doctor about the relevant data necessary for a differential diagnosis.

As stated several times in this book, in our opinion real progress in this field can be expected only if psycho-analysts can be moved to take part in the research. Our—at times perhaps too severe—strictures of the psycho-analytic interview techniques are intended to awaken self-criticism and interest in our colleagues for this most important and rewarding field.

2

After having shown up—perhaps in somewhat exaggerated form, but not, we hope, altogether unfairly—the shortcomings of our colleagues, it is high time to disclose our own ideas about the diagnostic interview and to accept criticism on the same terms that we have used against others.

We shall leave out of our discussion the question of diagnosing an organic condition. There are many reasons that justify this proposition: the methods for diagnosing organic conditions are fairly reliable and largely unequivocal; since the conditions to be diagnosed belong to the field of one-person biology, traditional diagnostic terms are adequate to describe them; though an organic diagnosis has to be taken into account when contemplating psychotherapy, in the last instance it is the patient's potentiality for developing and maintaining human relationships that decides the issue.

The chief aim of the psychiatric interview, as of every medical examination, is diagnosis; unfortunately in our case this is merely a portmanteau word, and so we must ask, diagnosis of what and in what terms? We have pointed out many times in this book that neither academic psychiatry nor psycho-analysis has been able to devise a real classification of mental illnesses amounting to a kind of natural system; hence attaching a diagnostic label to the patient as a result of our interview is only of very limited value. Moreover, as discussed in the previous chapter, our diagnostic labels have been borrowed from anatomy and physiology and are, therefore, signally inadequate for the description of the patient's potentialities to develop human relationships, which are the factors that determine the patient's response to any kind of psychotherapy.

There is, as yet, no reliable technique for the appraisal of these potentialities; in consequence, in order to obtain some idea of them, a round-about and rather cumbersome method is used. The interviewer tries to assess the stability, strength, and integrity of the patient's ego structure, the firmness or laxity of his libido organization, the flexibility or rigidity of his character defences, and last, but not least, the 'depth' of his neurotic disturbances; the sum total of these data is customarily described as the psychopathology or psychodynamics of the particular patient. It is hoped that in the possession of these assessments the psychiatrist will be able to form an opinion about the patient's prospects if psychotherapy is attempted.

This general assessment, however, is a formidable task; partly because our ideas of these quantitative factors and their influence on the patient's prognosis are rather vague, and partly because we have only equally vague techniques for gauging them from our observations during the interview. Thus in practice one is content to establish, tentatively, the chronology and nature of the traumata that the patient has had to endure, chiefly but not exclusively in his childhood, together with the corresponding fixations and reaction-formations that he had to erect for coping with them. It is hoped, though hardly ever explicitly stated, that the last-mentioned set of data will constitute a sufficiently firm basis for drawing reliable inferences from it about the second set, the psychodynamic structure of the patient's character and illness, and that on the basis of this latter, the patient's prospects for psychotherapy can be properly estimated.

Whether all the factors mentioned above are explicitly assessed on the basis of the psychiatric interview or whether the assessment is only implied or even merely glossed over, makes hardly any real difference, because not these factors but the findings about the patient's potentiality to form and maintain relationships are the basis for or against recommending psychotherapy. Furthermore, our first set of data, twice removed from what we really want to know, is mainly about traumata, that is, events belonging to the field of two-person psychology, and about their possible effects. We then infer from them the psychopathology of the patient's illness and personality and express our inferences in the language of psychodynamics, which belongs largely to the field of one-person psychology. In a final step, then, we try to predict on this basis how the patient will respond to psychotherapy, which is an essentially two-person relationship.

This complicated procedure is the result of a historical development: psycho-analytic theory, the prototype and model of all dynamic psychology, was profoundly influenced in its early stages by the mechanistic idea of physiology, an essentially one-body science. As we have pointed out many times, the psychiatric interview is an interaction between two actors. Thus if we wish to improve the reliability of the techniques used in it, and define more exactly the standards by which its achievements can be measured, it will be a simpler and more promising proposition to study—instead of the complex three-stage procedure just described—how the contributions of each actor influence the interaction. It is probable that the present comparative neglect of this field is due to the fact that until recently the interviewer's contributions have not been properly examined. In order to emphasize this important difference we shall try to describe the interview from the point of view of each of the two actors separately, although it will prove impossible to keep either description restricted to one of the actors only. To a large extent we discussed these processes in Chapter 10, 'Understanding People Professionally', and Chapter 11, 'Enabling People to Understand Themselves', so that a short summary may suffice here.

For the *doctor*, the first aim is to create an atmosphere in which the patient can reveal himself or, at any rate, enough of himself to enable the doctor to be confident that his assessment of the patient's state and his potentialities for developing human relationships, arrived at on the basis of his observations, will be fairly reliable. The second aim is to form an opinion whether anything, and if so what, should be done in the case; the third aim is to help the patient to see that the doctor's conclusions and recommendations have followed logically from what has happened during the interview—in fact what had happened and was happening in his (the patient's) life. If this can be achieved, it may form a sensible basis for the important decision as to what sort of therapy, if any, should be undertaken in his case.

From the *patient's* point of view, the interview should be an impressive experience of being given the opportunity of revealing himself, of being understood, and of being helped to see himself— his past and present problems—in a new light. If possible, this new insight should enable him—and that is the second aim—to decide for himself what his next move ought to be and to carry out this decision; should this prove too much, the patient should at least be able to see why the doctor had to decide in the way he did, accept this decision as sensible and co-operate with it.[1]

The fact is that, no matter whether it is readily admitted or not, all the factors that form the basis of our understanding of the interaction between patient and doctor, and are used in the assessment of the patient's potentialities to form human relationships, were discovered originally by Freud. Moreover, it is we psycho-analysts who since have constantly scrutinized, refined, and developed them, while hardly anybody else outside our ranks has contributed anything significant to this development. We may even say that it is unlikely that this might happen in the foreseeable future as all the ideas that

---

[1] The fact that a decision must be taken at the end of the interview is another cardinal difference from the psychological test, which, in principle, is restricted to observations and inferences drawn from them. Furthermore, the task of drawing inferences rests solely with the psychologist and is usually undertaken after the test proper, and in the patient's absence; it may even happen—in fact it often does—that the patient will never know what the results of his test were, since they are communicated only to the referring doctor. A procedure of this kind would be most unsatisfactory in a psychiatric interview, since it would mean defeating one of its principal aims.

form the basis of these developments have been derived from observations within the psycho-analytic situation. Theoretically it is possible that in the future three other fields might contribute to the knowledge of these factors. These are observations of very young children, of highly regressed psychotics, and of people having bodily illnesses. But until now these fields have yielded mainly confirmation and criticism of analytic findings but hardly any new ideas. Thus any further development must be expected in the first place from analysts. In the next chapter we shall try to sketch out various aspects of the problems encountered by us in our invesitigation of the psychiatric interview, which in our opinion badly need, and would greatly benefit from, a proper study by analysts.

CHAPTER 15

Analytic Survey of Interview Techniques

For presentation of the many unsolved problems that we encountered in our study of the psychiatric interview we had to devise some system. The chosen system is modelled on the various roles in which the psychologist functions during a projective test. Although we are aware that—because of the cardinal differences discussed in Chapters 13 and 14—this system is to some extent alien to the psychiatric interview, we had to use it for want of better.

The psychologist's five roles are:
(a) preparation of the patient,
(b) administration of the test, which we propose to call the presenting of stimuli,
(c) recording the patient's responses,
(d) evaluation, to which one must add
(e) devising and validating the test.

Taking this as our model we shall discuss the problems of the psychiatric interview under the following headings:
(1) preparation of the patient,
(2) creating an atmosphere,
(3) selection and presentation of stimuli,
(4) plan of the interview,
(5) duration,
(6) interaction between the patient's transference and the doctor's counter-transference,
(7) interventions and interpretations,
(8) recording and reporting,
(9) criteria for the completeness of the interview,
(10) integrating the physical and the psychiatric examinations,
(11) ending the interview.

Unfortunately all these classes are artificial, based largely on extrinsic criteria. This means that when discussing phenomena clearly belonging to one class, we shall not be able to prevent the argument from overflowing into several other classes. This caused us considerable difficulties while arranging our material, and we are afraid that we cannot save our readers altogether from encountering the same trouble.

As we have said before, we consider the interview essentially as an interaction between patient and doctor. Our existing scientific language is most unsuitable for the description of situations involving more than one person, consequently time and again we were forced, against our liking, to restrict our description to the role and function of one person only. In most such cases we concentrated on the doctor but, naturally, this does not mean that we think the patient's role negligible. It only means that we had to choose and, since the principal topic of this book is the doctor's technique, our focus was chiefly on him.

(1) We mentioned in Chapters 12 and 13 that every psychological interview must start with *a preparatory period*, the aim of which is to put the patient at ease and to win his co-operation. The methods developed for achieving the same aim in the psychiatric interview are largely empirical; the dynamic processes involved have hardly been examined.

To show the complexity of the problem we shall quote two special aspects out of the many that we have met during our research. Most doctors start the diagnostic interview, in contrast to the therapeutic one, by enquiring about certain objective facts, such as: age, number of siblings, marital status, number of children, relation to parents, occupation, previous illnesses, etc. In a way this is a sensible routine as it supplies the doctor with some useful information, and on the other hand has a reassuring effect on the patient, since it implies that the doctor is interested in the environment as well, that is, in what fate and other people have done to the patient, and views the patient as an unhappy and possibly innocent victim of external circumstances, as was already mentioned in another context in Chapter 12. On the other hand, the real aim of a psychiatric interview is to find out what is and has been going on inside the patient, what his contributions to his own fate have been; an enquiry of this kind is bound to cause some anxiety and strain. However, if the interview is to yield results, the patient must be induced to tolerate some strain and, if one spends too much time on external circumstances, possibly too little will be left for obtaining sufficient information about the patient's internal problems. Apart from the difficulty about time, the technical problem is how and when to switch over from the non-dangerous and possibly reassuring investigation of external, objective facts to the more tense area of the patient's internal life.

Some patients come to the interview with the insight that they are suffering from some psychiatric condition, know already that they need help, and are asking for it. These people need no preparation, they may even resent it if the doctor should waste too much time with irrelevant external data; the atmosphere in which the patient can reveal himself need not be created, it is there, brought along by the patient. The doctor must recognize this fact and act accordingly, while constantly watching whether the apparent insight and co-operation do not mask something that the patient does not want to or is afraid to reveal. On the other hand, it is naturally unprofitable—it may even be harmful—if the doctor is too suspicious with an earnestly co-operative patient.

(2) This leads us to the second group of problems, which may be called *creating and maintaining a suitable atmosphere* in which the patient can reveal enough of himself to be understood by the psychiatrist. Some aspects of this have already been discussed in Chapters 10 and 11.

As just mentioned, in a number of cases no special effort is needed by the psychiatrist since the patient comes driven by an insoluble problem and is willing and anxious to talk. However, this is not always so; some patients are over-anxious, others embarrassed, or have come reluctantly and resentfully under the pressure of their environment, are suspicious of anybody prying into their secrets, or try to drown any cue in a flood of words. Here we are faced with the technical problem as to the cases in which it is advisable to let the patient run the interview and those in which it is more profitable to induce him, or even to press him, to do what we want him to do, that is, to let the interview be run by ourselves.

Many secondary problems arise here which are, so to speak, special cases of the previous one. To quote a few: is it permissible and profitable to let the patient 'stew', in the hope that the increasing tension will enable him to overcome some of his resistance on his own, and in this way reveal some of his habitual working patterns? On the other hand, we must not forget that this procedure amounts almost to premeditated cruelty, to watch somebody in distress and not to do anything to relieve it. If so, is it advisable to relieve the distress, that is, to 'reassure' the patient? Obviously a doctor constantly reassuring whenever he notices that his patient is under some strain will obtain different material from that which his colleague would obtain who watches passively and allows the patient to 'stew' or to run the show. Yet another atmosphere will be created when the doctor understands the problem and the difficulties, and conveys this understanding to the patient by an interpretation in the early stages of the interview; furthermore, the interpretation can be chosen so that it should allay or, on the contrary, provoke some anxiety. We all use these and similar techniques on a purely empirical basis, tackling the problems presented by the case without the help of properly validated knowledge. We would add that a similar technical dilemma has to be solved when the patient is either over-talkative or is reluctant to speak, etc.

But whatever technique the doctor decides to use, his interaction with the patient will create a specific atmosphere. A proper study of these different atmospheres, their suitability or unsuitability for diagnostic purposes, and the techniques needed to create, change, or maintain them, would be most rewarding.

(3) We call the next group of problems *selection and presentation of stimuli*. We refer here to Chapters 13 and 14 in which this field was surveyed up to a point. To continue with the comparison between the psychological test and the psychiatric interview: the Object Relations Test,[1] for instance, contains in an orderly manner an equal number of cards representing one-person, two-person three-person, and group situations, respectively. Moreover, all these were devised so that one set should elicit responses from the more superficial layers of the mind, another set from the deeper layers, and the third should stimulate emotional responses; and, lastly, it contains a blank card which is experienced by the patient either as an inviting or a frightening stimulus.

From this angle the interviewing doctor represents rather a poor and unsystematically assorted collection of stimuli; however sympathetic, understanding, and adaptable he may be, he is definitely one person only, has a definite age, sex, and so on, and thus his potential as a stimulus is sorely limited. Still, as everyday clinical experience proves, the results of a psychiatric interview are, to say the least, comparable with those of a projective test. We are prepared for a number of psychiatrists, under the influence of the denial and idealization discussed in Chapter 14, to refuse to see any problem here. Nevertheless, we think that a comparative study of the stimuli offered, on the one hand during a psychological test, and on the other during a psychiatric interview, would yield interesting material for the understanding of these two important situations. What is needed for this study is an uncompetitive, trusting co-operation between a reliable psychologist and a sensible psychiatrist, a condition not easily come by.

[1] H. Phillipson.

(4) The next group of problems may be considered as one problem only, though with many special cases. It may be called the influence of the setting on the *plan of the interview* and on the techniques used.

Evidently the plan of the interview must be different in the case of a patient who may continue, and develop without any break, the relationship started with his interviewer, into a therapeutic situation. The plan must be somewhat modified if he has to wait for the beginning of proper therapy for some time. Yet a different plan will be needed aiming at different emotional involvements if the interviewer intends to refer the patient for therapy to one of his colleagues. Then there is the fourth variety, equally important, where the interviewer is expected to give some advice to the therapist; when, for instance, the therapist is a candidate in training, a junior to the interviewer, or—as happened in our Tavistock scheme—a general practitioner responsible for the treatment. The advice may be about how to handle the patient, what to look for in the emerging material, and what possible pitfalls and obstacles the therapist should try to watch and avoid. Of course, there are many more varieties, among them the sad case in which no therapy can be offered to the patient, and its opposite, when the interview shows that no therapy is needed.

In the first variety, when the doctor knows that the interview will continue as therapy, he may allow all sorts of emotions to emerge, confident that he will be able to cope with them in due course. There will be some difference in his handling of the emotional material according to whether he intends to start the treatment immediately or has to ask the patient to wait some time. When the interviewer intends to refer the case to one of his colleagues, common sense suggests that he should avoid as far as possible involving the patient in any intensive relationship with himself; this suggestion, however, must be qualified in so far as the patient must be impressed by the interview to the extent of being able to accept the doctor's recommendations. It often happens that this miscarries, which proves how difficult it is to steer a middle course. For instance, we know that—as was mentioned in the previous chapter—a fairly high proportion of the patients whom we refer to one of our colleagues fail to act upon our recommendation. Conversely this means that in this respect our interview techniques are not as good as they ought to be.

The task of the interviewer with patients whom he has to get to know sufficiently to give some advice to their future therapist, is still more difficult, though possibly the difficulty is basically the same. On the one hand the interviewer must watch carefully that the patient should not become too attached, that is, should remain free enough to accept the other therapist; on the other hand he must make

191

a contact good enough to obtain a reliable picture of the patient's personality and problems.

We cannot but repeat that all these are everyday problems, that they are dealt with on a purely empirical basis, and that they are in very bad need of proper study.

(5) Although logically this group belongs to the previous one, for the sake of convenience we classified it separately. It contains the problems centred around the *duration of the interview* which, in fact, is part of the plan of the interview.

The first problem that belongs to this subgroup is *physical time*. Doctors vary greatly in the amount of time they consider adequate for a proper psychiatric assessment of the average patient: some feel that 30 to 45 minutes are sufficient; others like to budget an hour to an hour and a half; and others prefer to see the patient, if possible, on two occasions for about an hour each time. But whatever the doctor's predilections—and the pressure of external circumstances—may be, the time available is always limited and is either pre-determined by the doctor's personality, or varied, within limits, by the doctor's response to the patient's needs; in either case this means by the doctor's counter-transference, kept in check by the exigencies of reality.

Apart from the time limit set by the doctor's customary routine (and varied within limits by the exigencies of the case) there are two more factors, both psychological, that play an important part in determining the duration of the interview. These are the doctor's *scientific and emotional curiosity*, which must be satisfied by the material produced, and *his need for security*, which prompts him to go on with the interview till he may feel that he has found out enough about the patient to be fairly sure of his diagnosis.

Of course we do not wish to say that the patient has no influence on the duration of the diagnostic period. Naturally he has, and a very great one. What we would stress in this section is that the duration of the interview is determined by an interaction between patient and doctor and exerts an influence on the whole structure of the interview. Though some of our readers may not agree, we think it must be accepted that limiting the time cannot but have a profound influence on the patient's responses, i.e. it acts as a stimulus, presented by the doctor.

(6) Because of the central position of the next group of problems, it is well-nigh impossible to delimit it either towards the previous or the following groups. It may be called *interaction between transference*

and counter-transference which corresponds roughly to the technique of administration in the psychological test. We use the words transference and counter-transference here to describe all the feelings and emotions, whether conscious or unconscious, that are called into play and operate in the transactions between the doctor and his patient; the transference stemming from the patient, and the counter-transference from the doctor. Several of the cases reported, not only those in Chapter 6, demonstrate how difficult it is at times not to respond emotionally to the situation created by the patient. Of course, every doctor will try hard to control his emotions or, at any rate, to keep them within limits, nevertheless it will be partly on the basis of his emotions that he will decide on his behaviour towards the patient.

We propose the thesis that the doctor's behaviour—no matter whether imperturbably calm, sympathetically objective, strictly controlled, slightly irritated, somewhat defeated by the patient's brick-wall resistance, trying to close the interview because the pre-arranged time has been greatly overrun, etc. etc.—acts also like the stimuli presented by the tester, and that the patient will respond to it in his individual way. If this is so, then we must accept also that the course of the interview may from this angle be described as an interaction between the patient's transference and the doctor's counter-transference. This is an enormous field of study of which we have been able to explore but the fringes.

Here are a few examples of the problems that we have isolated. Whereas a projective test must start with a period of preparation, this—as mentioned in Section (1) of this chapter—is not unconditional in the psychiatric interview. One may even ask whether a period of preparation in the psychiatric interview is necessary, advisable only, or even contra-indicated. After all, a preparation is an intervention dictated partly by the doctor's counter-transference, and it may be argued that a much more revealing picture of the patient may be obtained if one interferes with him as little as possible.

A further problem is caused by the lack of standardization. Whereas the psychologist, after having carefully devised and validated an appropriate set of stimuli, may restrict himself during the test to administering them in their pre-arranged order, the psychiatrist has no standard set. He has to devise the stimuli, that is, his own behaviour, on the spur of the moment under the influence of the patient's responses to the stimuli presented previously; moreover, as yet there is no possibility for the doctor to devise a standardized sequence of stimuli, still less to validate them. It is even questionable whether it is advisable during a psychiatric interview to vary the stimulus, that is, the doctor's behaviour, to any great extent; on the whole, clinical experience suggests that a not too rigidly consistent behaviour creates perhaps the best conditions for a successful interview.

On the other hand, it is fair to say that doctors vary considerably in their interview techniques; moreover, the same doctor unquestionably adapts his technique to the individual patient in the early phases of the interview. We would add in parenthesis that these adaptations, as well as the doctor's basic interview technique, are prompted partly by the exigencies of the individual case but also, and to a large extent, by the doctor's individuality; that is why we talk about the interaction of the patient's transference and the doctor's countertransference. The study of this interaction offers a vast field for research with the ultimate aim of devising for use in psychiatric interviews something similar to the classical medical examination.

However, we must add several important riders. Already the Romans knew well: *Si duo faciunt idem, non est idem* which, in our case, is true for both partners. Exactly the same words and the same behaviour would have utterly different meanings if used by two different patients, and in the same way exactly the same words and the same behaviour would have utterly different effects if used by the same doctor in the presence of two different patients. This simple truism must be constantly borne in mind by anyone who attempts to devise a standardized form of interviewing.

The other rider is about the opposite problem. It will be easily agreed that for a reliable diagnosis the doctor should aim at obtaining as wide a spectrum of the patient's habitual responses as possible within the limits of the interview. This, conversely, means that he should devise his stimuli, presented during the interview, so that they potentially activate responses from all the layers, structures, and instances in the patient's mind. But when we ask what qualities the stimuli should have in order to achieve this and, in particular, on what basis to decide whether the patient's responses, elicited by the doctor, may be considered as complete or, at any rate, fairly representative, we cannot find any answer in either the psychiatric or psycho-analytic literature. We have again to admit that our technique has only a shaky empirical foundation.

Exactly the same situation meets us when we enquire whether—in order to elicit a more complete spectrum of responses—it is advisable for the doctor to present a wide variety of stimuli or, on the contrary, remain relatively unchanging and unchangeable. Under varying the stimuli presented, we classify: deliberate or spontaneous changes in the doctor's behaviour, enquiring about topics avoided or omitted by the patient, accepting tacitly or explicitly that certain topics will not to be touched upon, etc. etc., up to fully fledged interpretations which may be either anxiety provoking or allaying.

(7) With this we reach our next group of problems: deliberate *interventions* including *interpretations*, which is only a special case belonging undoubtedly to the previous group, but which, because of its importance, is better treated by itself.

However passive the doctor's habitual behaviour in an interview may be, it cannot be altogether passive. At some points in the interview he must intervene, i.e. he must come out of his passivity. To mention a few possible interventions: he may ask questions, utter encouraging or discouraging noises (like 'hm'), or even phrases and sentences, give advice or reassurance and, last but not least, he may express his understanding or switch the patient's attention from one topic to another by some interpretation. To avoid misunderstandings it is worth while to state that, for instance, offering treatment to the patient is unquestionably a piece of advice because, however carefully the doctor words it, it means 'in my opinion this is the best thing for you to do'. In the same way, offering, or accepting the patient for, treatment is tantamount to reassurance as it inevitably implies that we do not consider his condition hopeless.

Of course interventions should be kept to a minimum, or at least to an optimum. Unfortunately we have no criteria to determine what is sufficient or satisfactory, and what is not. Being psycho-analysts, we are principally interested in interpretations and their function during the interview.

Even this limited problem has innumerable facets and this makes a systematic discussion impossible. Let us therefore start with the question that in another context has already been asked in Chapter 13. Has the patient the absolute right to leave the interview untouched, undisturbed, or only unchanged? To put the same question in different words: has he agreed—implicitly—by asking for an interview that he might be influenced, stirred up, or even possibly considerably changed by it? Should this question fail to be answered in the affirmative we must enquire further: at what point does the unwarranted violation of a patient's integrity start?

Yet another formulation of the same problem runs as follows. Is it advisable or desirable that a consultation should amount to nothing more than a diagnostic examination, or should it include some sort of therapy, e.g. some highly mitigated form of psychoanalysis? Our last version asks in fact whether the patient has an absolute sovereign right to his own unconscious and, if not, who is to decide what the limits of his rights are? Unfortunately there is no answer available to any of these formulations. The only honest answer is that we do not know. What happens in practice may be described as cautious empiricism seasoned on occasions by some adventurous experimenting.

We must not forget, however, that every interpretation—even if it is described as clarification, confrontation, summing up, etc.— aims at making the patient aware of something that he has kept away from himself. In this respect it does not make much difference if we describe this keeping away as being unaware of something, not realizing it, denying it, or repressing it. The aim of the interpretation remains the same, to extend the patient's consciousness—which, in principle, is therapy.

This is about as far as our experience allows us to go. In Parts II and III we have examined some aspects of this extending of the consciousness in more detail. Here we wish to stress that, perhaps contrary to general belief, this should be one aim of a psychiatric interview and, if it cannot be achieved, the interview must be considered a failure, or only partially successful. After all, the patient has come with a problem—for instance, whether he should have psychotherapy or not—and at the end of the interview either he will be able to decide about it or the doctor must make this important decision. We think we may all agree that the former is the far more desirable outcome, but it can be achieved only if the interview has helped the patient to take a responsible decision in a matter which was impossible for him until now. This cannot be done without some change in him, and the basis of this change is his new impressive experience that he received from the interview, the chief factors of which are perhaps that he was first understood and was then helped to understand himself better; both having been discussed in Chapters 10 and 11.

(8) A subsidiary aim of every interview is to enable the doctor to produce—on the model of a medical record—*a record about the patient's state* which can be confirmed by any one of his colleagues with equal training if the interview is repeated. In fact, this is the standard in every field of medicine, but the situation is not so simple in psychiatry. It is highly unlikely that a medical examination, however searching, will permanently change any of the patient's functions or symptoms. There may be a few rare exceptions such as an exploratory laparotomy, but on the whole this statement holds true. On the contrary, some permanent change may be the result of a psychiatric interview, as is convincingly shown by the two cases quoted in Chapter 3.

The reason for this difference between medical and psychiatric examination—as discussed in Chapter 13 and in the previous section —is inherent in the situation. Let us take, as an illustration, the case of an inhibited young girl who bites her nails, pulls out her hair, has frightening nightmares, and is unable to concentrate at school; it is safe to assume that she is so absorbed in the struggle against her violent sexual fantasies, that insufficient energy is left over to cope with external problems and that at times she cannot but turn the violence against herself. But if one wishes to verify this assumption, the only way is to make her talk about her violent fantasies and her struggle with them; this, however, means reducing or breaking down her inhibitions, which inevitably leads to a change in her; though it is not easy to predict what the ultimate effect of such an interview will be—an easing of the repression or, on the contrary, a further reinforcement of her defences after she realized that, in spite of her efforts, an outsider was able to discover some of her guilty secrets. Many examples of this kind could be quoted, showing that the psychiatric interview, however expertly and cautiously conducted, may provoke changes in the patient. Consequently, if it is repeated, it may yield different results.

This is a complication that is always present—though its effects may vary greatly. Some interviews do not amount to more than a medical examination; others are in fact therapeutic interventions, either with good or with not so good results. However, in the same way as a physician can piece together with reasonable probability, on the basis of his findings, what the patient's state might have been before a therapeutic intervention, say, an operation, so a psychiatrist can infer, from the data of a subsequent interview, what the situation was that faced his colleague in the previous one. Many discrepancies between psychiatric opinions are due to forgetting, disregarding, or neglecting this important fact.

The next problem in this group is about what to record. If we take as our model the classical medical examination, then the unequivocal answer is that we have to record every examination performed and the results obtained, which then should lead to a diagnostic conclusion and to therapeutic recommendations. All this should be recorded in an efficient shorthand version but so that the reader should have no doubt which examinations were performed, what were the results obtained, and how the doctor arrived at his diagnostic conclusions. For instance, if the record runs 'lancinating pains, ataxic gait, pupils do not react to light, grossly exaggerated knee-jerks, Wasserman positive in serum and liquor; diagnosis: tabes', no doctor will have any doubt which examinations were performed, what results they yielded, and how the diagnosis was arrived at.

In the field of psychiatry, apart from a few illnesses which only rarely concern a non-psychiatrist, facilities for this way of thinking and recording simply do not as yet exist. We have only very vague ideas as to what sort of 'examinations' should constitute the psychiatric interview, and no established and generally accepted shorthand for recording their results. Our notions about the nature of illnesses are not based on proper aetiological knowledge and are thus somewhat shaky and subject to disquieting changes according to the fashion of the time. In these circumstances it is no wonder that our psychiatric records are neither uniform nor concise, often do not contain the information that one is seeking, are difficult to judge as to whether or not the examinations made have covered reliably all the aspects of the case, and thus on the whole are rather unsatisfactory.

To show how difficult it is to do the right thing in this field, let us return to the case of the young girl mentioned at the beginning of this section. Will it be sufficient if the doctor records an exhaustive list of her symptoms, his own ideas about their meaning, together with a few corroborative facts that he picked up during the interview? Or should he try to reduce her inhibitions and defences so that she may be able to produce some of her fantasies to confirm the doctor's ideas? Or must he go further and try to find out the cause of the disproportion between the violence of her fantasies and the strength of her ego-structure, and how this cause is related to the way she was brought up, say, to her oedipus complex? Or must he go still further and try to discover something about her earliest relationship to her environment and all that is connected with it, which may be called the family tradition of handling children?

These are only a few possibilities; in reality there are many more problems to account for. But even if we had agreed at what point a reliable psychiatric examination should stop, we have not solved yet the problem of what examinations will yield reliable material for our questions. In medicine, for instance, we have some idea what sort of differences and agreement to expect when we determine the size of the heart by percussion and by screening. This knowledge was achieved only through comparing the results of these two different methods of examination. Before this comparison can be made, however, the two examinations themselves have to be fairly well standardized. In the field of psychiatry we have not reached the stage where the various 'examinations' could be standardized and thus we have no possibilities yet for a reliable comparison of their results.

One more short remark before we leave this group of problems, about the length of the report. Ideally a report should be concise, containing nothing but the relevant facts about the patient's life and an account of the relevant interactions between patient and doctor in the interview. Unfortunately we have as yet no criteria on which to decide the facts and observations that are relevant and those that are not. This uncertainty about knowing what to look for gives rise to anxiety, and some doctors defend themselves against it by long reports. On the other hand, a short report runs the risk of omitting data and observations which might be needed by the reader. Thus we come to the 'impasse between long, almost verbatim reports, and the short ones which contain hardly anything but the doctor's conclusions.

To make the situation still more difficult one could ask, does the fact that the doctor cannot write a concise report show anything relevant about (1) the patient, (2) the doctor, (3) the shallowness of the interaction between them, or (4) about the present sad state of knowledge in psychiatry?

Of course every report is written with an eye on the prospective reader. This is true of all professional reports, medical among them. The situation is somewhat more complicated in the case of a psychiatric report since here not only its objective content will matter but also its psychological effects. We mention this factor for the sake of completeness but we will not discuss it in detail.

(9) The next group comprises difficulties about reliable criteria on the basis of which one could judge whether the interview had got hold of enough of *the relevant factors* for a proper diagnosis. Before discussing them we would like to use this opportunity to show some of the difficulties that confronted us when we tried to devise a system for presenting our problems. So let us ask what should have been the proper place for this group. Of course no doctor would close an interview before satisfying himself that he had been able to assess the patient's problem. Consequently the problem of criteria ought to be discussed before the group of problems concerned with the duration of the interview. Perhaps the same could be said about its relation to the plan of the interview which was discussed in Section (4). Similarly no doctor would hazard an unnecessary interpretation when he had been satisfied that no further material would be needed for his diagnosis, therefore this section should have preceded that on interpretations; and lastly, recording and reporting should certainly start after the interview has been completed according to the doctor's criteria, thus the order of these two sections should have been reversed. The reason why we put it in its present place was that we thought that recording should be going on throughout the interview— of course only in the doctor's mind—thus the criteria for termination

should come after it. However, we are fully aware that our choice is arbitrary, but we have to add that practically the same could be said about the placing of all the other groups in our system.

The question of criteria is closely linked with several of the previous groups, foremost among them with that on recording. The classical medical examination is so well standardized that routine record sheets could be easily devised which then mercilessly betray any doctor who tries to get away with an incomplete examination. Although innumerable attempts have been made to devise something similar in psychological medicine, all these attempts proved only partially successful.

This is a bitter and hard fact which, according to our experience, doctors find very difficult to accept. The chief reason for this bitter fact is that it is much more difficult to prove that a particular psychiatric interview was patchy, full of holes, or that it was self-contradictory, than is the case with a medical examination. Let us assume that after finishing a conscientious interview the doctor notices that the patient hardly mentioned his father. Does this mean that his father was an insignificant man who was possibly overshadowed by an important mother, or that the patient is so anxious about his precarious idealization of his father that he hardly dares mention his name, or that the patient's hatred of his father is overwhelming, or last, but not least, that the doctor's technique was faulty? We have mentioned in Chapter 6 that in one of our attempts at devising a reliable record form we tried to overcome this difficulty by printing in bold letters in the right-hand top corner of the record sheet: *Negative findings must be explicitly stated*. In spite of our precaution, time and again we caught out one or the other member of the research team neglecting this instruction when using this record sheet.

How to decide whether an interview was sufficiently complete or not is the one of all the many problems thrown up in this chapter of which we know perhaps the least. In spite of all this we, like any other psychiatrist, conduct interviews and have to judge whether our results are acceptable or not. Although we are fully aware that they do not amount to much, here are the questions that we ask ourselves when we try to decide whether our interview was successful or failed.

The first is about internal evidence. Does the material produced by the patient hang together, does it fit into an understandable story, or are there internal contradictions? Some aspects of this problem have already been discussed in Chapter 10, on 'Understanding People Professionally'.

The second question is whether the picture emerging in the doctor's mind will or will not match the picture of the illness that the patient brought into the interview. This is an important criterion, and some of its implications were discussed in Chapters 10–12.

The third question is whether the patient has learned something new about himself and the picture of his illness that he brought along to the interview, and whether the something new makes sense to him or not. This topic, too, was discussed previously in Chapters 11 and 12.

The next question is whether this new light will enable the patient to assess his present situation more correctly than previously and whether he will now be able to decide what his next step should be, or, at least, to accept the doctor's recommendations as a sensible proposition.

Time and again there will occur interviews after which the patient will be able neither to decide for himself nor to accept what the doctor proposes. Most of them should be considered as failures. The commonest cause of these failures is that the doctor was carried away by his diagnostic discovery and forgot to see to it that the patient followed him. However, there are a few cases in which the criteria enumerated above cannot be achieved. In order to elevate them from the class 'failures' to the class 'qualified successful interviews', the doctor must be able on the basis of his findings to understand why his recommendations had to be rejected. Unfortunately it is very easy to be somewhat kind to oneself, and so we recommend using this escape paragraph cautiously.

(10) This section is about the problem how best to *integrate the psychiatric interview into the medical examination*. Of course, the ideal medical examination should include both the patient's physical examination and the psychiatric interview in one consultation. For the time being this integration is rather difficult. The main reason lies in the doctor's previous training, in which it was really drummed into him how to take a medical history, how to conduct a physical examination, and how to arrive on the basis of his findings at a fairly reliable physical diagnosis. Thus medical history-taking and physical examination have become almost automatic skills, a kind of second nature to every doctor. These skills, however, presuppose a setting according to the pattern of one-person biology.

The interview technique that we advocate is based on the study of the interaction between patient and doctor, that is, of a two-person relationship. The physical examination does not lend itself as a good starting point for this study. In our opinion this is why most doctors divide the consultation into two parts. During the first, the physical examination is carried out in the traditional way, and in the second, after the patient has rearranged his clothes and sat down in front of the doctor, the psychiatric interview follows.

This, however, is far from being an absolute rule. We know doctors who continue the psychiatric interview while the patient is on the examination couch. On the other hand, most gynaecologists in our experience after some preparation put the patient on the examination table, finish the gynaecological investigation, and then start talking to the patient after she has been dressed again. Apparently a number of paediatricians adopt a similar technique; after due preparation they physically examine the child and then talk to the mother—but hardly to the child.

The reverse problem meets us when we examine the habitual course of an interview by a psychotherapist or a psycho-analyst. The difficulty of switching over from a psychological to a physical examination is very great for the doctor because of the fantastic and unreal but most intimate content and intense emotional atmosphere of a psychiatric interview, which make him feel that it would be a shock to his patient to be forced to change over abruptly from this world to the tangible and realistic world of his physical body. In consequence a physical examination is, as a rule, completely omitted. Should the interviewer think that the physical side of the symptoms needs clarification, the patient—almost invariably—will be referred to another doctor. The task of integrating the two examinations is in this way avoided and one has to reassure oneself by using various theoretical considerations that it is in the patient's interest to keep mind and body apart. Experiences such as reported in Chapter 2 show that this is not necessarily true. A further consequence of this clean separation is that for psychiatrists, and especially psycho-analysts, direct physical contact with the patient's body is practically anathema. This general attitude is, on the whole, wise and well-founded, but its inevitable consequence is that these doctors do not have any direct experience with this problem, though they are fully aware of the importance of the relation between the body and the mind.

We would mention that a group of doctors in charge of marital problem clinics of the Family Planning Association have studied the possibility of combining physical and psychological examinations for therapeutic purposes in cases of non-consummation of a marriage. The results of this—truly psychosomatic—approach are most promising. The experiences are being written up and, we hope, will be ready for publication shortly.

Let us repeat again, this is a vast field, most important for everyday practice, and in bad need of proper investigation and research.

(11) To end this chapter, we think we ought to mention, however briefly, two more, interrelated, problems. As discussed in Chapters 10 and 11, in most interviews, especially in those considered successful, the patient gets something valuable. It may be new insight, a somewhat more realistic assessment of his problems and his own personality; it may be a memorable experience of being understood and in this way learning something really new about himself, and so on. As a rule this has to be paid for by accepting and tolerating some strain, or even a painful realization. All of us doctors know that these two dynamic processes exist, and all of us watch carefully that the patient's gains and the price he has to pay for them should be in a reasonable proportion. It is also known that certain types of patients are very sensitive or touchy, their stability is so precarious that they can tolerate only a small increase of strain; that others are so well defended that they can take a good deal without turning a hair; and that there are mixed types, touchy in some respects and indifferent in others.

However, all this is only crude empirical knowledge and it would be a most worth while study to find out what sort, and what intensity, of strain produces the most profitable results in which patient. The situation is still more complex because we have some idea that the ways in which the patient is subjected to strains and then helped or not helped during the interview to bear them will considerably influence his ultimate reaction.

The other problem, closely related to the previous one, is *how to end the interview*. Should the doctor try to round it off, summing up in a somewhat doctrinaire manner the chief points elicited, showing in logical order the steps that led to *his* conclusions and to *his* recommendations; should he leave all this to the patient, or should he try to induce the patient to undertake the summing up of what was achieved in the joint work?

What we wish to stress is that the way the doctor terminates the interview will influence the patient towards or against what the doctor helped him to experience. Thus these two problems—balancing the gains and the strains in the course of an interview and the method of terminating it—belong to a borderland, they end the diagnostic period and lead the way towards therapy. They, too, certainly offer a rewarding field for research.

We started Chapter 13 by reassuring our non-psychiatrist colleagues that, contrary to their expectations, psychiatrists have not got many trade secrets about how to conduct an interview. We hope that the last three chapters will have convinced them that this is really so.

The psychiatric interview, in contrast with the clinical examination, has as yet no standardized drill; in fact its many problems are, on the whole, disregarded, pushed on one side, or glossed over. It is quite possible that this chapter is the first published attempt at a more or less systematic survey of this field.

Yet there is some truth in our colleagues' expectation. The trade secret that they suspect is the familiarity that a psycho-analyst acquires during his training with the unconscious and its seemingly irrational mechanisms. This familiarity enables him to understand connections and situations which appear nonsensical or baffling to a doctor not trained in this way.

We must not forget, however, that this difference, though considerable, does not amount to an absolute 'yes' or 'no'. As the case histories quoted in this book show, it is within the possibility of any doctor to become familiar with some ways of the unconscious mind. Of course, it cannot be expected that he will reach the same degree of familiarity reached by the analyst during his many years of training and practising; consequently in a way some techniques in interviewing will remain for ever a kind of trade secret or esoteric knowledge.

This, however, is only one side of the picture. The other side is that doctors know a good deal about events and phenomena that are unknown and even inaccessible to psycho-analysts. Thus we would like to end this chapter with our refrain, that real progress in this field can be expected only if doctors, that is, general practitioners and specialists on the one hand, and analysts on the other, join hands as equals to study the many problems still facing us.

CONCLUSIONS

The Autogenous and the Iatrogenous Illness

We stated in the Introduction that present knowledge is as yet insufficient for a systematic presentation of the field of psychotherapy. In consequence what we aimed at in this book was to clear the ground of some of the most obstructive prejudices and misconceptions and then establish a few reliable working principles which at some later date may be incorporated in a systematic building. We tried to avoid as far as possible any controversial issues and to discuss only topics about which some consensus of opinion could be expected.

In our opinion perhaps the most important factor that has prevented the development of a proper psychotherapeutic methodology in medicine has been the half-truth that psychiatrists can advise general practitioners and non-psychiatric specialists what to do and what not to do in any given case. We devoted the whole of Part I to showing that the setting in which the therapy is carried out determines, to a large extent, the techniques used and the results obtained. As psychiatrists, and for that matter psycho-analysts, are familiar only with techniques determined by their own individual settings, their well-meant advice and guidance, instead of furthering, inhibited the development of a systematic psychotherapeutic methodology. We hope that the evidence we have presented will be convincing enough to show that each medical setting has its own possibilities and limitations and, instead of a wholesale importation of alien techniques, each branch of medicine ought to aim at developing its own psychotherapeutic techniques congenial to its setting.

There are, however, basic problems which are met almost in identical form no matter in what setting the psychotherapy is carried out. In organic medicine it is taken for granted that it is the doctor who examines the patient, makes the diagnosis, and prescribes the treatment. This traditional procedure, well proven in organic medicine, was imported wholesale without any further examination into psychotherapy and psychodiagnosis, causing unnecessary obstructions and difficulties. We tried to show in Part II that a number of these difficulties can be avoided if techniques are developed that are natural consequences of the psychotherapeutic setting, just in the same way as the traditional procedure is a natural consequence of the setting in organic medicine. We hope that the techniques we have isolated and described—examination by the patient, watching the influence of the doctor's emotions, avoiding the temptation of treating the absent patient in place of the present one, etc.—will be found generally acceptable and may constitute the first steps towards a systematic psychotherapy.

We concluded Part II with an examination of the place of psychotherapy in medicine and reached the opinion that it is determined by two basic differences. In organic medicine the doctor's task is mainly intellectual, he need not watch carefully what his own emotional involvement is or what the patient feels, indeed for a number of surgical and medical procedures the patient may preferably be anaesthetized. Of course, no psychotherapy can be carried out with an anaesthetized patient; here, in addition to the intellectual problems encountered, the emerging emotions both in the patient and in the doctor must be carefully observed and understood. The other cardinal difference is that in organic medicine it is sufficient if the therapy makes sense to the doctor; what is required from the patient is merely that he should reliably carry out the doctor's prescriptions. Contrariwise in psychological medicine it is essential that the therapy should make sense both to the patient and to the doctor.

In Part III we tried to analyse this complex interaction between the doctor and his patient. In somewhat simplified form one may say that this 'sense' depends on two part-functions: first the doctor must understand his patient, and then enable the patient to understand himself. It was from this angle that we examined the various forms of psychotherapy and in Part IV the specific nature of the psychiatric interview and its many unsolved problems.

We hope that two main themes will clearly emerge from our book, the second representing a special case of the first. The first theme is about the nature of the psychotherapeutic process. On the basis of our experience with the various forms of psychotherapy, we think that the prevailing theoretical approach, regarding it merely as a therapy *of* the individual patient by any doctor using standardized correct techniques, is limited, and a real progress in our understanding may be expected only if it becomes generally accepted that *psychotherapy is essentially an interaction* between a particular patient and his doctor. Consequently, we decided to centre our discussion on the doctor's technique and, in fact, have hardly mentioned in this book the patient's psychopathology or psychodynamics.

This is contrary to the practice of most authors who set out to write about psychotherapy; their discussion centres, as a rule, around psychopathology, and their case histories describe well-organized syndromes and often illnesses rather than individual patients. Little is then said, or indeed can be said, about psychotherapy except perhaps to advise it in one case and not in another. It is very tempting to think that, if the psychopathology of a patient is understood, the rest will follow, and there is no need to examine the therapeutic processes themselves. How the doctor conducts the psychotherapy is apparently his own affair once a well differentiated diagnosis in psychodynamic terms has been made. We have not fallen into this trap but our readers may feel that we have fallen into the other by describing in detail what happens during therapy to the doctor rather than to the patient; it could legitimately be said against us that there can be no therapy worth its name unless the cause of the illness is understood. We must plead guilty to this charge since, as we have just stated, we have not paid much attention to the aetiology of the illnesses—but perhaps we may take the fact that our plan could be carried out and yielded some acceptable results as a proof that our view may have some validity.

Our second theme needs some introduction. We have just pointed out that it is generally believed that the first task of a doctor is to arrive at the aetiological diagnosis of the patient's complaints. It is believed that, if this can be done, the treatment prescribed will be to the point and effective. Unfortunately even in organic medicine it is not always possible to arrive at a veritable diagnosis; in its place, not so seldom, a *spurious diagnosis* is adopted, mimicking the real thing. This is a serious risk since patients and doctors may then be tempted to treat the spurious aetiology, a futile endeavour which leads to a waste of time, money, and effort and, as a rule, causes a good deal of pain, disappointment, and even despair to the patient.

This danger is always present. It is smallest in the case of patients whose illness is of the type of an accident as discussed in Chapter 9. The less the illness resembles this type, the greater will be the danger of a spurious diagnosis. However, this danger may be considerably reduced if doctors bear in mind that *in every patient they have to cope with two illnesses—instead of one*. When the patient arrives at the doctor's rooms complaining—we leave the verb intentionally without an object—he has already created out of his new sensations, fears, suspicions, and pains, a more or less stable picture, which may be called the *autogenous illness*. While taking a medical history, listening to, and examining his patient, the doctor too creates out of all these elements a more or less stable picture, which may be called—

sit venia verbo—the *iatrogenous illness*. Hospital medicine confidently believes that if the more realistic iatrogenous illness can be cured, both illnesses will disappear for good. In cases in which a proper aetiological diagnosis can be established—provided the diagnosed illness is curable—this often, but by no means always, does in fact happen.

In scientific medicine, especially since the establishment of pathological anatomy as the highest court of appeal for any medical problem, practically all attention has been concentrated on the study of the iatrogenous illness, while the autogenous illness, which often has no anatomical basis, has been more and more considered as an irritating but largely irrelevant nuisance. In consequence neither its diagnosis, nor its therapy, has been regarded worthy of serious study, although its existence forced doctors to develop, shamefacedly, some empirical, not quite sincere, not even quite honest techniques to counteract its influence.

An obvious precondition for remedying this situation is that doctors must learn to diagnose not only the patient's 'real' iatrogenous, but also his autogenous illness, and find out what sort of help will be needed for both. Attaching to the patient diagnostic labels, such as neurosis, stress disorder, psychosomatic condition, may reassure and help us doctors, but hardly the patient.

An important initial task in psychological diagnosis is to establish some connection between what the patient feels he has come about (autogenous illness) and what the doctor has been able to understand about the patient's condition (iatrogenous illness). This connection must make sense to both of them, and it must satisfy the patient emotionally, otherwise he will feel not understood, disappointed, irritated, let down. As medicine well knows, these feelings may prevail even in patients whose 'real' illness has been efficiently and properly treated, or even cured. Returning to our field of psychological medicine, here is the explanation why mere listening to the patient's story, even in a most sympathetic way, is only seldom sufficient therapy, in the same way as compelling the patient to listen to one's own ideas hardly ever is. It is easy to point this out, but in practice it is not so easy to escape the Scylla of mere sympathetic listening as well as the Charybdis of being carried away by one's own 'scientific' ideas.

We have learned a good deal about the iatrogenous illness, which is customarily described in psychological medicine as the patient's psychopathology or psychodynamics; our knowledge of the autogenous illness is much less systematic, in a somewhat condescending way it is dealt with under the heading: subjective symptomatology.

The iatrogenous picture of an illness is always expressed explicitly in words; and in medicine, organic as well as psychological, no effort has been spared to make these words, and the ideas behind them, precise, unequivocal, and capable of verification by experiment and observation. We would stress that all these functions—description by precise words, experimentation, observation—are carried out by the doctor for whom the phenomena in question are external events. This condition does not obtain for the autogenous illness, which rests almost entirely on subjective, that is internal, phenomena, and these are never unequivocal or precise. Words are notoriously inadequate for describing the internal world, except if they are used by a poet. While the iatrogenous illness is built up of perceptions obtained as far as possible through the projective senses, chiefly sight and hearing, and to a minor extent touch, the autogenous illness uses perceptions through the more primitive senses, such as pain, general body sensations, etc.

All this creates signal differences between the two pictures. The autogenous picture is hazy and vague; the words in which it is expressed may even change, to the utmost exasperation of the doctor, though possibly the substance of the illness has remained the same; no wonder then that doctors, scientists as well as practitioners, have paid more attention to the more stable and more reliable iatrogenous picture. It would be an important question which of the two illnesses is more relevant; in a case of a perforated appendix, a hypoglycemic attack, an operable cancer, undoubtedly the iatrogenous, but will the same be true for every complaint presented to the doctor? Is there a 'real' illness, a *Ding an und für sich*, apart from the two pictures? If so, which of the two is a truer picture, nearer to the real thing, and in which case? For instance, if only a spurious diagnosis can be established, will the iatrogenous illness be nearer the truth than the autogenous illness? We mention all these fundamental problems only for the sake of completeness since we cannot offer proper solutions, though we have been studying them for some time.

But however great the differences between the two illnesses may be, this two-fold function—recognizing the existence of these two illnesses and then integrating them into something that makes sense—represents a significant special aspect of the interaction between doctor and patient during psychotherapy, the one that we described a few paragraphs above as our second theme. For the sake of brevity we propose to call it 'matching'. Up to this point we have limited our discussion to its importance for psychological diagnosis but we think that its importance for psychotherapy proper is equally great.

We have already dealt with some aspects of this matching function

P 209

when we discussed in Chapters 10 and 11 'Understanding People Professionally' and 'Enabling People to Understand Themselves'. Viewed from this angle every interpretation or, for that matter, clarification, confrontation, etc. used in psychotherapy rests on these two fundamental functions, that is, on 'matching'—recognizing a new and hitherto hidden part of the patient's autogenous illness, developing further the iatrogenic picture of the illness by fitting this new bit into it, and then trying to integrate the two by communicating the new discovery to the patient in some form or other.

Not much attention was paid to the therapeutic effect of the therapist's choice of words for this purpose till the emergence of the various schools in psychotherapy and, in particular, in psychoanalysis. Comparison of the case histories described by the various schools shows that—in addition to the common words and phrases—each school has developed its own terms and, still more important, can apparently describe and observe phenomena and processes that are not described, and perhaps not even observed, by another school. This applies equally to diagnosis and to therapy. A number of complex problems arise here: Do these therapeutic processes occur only if the patient is treated in the way advocated by that particular school? Are these processes ubiquitous, though observed only by the school that has developed words for describing them? If observed and properly dealt with, do they lead to different results, and are these results significantly better or worse than those of the other schools? No final answer is as yet available to any of these questions, though in recent years more and more attention has been paid to them.

In our view this whole group of problems represents only a special case of the general problem of 'matching', which happens at every step in psychotherapy. Unfortunately we do not know enough about why certain ways of matching—whether done by words or by non-verbal means of communication—are therapeutic in one case while others are ineffective, though various theories have been proposed to answer this problem. To mention a few: corrective emotional experience, non-directive counselling, and last, but not least, the theory of interpretation in psycho-analysis. In our view, all these formulations describe one or the other aspect of the same process: the doctor enables his patient to see a part of the external or his own internal world and his role in them in a different way, which in turn will lead to a different relationship between the patient and that part of the world.

The process that we termed 'matching' is implied by the sentence: 'the doctor enables his patient to see differently'. To state it explicitly —even though we have to repeat ourselves—(*a*) the doctor recognizes

210

the two illnesses and matches them first for himself so that they make sense together for him, (*b*) expresses his findings, in the main, in words which are directed so that (*c*) the patient should be able to match the doctor's ideas and feeling, that is, the iatrogenous illness with his own autogenous illness so that the two should make sense to him too.

We think that psychotherapy in medicine is in a particularly favourable position to contribute valuable clinical observations to the study of this therapeutic interaction, because in most medical cases both the autogenous and the iatrogenous illness are more vivid, more tangible, and better isolated from each other than in psychiatry proper. In our view this will make the study of the two illnesses and their interaction considerably easier, and we see this book as a contribution to this study.

We know that some steps in this train of thought are not quite certain or are somewhat over-simplified, and thus in need of re-examination and of being made more precise. Evidently this cannot be done here. In concluding our book, a progress report of our various research projects, we wanted to indicate the direction of our ideas of the day, that is, the point we have reached and the direction that may possibly be taken by our future research.

APPENDIX

Follow-Up Reports

In psycho-analysis we have learned to consider the subsequent dream as a proof whether the interpretation of the preceding dream was correct or otherwise. In our opinion a working principle of this kind should be adopted also by medicine. This means evidently that merely following up the course of one illness is not satisfactory. In many cases one illness, offered by the patient to the medical profession, which did not meet with a constructive reception, that is, could not elicit a satisfying answer, will be replaced—as many cases taught us—by another 'offer' seemingly independent of the first. We think therefore that the whole patient has to be followed up in order to find out whether our treatment helped him to solve his problem or only forced him to change his symptoms. To show the usefulness of this approach it was decided to follow up each case reported in this book till August 1960.

CASE 1. MRS. Q. (reported by Dr. M.)

As the years passed Mrs. Q. became more and more independent. Parallel with this she felt that her marriage was increasingly unsatisfactory, especially so sexually. She struck up a friendship with another man, an Indian, who is kind, generous, very fond of her and treats her gently. Thus he is utterly different from her husband. After some time she decided to leave her husband and to ask for a divorce on grounds of cruelty.

First she moved with her child to her parents but remained on the doctor's list. The parents did not approve of her affair and refused to look after her child, insisting that this was Mrs. Q's duty. On the other hand they were willing to allow her to stay in their house. Under these circumstances she had to accept support from her Indian friend.

During this period Mrs. Q. came occasionally to tell the doctor about developments and eventually asked him to be a witness in the divorce proceedings, which he accepted. Mr. Q., however, defended the suit, promised at the hearing to mend his ways and offered reconciliation, which Mrs. Q. refused. Under these circumstances the judge did not grant a divorce but gave the custody of the child to Mrs. Q.

Now she is living with her friend, officially as his housekeeper, facing the difficulties of her position amazingly well, and she hopes to have a child by him in due course.

She has had no illnesses in recent years. No further work has been done about her jealousy of her sister and sister-in-law, in fact the doctor thinks that she sees very little, if anything, of them.

In the doctor's opinion she certainly has become more mature, dresses neatly, and is no longer sluttish. She knows that if her husband can prove adultery her son may be taken away from her. She says that she loves him very much but feels that she should not sacrifice her life and independence completely to him. She had to make a difficult decision whether to stay with her parents, who did not treat her very well, and be sure that she could keep her child, or go and live with her friend and risk losing the child. After long consideration and without any outside help she decided on the second choice.

This is a complex situation, difficult to judge, so let us first take the facts. Mrs. Q., for the first time in her life, lives with a congenial companion in a satisfactory sexual relationship. She has become independent, does not rely any more on either her mother or her somewhat uncouth husband and was able to make up her own mind in a difficult situation. She can look after herself and her appearance is that of a woman of her status. When we compare this picture with the condition in which she originally presented herself in 1952 to her doctor, we cannot but admit that she has improved beyond recognition.

On the other hand, it must be counted against the improvement that she could not make a success of her marriage, neither could she arrange her affairs so that her husband acquiesced in a divorce or that she could have proved her case against him. In these respects she has definitely failed. Then there is the most complex problem of choosing an Indian as her partner. We cannot judge whether in her social circle even a legal marriage with an Indian is acceptable and must leave this question undecided; in consequence only some more years of follow-up will show whether her recent choice of partner was neurotic or sensible.

Even allowing for this uncertainty we think that it can be claimed that this case was on the whole correctly treated. True, possibly the doctor could have intervened when he was first informed about the impending break-up of the marriage. This is another difficult problem

213

in this kind of therapeutic relationship. Should every breakdown of a marriage be considered as a symptom of some illness and be treated as such, or is it beyond the confines of medical responsibility? There are no hard and fast rules in this field; some breakdowns are definitely neurotic and ought to be treated, others are definitely not. In this case the doctor decided to remain a passive observer and only a further follow-up will tell us whether he was right or wrong. In any case there can be no doubt that his functioning in his many and varied roles as general practitioner, as psychotherapist, as obstetrician, then again as a general practitioner, and so on, has considerably helped Mrs. Q. to reach the state in which she is now.

CASE 2. MR. V.

Dr H. reported as follows:

Mr. V. has not consulted either me or any of my partners for some considerable time, nor does he come to the surgery. On the other hand, a fairly good contact has been re-established between myself and his wife. She is employed as a cashier at my greengrocer's where I shop regularly, when she has always been anxious to be helpful to me. She comes only rarely to the surgery but consults us occasionally for her two younger children.

The last time she came bringing the two younger children, she was accompanied by her husband. This happened about two months ago. On that occasion she came alone into the consulting room, leaving her husband in the waiting room. When I asked her about him she reported that he was very well and added that he had just said to her that he must have made a good job of decorating the waiting room since it was still in such a good condition.

I learned from his mother-in-law, who is also my patient, that he is doing extremely well. He threw out his former partner and took his younger brother as a junior partner into the business; they are now employing a staff of twelve; Mr. V. rarely does any decorating himself these days, his time is mainly taken up by administrative work.

They are buying a house outside London and intend to move there next year.

COMMENTS BY DR. H.

I feel I would like to have another talk with this patient, the reason being that I do not consider the case finished. In my view things started to go wrong when I made the mistake of employing him to decorate my new house. The fact that he was made to do things for a woman, as he used to do in his childhood for his mother, reinforced his experiencing me as a mother figure; this was then further intensified when my husband criticized Mr. V's work as Mr. V's father used to do. Having failed to make these interpretations to the patient, I cannot consider the treatment as having been properly completed in spite of all the real successes achieved by Mr. V. in his marriage and in his business.

Perhaps an important cause of his not coming to the surgery is fear of further criticism. That he had to comment on the excellent condition of his work appears to be in good agreement with my idea.

This report well illustrates how strict our standards are that we use for judging the results of any treatment. When Mr. V's present state is compared with that of 1953, when he was given up with a very poor prognosis by a teaching hospital, the therapy cannot but be judged as highly successful. Then he was constantly ill, could not keep his job, had violent quarrels with his wife who seriously considered leaving him, and his daughter was badly enuretic. He has now three normal children, a satisfied wife, and has been highly successful in his business. Furthermore, he has had no illnesses for several years, has not even consulted his doctors, and still Dr. H. is not really satisfied with her work and seriously considers rounding it off by asking Mr. V. for a long interview.

Although her idea about why Mr. V. has kept away from her is plausible, we think that a more important factor was what we characterized in our discussion in Chapter 2 as change of atmosphere between patient and doctor. We predicted then, in summer 1958, that unless the doctor was able to reconstitute the old atmosphere Mr. V. would drift away from her. Apparently this is what has happened.

CASE 3. MISS I.
The doctor reports:
I have seen her on only a few occasions since last report (that is 1958). She seems to be a happy, well balanced, young married woman, devoted to her husband of whom she speaks very well. Except for the fact that she still has no family one would be justified in describing her treatment as a complete success.

We fully agree with the doctor and would strongly recommend that on the next occasion when he sees her he should broach this subject, and if he cannot clarify it to his satisfaction the patient should be referred for another psychiatric interview.

CASE 4. MR. N.
The doctor reports:
The family seem to be well. Complaints are rare and strictly 'organic'.

The children are two wonderful specimens, the boy a six foot athletic type as normal as one could wish for, and the girl is pretty, brilliant academically, captain of the school, top girl, etc. with never a complaint of any sort. Mr. N. does not present any depression or anxiety. He tells me everything is normal sexually and he has got over that phase. If I have any doubt at all it is with Mrs. N. who, on the rare occasions I have seen her, in spite of her 'all's well' protestations, has made me suspect a very mild undercurrent of 'something or other'. I have not pursued it as I would hesitate to disturb such a family as they are now. I may also add that my relationship with the whole family is excellent, even better than prior to the psychiatric interview. I am a real family friend who was truly interested in them and sent them to the best place for advice.

Apparently our assessment of this family was somewhat cautious. The boy was able to get through his difficulties and has developed well. Mr. N. has maintained his improvement and there has been no relapse or even a threat of relapse. Even Mrs. N. has stopped complaining about tiredness, depression, and headaches, yet there is this 'undercurrent of something or other'; possibly it is she who has to bear the brunt of her husband's suppressed aggressiveness which is so characteristic of a well controlled obsessional man. Thus this case could have been used in Chapter 8 to illustrate the doctor's responsibility. If he decides on a policy of wait and see, it means that he will 'teach' that women must put up with their husbands' peculiarities even though they are heavily taxed thereby. On the other hand, if he decides to go further he would 'teach' that wives need not tolerate their husbands' obsessional world even though this might disturb the peace and upset a possibly finely balanced equilibrium.

CASE 5. MRS. L.
The family left the district in 1957. At that time Mrs. L. was definitely better though being left alone in the house was still a problem to her. She felt that perhaps she could tolerate a train journey but avoided testing this out. When taking her leave she was most grateful for everything her doctor had done for her and even offered to pay for the many consultations which the doctor—though regretfully—had to refuse.

In January 1958 Mr. L., being in the district, visited the doctor and told him that his wife 'is pretty well with no obvious difficulties; she has not tested her reaction to a train journey but Mr. L. thinks she would be all right'. The doctor has not heard from them since.

In our opinion this is a classical case. A conscientious doctor sparing no effort, a most grateful, appreciative, and co-operative patient—and yet no real change, because the whole examination had been carried out by the doctor with the patient taking hardly any part in it.

CASE 6. MRS. X.

Our optimistic prediction in this case was apparently not justified. She was seen in early February 1960 by the Registrar who, at the end of the interview, referred her to the Gynaecological Department of his hospital for contraceptive advice. Unfortunately she could not be given an appointment before the end of April, the waiting list being so long. While waiting for her appointment she came again to see the Registrar in March. She was quite well then and was intending to keep the appointment. In fact she did not turn up, nor did she answer a letter by the Gynaecological Department and another written in the summer by the Registrar.

One can think of two possible reasons why Mrs. X. failed to keep her appointment and had since apparently disappeared. The easier is to put the blame on the inhuman waiting list. Patients need treatment when they need it and not when their turn arrives according to the waiting list and the various priorities. It is quite possible that Mrs. X. would have willingly accepted examination and advice in February while she was still under the impact of the interview. In April all the effect of this interview may have vanished and the examination seemed to her a threat of further unpleasantness; in this case her failure to answer the various letters may be explained by her uneasiness; though she knows that something ought to be done about her sexual and marital life, she rejected the offer of help and now she cannot see what to do.

The other reason may lie in some technical fault in her referral. There are so many possibilities here that we would like to single out only the principal ones. The idea of the referral probably did not grow out of the joint examination by patient and doctor of her whole life situation, it was only the doctor who reached this conclusion and presented it to his patient. Especially when the examination raises some guilt feelings in patients, they may obediently agree to their doctor's proposition, often even act upon it and appear for the psychiatric consultation, but after having eased their guilt they disappear after one or two interviews. This is a type fairly well known to us. The other fault may be in the doctor's apparent lack of interest in her. After all, what else could she think of her doctor who stirred up her interest and anxiety by his examination and then let her stew for about two months without doing anything for her? Her visit in March would certainly fit well into this picture.

217

Whatever may be the reason for her disappearance, it is quite possible that in due course yet another 'illness' will be produced and she will be referred again for examination and advice to the same Department, but it is rather doubtful whether she will find the same Registrar.

POSTSCRIPT IN OCTOBER 1960

We finished the manuscript of this book in September but decided —because of its interest—to include this additional piece of follow-up. The Registrar reported in writing on 19th October 1960 as follows:

Mrs. X. turned up in my Out-Patients' Clinic to-day, and so I am at last able to give you some follow-up data about her. She did not go to the gynaecologist because she was frightened to do so. I could not really discover why she came to see me to-day but I think it was because her father has just been found to have pulmonary tuberculosis and she wanted to know whether the family ought to have a chest x-ray. I am pleased to say that she is very much better. She tells me that she is no longer depressed and she attributes her improvement to improved relationship with her husband. He is using a sheath for the first time, and she is better able to 'relax', as she put it. I really think she is much better and I have not made another appointment to see her.

There are so many interesting points in this short follow-up report that it was not easy to resist the temptation to write a whole chapter on it.

First there is the change of 'offer'. This time it is anxiety about a possible tuberculosis infection, but it is not very difficult to discover behind it the general anxiety that something might not be quite right with herself and that this something might be connected with her relationship to her parents, in particular to her father. A further possible motive for this 'offer' is an attempt to attract the Registrar's attention away from her marital problems to a more presentable field like a tuberculous infection.

Possibly the chief reason for her coming was her need to reassure herself against her guilt feelings which had been stirred up by her not keeping the appointment and not answering the letters. Her appearance when she was not expected is therefore a kind of compromise; she has come but in her own sweet time and well sheltered by impressive and acceptable disguises.

The same flavour of acceptable compromise pervades her report about the changes in her marital life. Although she has not gone as far as the doctor advised her to, everything is much better now; she is not depressed any more, her husband is more co-operative, she is better able to 'relax', etc. Almost certainly what she wanted to convey was something like this: 'I am a sensible woman, I have done as much as I can be expected to do, I am most appreciative of your help but please let us stop here.' As the report shows the doctor in fact agreed.

It is gratifying for us to see that our analysis of the possible effects of the 'examination by the patient' has been, on the whole, correct. Mrs. X. has been enabled to understand herself better and on the basis of this understanding has been able to do something about her life. This understanding, however, is apparently not deep enough to free her sufficiently not to be frightened by a possibly searching gynaecological examination. It is fair to assume that in February the impact of her new discovery would have been strong enough to overcome this anxiety but with the passing of time this impact diminished and her defences became reinforced.

And last, but not least, here we have another instance which proves that no doctor can evade or circumvent his function to teach. Our Registrar had the choice either to agree with the patient's 'offer' or to probe further in order to find out why she is still frightened of a gynaecological examination. He chose to agree and for Mrs. X. this will be his teaching. Only a further follow-up of at least five to ten years can tell us what the consequences of his decision will be and thus enable us to decide whether or not he taught wisely.

CASE 7. MR. G.
The doctor reported in August 1960:
Mr. G. has continued to call about every six weeks for his Nembutal and antacid prescriptions. On 2nd May (while I was on holiday) one of my partners was called to his house for 'severe indigestion'. He prescribed an antispasmodic and I saw him a week later myself. I signed him off on 20th May. Apart from this he has remained at work. He heard of a new remedy for 'restless legs' from a friend and had a short trial of it, with no benefit after the first night.

Although the reported episode is undoubtedly a slight relapse, spoiling Mr. G's excellent record which started abruptly with the interview in November 1958, his present state is still incomparably better than it used to be. Whereas in the previous six and a half years he missed roughly one day out of every six for illness, since January 1959, that is, in the last twenty months, he has missed only eighteen days, which is less than one in thirty; thus the general improvement which we predicted has been maintained.

While this is true for the present, we are not so confident about the future. Our reason is that apparently the doctor is not able or is not prepared to maintain the personal relationship that means so much to Mr. G. and is perhaps sliding back into the relationship which prevailed before the interview in November 1958. His report speaks only of physical symptoms, of drugs prescribed and of certificates given, but does not mention at all Mr. G's 'relationship to his work and the world in general'. We have met this development in our Case 2; there the changed relationship resulted in the patient drifting away from his doctor. This is the danger in this case too and if the doctor does not restore the situation soon, it might happen that either Mr. G's indigestion will become worse or, somehow or other, he will change over to one of the other doctors in the partnership.

CASE 8. MRS. C.

The doctor reported about this patient to the seminar at the end of July 1960 as follows:—

I have seen her again after a long interval. She isn't pregnant yet. She has been attending the subfertility clinic regularly, but not on the days I am there. This time she turned up on my day and asked Sister if she could see me. Sister said to me: 'You won't recognize her, she has changed so much'. She looks young and cheerful. Having routine tests, tubes all right, biopsy all right, fairly good post-coital test, but the husband hasn't got a terribly good sperm count, it is only reasonable. Sister told me that the mucus was a bit scanty and Mrs. C. was having pills to increase it. I don't know why she can't get pregnant. True, I didn't see the notes, only the patient. I started, 'You are not pregnant yet', and she said, 'No, but I am not too worried about this. I am trying to be sensible about it and not get myself into a state'. She added that her husband and she get on much better now and she enjoys intercourse. 'Do you remember when I tried to be sick when you talked about it? Do you know, if I met a woman who was as idiotic as I was, I could convince her that it was nice.' In the subfertility clinic at first she kicked up a fuss but now she is sensible and does what she is told. She still feels frightened but tells herself she can do it. She is much more confident all round. I asked, 'What do you think helped?' She said, 'I think it was just that you nagged at me. I thought, if this doctor is so persistent and so patient and so determined to see me again, it makes me feel at least I am worth bothering about.' I asked, didn't she feel that before? She said, 'No, it was because you went on and said you wanted to see me again.

It made me feel that I myself was worth something.' I thought that was quite interesting. She said, 'Strangely, I get on much better with my parents now'. She had expressed great antagonism towards them before. She said, 'I felt there was a wall, and my parents were on the other side of it, and my husband was on the other side too with them. When I broke down the barrier with my husband, I suddenly made better contact with my parents, and I am getting on quite reasonably with them now.'

The treatment took place early in 1958, thus the follow-up is longer than two years. The improvement achieved seems to be permanent, and we started the discussion in the seminar by congratulating the doctor on his successful treatment. Then the discussion veered round and we examined in detail what happened in the interview just reported. Soon it became clear that, figuratively speaking, the doctor was basking in the patient's gratitude and appreciation, forgetting in the pleasant atmosphere to examine what was really happening. When we challenged him on this point he replied, 'Mrs. C. was not thinking of our talk as a professional interview, she was just telling me what was going on in her life.' This was, of course, unacceptable and it was pointed out that it is only the doctor who can make a talk unprofessional, never the patient.

We cannot relate here the whole of the discussion but we would like to report its main results. First, after a very successful and intense period of treatment in 1958, the patient was handed over to the subfertility clinic where she received exclusively physical treatment. After two years and after overcoming some considerable administrative difficulties, Mrs. C. managed again to see her original doctor. Her gratitude and the somewhat exaggeratedly beautiful description of her life were then accepted by the doctor at their face value and neither patient nor doctor cared to examine why she wanted to talk to the doctor, why she painted everything so beautifully, or what the possible psychological difficulties were that prevented her becoming pregnant. Instead, as is well demonstrated by the doctor's report, both of them concentrated on a possible physical cause and its treatment. From this angle the talk can be described as a shutting out interview.

When we reached this point the doctor recalled a few more features of the interview and was able to piece them together himself. He saw then that the patient treated him as an idealized parent figure who must be kept entirely good, while all the criticism and aggressiveness must be directed against other people. He realized also that he colluded with the patient during the interview in that he accepted with pleasure

221

the praise and appreciation and, so to speak, agreed that the various aggressive and critical remarks made during the interview had nothing to do with him.

With that we have arrived at the dilemma discussed in Chapter 8. Should the doctor try to remain the idealized figure who is patient, knows everything, and to whom the patient can return from time to time, or should he make the patient see how she splits off her aggressiveness, directing it towards other people and possibly towards the treatment? The doctor decided for the latter policy and we must await further developments.

CASE 9. MRS. P.
The doctor has not seen Mrs. P. since the last interview, that is, June 1960, neither has any of his partners. As the follow-up is too short, not quite three months, it does not allow us to draw any conclusions.

CASE 10. MISS F.
Dr. G. reports:
There has been a further call for help in the nature of severe generalized headaches and I am at present attempting a psychotherapeutic approach.

Unquestionably another 'offer', but this time, perhaps helped by our discussion at the seminar, the doctor is apparently trying not to act upon his emotions but to examine the whole situation *with* his patient.

CASE 11. JOHN K.
The doctor reported as follows:
John came once during the holiday, during a busy evening surgery. He was very non-committal and said that he could not come during the afternoons as he was working at his uncle's. He would come back when the work was not so heavy. He felt better and everything was fine in this best of possible worlds. He was greatly relieved when I let him go.

A week later I was called again to the K's. John had another bad asthma attack. He was again lying on the couch, very reluctant to say anything, often did not answer questions at all, and I just could not get anywhere with him. Mrs. K. was very guilt-stricken and I asked her to come and see me.

She came a few days later during the afternoon and complained of

John's aggressive and resentful attitude towards her. She said she did not make her children cling to her as I might think. John still keeps bad company at the billiard hall, and a neighbour told her that he saw John play with the girls in the park (i.e. with a set of rather loose teenagers). He is very easily led by others.

She had trouble with some of her other children too. She married her husband, widowed when his wife gave birth to Bertha, when Bertha was four years old. They got on very well until somebody told the girl that she was not Mrs. K's child. Bertha is happily married now and has three children herself.

Muriel, her own daughter, 24 years old, studied dispensing and suddenly decided four years ago to marry a labourer. When mother remonstrated with her, she became pregnant and got married. Muriel's husband drinks and ill-treats her, and she has just left him. I know Muriel well, she came to tell me about her troubles, she is frigid, her husband nearly impotent.

Freddy, the eldest of her sons, 22 years, lives at home. He has no time for girls. He went in for a trade, but she took him off it, he looked so ill; he is now an unskilled building labourer.

Peter, the other boy, and her husband were never mentioned.

She always stays awake when one of her children is out, she just cannot sleep, even when Freddy (22 years) is out, though he is a good boy.

I felt that Mrs. K. and John would be too much for me. I suggested referring John for psychiatric treatment, and she was very agreeable.

I saw John later and he also agreed, though I do not think he saw the implications. He thought it was for treatment of his asthma.

It is quite possible that the doctor was right in his final assessment that the treatment of either John or his mother would be beyond his technical possibilities. Some people might even say that it would have been much better for everyone concerned if he had reached these conclusions some years before. The trouble with both these criticisms is that although they are partly true they miss the real issue.

First, it is quite clear, both from the case history and from the follow-up, that the doctor has never succeeded in examining the real patient, John, and still less in inducing John to examine himself. In this respect the case is reminiscent of Mrs. L., Case 5, where too the doctor knew all the details but the whole thing did not make sense to anyone.

Instead of occupying himself with the present patient the doctor turned all his attention to John's mother, Mrs. K., who in a way was always an absent patient. True the decision was not easy which of the two presenting partners should be considered the real one. We had a similar problem in Case 13 but there the doctor decided upon one of them—it was the wife—and never looked back. In consequence he was able to achieve considerable changes, first in the wife and, as the follow-up shows, in the husband as well. In contrast, in our case what the doctor succeeded in doing was apparently to collect a very complete list of the bad results of Mrs. K's handling of her children. This looks very much like a list of sins which was bound to increase Mrs. K's guilt feelings. It is common experience that the pressure of guilt feelings makes patients obedient but does not lead, as a rule, to much therapeutic change. Apparently this is what happened to Mrs. K; she simply had to accept the doctor's proposition to refer her son to a psychiatrist. We are rather doubtful, however, whether she will be able to change in any way her handling of her son, and still more doubtful about her ability to co-operate with the psychiatric treatment which almost certainly will increase the tension between mother and son, at any rate for some time.

We have the same doubts about John's acquiescence in being referred to a psychiatrist. The follow-up report shows eloquently that this decision was taken entirely by the doctor and did not grow out of a joint examination by patient and doctor of the whole situation. Although John's resentment and resistance were carefully and correctly diagnosed, they were not treated at all and the whole attention was directed to his mother whose past and present failings are described at considerable length. As John has not been prepared for what he should expect from psychiatric treatment, we are fairly certain that the psychiatrist will have considerable difficulties with him at the beginning, and we would not be surprised if for some reason or other John's treatment were not started at all or, if started, were interrupted after a very brief period. Thus John's referral is rather reminiscent of Mrs. X's, Case 6, possibly for the same reasons.

CASE 12. MRS. B.

The doctor reports:

Mr. B. did eventually ask for psychiatric treatment, but the report from the psychiatrist was that though he was in urgent need of help he did not persist, attending twice only. I have not seen the wife or husband professionally since, though I have occasionally met them together in the district when they chatted with me and gave a superficial appearance of being on good terms. A recent comment of another patient of mine who knew them well and who originally sent the wife to me was this: 'The Bs are giving a party, this is an

224

unprecedented event and we, her friends, all take it as a very encouraging sign.'

The follow-up confirms our assessment of the case. Unquestionably
the husband is ill and badly in need of treatment. It is doubtful,
however, whether much can be done for him, at any rate for the
time being. It is easy to see that if the doctor had persisted in treating
him, the absent patient, while attending to Mrs. B. he would not have
been able to achieve much more than the psychiatrist did; thus all
efforts, his as well as the couple's, would have been wasted. By changing his approach and concentrating on the present patient, Mrs. B.,
he was able to ease the situation as is shown by the follow-up.

CASE 13. MRS. D.
The doctor reports:
July 1959. Pregnancy confirmed by test, she could not wait for the
usual confirmation by pelvic examination.
April 1960. Normal easy confinement which she enjoyed, in early
March. Baby is a boy and both husband and wife are very pleased.
Mother-in-law died in January from carcinoma, and the 'atmosphere'
at home has been much more relaxed since then.
June 1960. Intercourse normal. Husband did not want his wife to use
contraceptives but preferred to do so himself. She has willingly
given way to his views. Both of them are thinking of starting a second
pregnancy soon. I saw the husband after the clinic when I went out
to admire the baby, whom they had brought to show me. He appeared
both in his manner and conversation to be more confident and determined, less shy and apologetic than at any time previously. I don't
think he has become 'for ever an obedient husband to his wife'.
They seem now to be reasonably well balanced.

Apparently our predictions were fairly correct though somewhat
over-cautious. If further follow-up proves that the doctor was right
in his assessment of Mr. D's present and future possibilities, then
the story of this couple will be an excellent proof of the importance
of treating always the present patient.

CASE 14. MRS. W.
After the psychiatric interview the patient was not seen by her doctor
for more than a year. She appeared again early in August 1960 and
the doctor reports:
Her symptom was pressure on top of her head. The second time
she was much better—all symptoms gone! ! She says she has been

much better able to cope with her domestic situation since she went to see the psychiatrist—the essence being that her husband is ill and needs her. He sounds even more ill to me than he was before. She told him she had been to see a psychiatrist, but would not tell him his name although she invited him to go with her to see the psychiatrist again. He laughed and did not believe she had been at first—but eventually accepted it as true. I think, in her way, she is trying to contribute but whether it could be called the right kind of contribution I don't know.

Thus it seems that the psychiatric interview did not have much effect, certainly not in the direction that would have enabled Mrs. W. to recognize that she too was ill and on that basis ask for help.

Instead of all this she took away from the interview—not what the psychiatrist intended to give her but what she wanted to get—that her husband was ill and needed her. This type of outcome is not at all rare and it would be a worthwhile research to examine what mechanisms the patients use to achieve it. On the other hand it must be stated too that the psychiatric interview had the result that for one year she did not ask for any further medical help. Unfortunately we do not know the real significance of this respite, whether it was that the interview frightened her so much or, on the contrary, whether it gave her an opportunity to talk about her innermost problems and so eased the pressure on her.

CASE 15. FAMILY F.

The doctor reports that his relationship with the whole family if possible has become still better. He then continues:

I can't plead any personality difficulty in opening up the problem if I wanted to. But right or wrong I have all along decided to leave things as they are. The first reason is I see the Fs much less often than before. All three members of the family present me with fewer physical complaints than before. The boy has grown into a lanky youth, his skin quickly got better, he does not worry about it, and never did, and it looks as if he is not allowing his parents to play any part in it. I see very little of the husband and the wife and they appear to have settled into a sort of equilibrium. How stable and happy I can only guess. My guess is that it is pretty stable and will last. As for happiness, I don't think I can prescribe an additional dose of that for them. If their life is not full of jollity, at any rate it does not look very miserable.

What determined me to leave things alone was the group discussion that interference might well lead to a break-up of the marriage, or

226

any rate a severe disturbance of the relationship between husband and wife. Many years ago there was a saying amongst budding young surgeons—'Never open an abdomen unless you are prepared to deal with anything you find in it.' Well that was rather my position. I felt I had no right to open up this case unless I had a strong conviction that I could close it in a better state than it was in before. I certainly could not do that more than ten years ago, and I don't think I could do it now, and I can't see that this is the sort of case that I could get any help with from elsewhere. I should have to shoulder it all myself. Even if I had the time, I think the job is too big for me, and the last step would be worse than the first. Of course, I may be completely wrong, and I should be very pleased at some future time to hear arguments to the contrary.

We think this report is an admirable description of the situation facing the doctor. The only thing we can add to it is that this is what the doctor decided to 'teach' to his patients. As he rightly points out, the results are not too bad and so perhaps it will not be so difficult for him and for the reader to realize that all, the good as well as the not so good, results were also conditioned by the 'teaching'.

CASE 16. MR. K.
The doctor reports:
I saw Mr. K., since December 1958, on the following occasions: (1) June 5th 1959. He was 'shaky'. Long interview followed. He was promoted three weeks previously and was now a foreman. It was also brought out that his father had died on June 10th—which date was near enough. This all added up to some obvious interpretations which he willingly accepted. It worked as usual and he did not consult me again until (2) April 5th 1960. This time: dyspepsia and depression—dyspepsia the first time for ages, but not very severe in fact. Actually when one spoke to him, anxiety was really the major symptom. Another long interview followed and again an acceptable precipitating cause was found. His sister had had a bad accident—she was severely burned—and was in hospital. Some more obvious interpretations with usual results. He had been to see me the evening before but my partner was there instead of me and this worried him. We agreed that if he wished to see me especially in this type of situation 'which you and I readily understand' (to which he nodded vigorous agreement) he could phone me for an appointment. This made him very happy—all was well. I have not seen him since.

This report confirms all our predictions. The relationship between doctor and patient is so good that if any trouble occurs Mr. K. can ask for help in full confidence that he will get it. Furthermore, the depression—or anxiety—is under control and any exacerbation can be speedily dealt with in joint work between a co-operative patient and an understanding doctor. The dyspepsia that plagued Mr. K. for many years was cured by the interview in March 1958 except for a slight exacerbation in more than two years which lasted only for a couple of days. Thus the situation is exactly what we expected.

In spite of the favourable follow-up which now extends for almost two and a half years, we are not quite confident about Mr. K's future for reasons that were fully discussed in Chapter 8.

Returning now to what we said in the first paragraph of this chapter, we think that the follow-up reports have amply proved that it is possible to predict the events fairly accurately on the basis of observations such as are described in this book.

Sixteen cases have been reported in detail. Of these, Case 9, because of the short period of follow-up, is unsuitable for this survey. Of the remaining fifteen, our predictions were proved to be incorrect in only one, Case 6, which leaves fourteen correctly predicted cases. Admittedly in Case 14 our prediction, though correct in direction, was somewhat optimistic, and in Cases 4, 13, and 15, the predictions, though correct in direction, were somewhat too cautious. In Cases 1, 2, 3, 5, 7, 8, 10, 11, 12, and 16, not only the direction of the patient's development was correctly predicted but also its nature and extent.

TABLE OF PREDICTIONS

Period too short	1	
Predictions incorrect	1	
Direction and extent of development predicted:		
(a) about correctly	10	
(b) too cautiously	3	
(c) too optimistically	1	14
Number of cases	16	

INDEX

aetiology, *xn*, 198, 207

aim, *see* goal

ambivalence, 114

analysis, *see* psycho-analysis

anger, doctor's, *see* emotions

attitude, doctor's, 138, 139, 158-9; *see also* emotions

behaviour, external readjustment of, 152; *see also* (psycho)therapy

biology, one- and two-person, 166, 167, 201

blood pressure, 166-7, 168

blurb, standard, 168, 172, 173, 174, 175

case histories, reasons for choice, xvi

cases:

(1) woman of 23, illustrating value of stable doctor-patient relationship, 12-16, 39, 212-14

(2) man of 26, with anxiety states, illustrating effect of change in doctor-patient relationship, 16-22, 39, 214-15

(3) woman of 25, depressive, illustrating improvement subsequent to consultant diagnostic interview, 27-30, 39, 215

(4) man of 34, obsessional, with symptom of impotence, illustrating improvement after diagnostic interview, 30-4, 39, 215-16

(5) woman of 42, with phobia of travelling alone, illustrating effect of exclusive examination by doctor, 50-2, 66-7, 121, 216-17

cases—*continued*

(6) woman of 36, with fear of pregnancy, illustrating effect of patient's co-operation with doctor in examination, 52-3, 121, 124, 217-19

(7) man of 53, illustrating effect of examination by patient, 55-60, 121, 122-4, 219-20

(8) woman of 28, illustrating effect of doctor's emotional involvement in case, 62-8, 172, 220-2

(9) woman of 56, asthmatic, illustrating doctor's difficulties from emotional involvement, 68-74, 222

(10) woman of 34, with pruritus vulvae, illustrating effect of doctor's emotions and futility of reassurance, 75-9, 222

(11) boy of 15, asthmatic, illustrating 'mutual seduction', 84-8, 222-4

(12) woman in 30s, illustrating effect of treating absent patients, 88-92, 224-5

(13) woman of 26, illustrating need of choice for treatment between present and absent patient, 93-8, 225

(14) woman of 55, with inadequate husband, illustrating need of treating both present and absent patient, 98-103, 225-6

(15) family of three, illustrating process of teaching patients to live with illness, 106-9, 226-7

(16) man of 34, dyspeptic, illustrating results of training patient to inhibit aggression, 110-13, 227-8

229

emotions, doctor's, 61ff, 172
  and diagnostic interview, 191, 193
  and double-blind experiment, 119
  part played by, 79-80, 137
  and psychiatric interview, 175-6
  as symptom of patient's illness, 61,
    66, 77, 81
  and understanding, 133, 137, 139
  see also attitude
empiricism, 4
examination:
  clinical, 164-5
  by doctor alone, 50, 66
  medical, structure of, 47
  by patient, 49ff, 74, 76, 92, 120
  physical and psychological, 49,
    166-7, 173, 202
  standardization of, 198
  see also diagnosis; interview;
    testing
experience:
  clinical, need of, xvi
  communication of, 141
  dynamic, 141
experiment, double-blind, 118-19,
  121, 126, 127

Family Discussion Bureau, 7, 68
Family Planning Association, vii,
  xv, 7, 202
fantasies:
  accepting patient's, 157-8
  internal, 157
  production at interview, 198
  understanding, 141, 149
findings, negative, need of stating,
  71, 200
follow-ups, 26, 68, 155
  and general practitioner, 125
  hospitals and restricted, 124
  need for, 39, 115
  reports of, 212ff
Freud, S., xii, xiii, xiv, 39, 71, 163,
  178, 185
friends, patient's, analyst's and
  doctor's relations with, 8
function, apostolic, 114

general practice:
  aim of, 128
  and hospitals, 128
  and scientific medicine, 123
  special aspects of, 11
  see also doctor
general practitioner(s), xiv, xv, 3-4,
  7, 14, 34, 124-5
  constant availability of, 14, 144
  and consultant, 26-7
  as psychotherapist, 14
  relation with patient, 8-10, 124-5,
    144; *see also* relationship:
    doctor-patient
  as teachers, 128
  versatility of, 14
  see also doctor
General Practitioners, College of,
  3-4
geometry, projective, 167
gifts, symbolic, 139
goal/aim:
  of interview, *see* interview
  therapeutic:
    behavioural or internal, 151-2
    technique and, 149-50
    two classes of, 151
group therapy, *see* (psycho)therapy:
  group
guilt feelings, 155, 217

hospitals:
  and comprehensive medicine, 126
  and general practice units, 128
  shortcomings of practice, 124
  teaching:
    and psychotherapy, ix, xi, 3-4,
      47, 116, 126-7, 129
Hutton, G., 168
hypnosis, xii, xiv

idealization, 83
  as defence, 178-9
  see also identification
identification, 135-6, 137, 138
  one-sided, 83
  with patient, 83, 84, 150

231

305143270P